P9-BEE-797

THE COP SHOP

THE

COP SHOP

...

TRUE CRIME ON

THE STREETS OF

CHICAGO

ROBERT BLAU

A WILLIAM PATRICK BOOK

Addison-Wesley Publishing Company

Reading, Massachusetts   Menlo Park, California   New York
Don Mills, Ontario   Wokingham, England   Amsterdam   Bonn
Sydney   Singapore   Tokyo   Madrid   San Juan
Paris   Seoul   Milan   Mexico City   Taipei

Many of the designations used by manufacturers and sellers to distinguish their products are claimed as trademarks. Where those designations appear in this book and Addison-Wesley was aware of a trademark claim, the designations have been printed in initial capital letters.

Grateful acknowledgment is made to the *Chicago Tribune* for permission to reprint previously published material by Robert Blau. Copyright © 1988, 1989, 1990, 1991 by the Chicago Tribune Company. All rights reserved.

Library of Congress Cataloging-in-Publication Data

Blau, Robert.
    The cop shop : true crime on the streets of Chicago / Robert Blau.
       p. cm.
    ISBN 0-201-58113-2
    1. Police—Illinois—Chicago. 2. Crime—Illinois—Chicago.
    3. Chicago (Ill.)—Social conditions. I. Title.
    HV8148.C4B43   1993
    364.9773'11—dc20   92-37611
                                                              CIP

Jacket design by Diana Coe
Text design by Richard Oriolo
Set in 11-point Baskerville by Clarinda Company

1 2 3 4 5 6 7 8 9-MA-9796959493
First printing, March 1993

For my grandparents,
Ilona and Eugene

Some men wish evil and accomplish it
But most men, when they work in that machine
Just let it happen somewhere in the wheels.

STEPHEN VINCENT BENÉT

C o n t e n t s

. . .

Acknowledgments

. . .

This project began over lunch with Hillel Levin, who encouraged me to write a book and put me in the able hands of my agent, Nat Sobel.

I am indebted to lovely Leah Eskin, who was not only a perfect friend, but one of the sharpest editors I have known. I am also grateful to David Jackson, Buzz Bissinger, and Rick Kogan, three of the finest writers and readers anywhere.

Bill Patrick, my editor at Addison-Wesley, kept the faith—even after reading my first draft.

Special thanks to Running Dog Ranch for its writer-in-residence program, and to my parents for enduring my long-distance kvetching. Les Harris, as always, sustained me with his friendship. Molly Daniels shared her inimitable method of getting past the blank page.

I owe thanks to those editors at the *Tribune* who thought I could hack it on the front lines. Ann Marie Lipinski, deputy managing editor, was a source of support and inspiration. Joel Kaplan served as my journalistic *sensei*. And thanks to Bill Kennedy, who taught me many things, most importantly that storytelling is honorable work.

P r o l o g u e

. . .

T he Book of Death sat atop the metal desk of an Irish
detective, who entered names with a ballpoint pen.

Between its red vinyl covers were legal-size pages, each
with a hand-drawn line down the center to accommodate
double the number of murder victims. Before each name
was a number, the running count.

This was the Chicago Police Department's official led-
ger, kept on the fifth floor of headquarters, without computer grids, without even index cards. There was something
almost dignified about the inscriptions written one at a time,
slowly, in a handsome script the detective had reserved for
wedding invitations and birthday cards.

Each name was followed by a simple code: "sh" for shot;

"st" for stabbed; "t" for trauma, which might have been delivered with any of a variety of objects, ranging from baseball bats to porcelain lamps.

In this city, with its muscular skyscrapers, overhead trains, and roller-bladed lake shore, every substance, manmade and organic, had been transformed into a weapon.

That year, fifty people had been killed with kitchen knives, thirty-nine with feet, hands, or fists, one each with a necktie, a tree limb, and a hatchet, two with concrete, two with hot water, and three with lighter fluid. The circumstances of their deaths were recorded in other files and grouped by time of day, by location, by relationship—husbands who murdered wives, girlfriends who murdered boyfriends, workers who murdered bosses, and people who killed people they didn't know at all.

As police reporter for the *Chicago Tribune,* it was my job to follow these acts of suffering and turn them into stories that could be served in the morning with breakfast. Epitaphs with orange juice. Victims remembered with varying degrees of hysteria and hoopla depending on the flare with which they had been undone.

One of my responsibilities was checking the latest totals every couple of months. I'd run down the stairs from the press room, singing aloud the melancholy words of "Who by Fire," a Leonard Cohen song based on a prayer recited on the Day of Atonement, when fates for the coming year are sealed.

"Does that include today?" I'd ask the detective after he'd given me the latest count. "You know we had one at about eleven o'clock on Seventy-fifth Street?"

And the follow-up: "How many last year at this time?"

He'd open the book for the previous year, run his finger down the pages, and announce the number.

The pages were lined with needless obituaries, shootings and stabbings for every imaginable reason, and occasionally for no reason at all. Yet when I started in the job in the spring of 1988, the simple math added up to surprisingly good news. The city was experiencing its lowest murder rate in two decades, 660 homicides by year's end.

"Not bad," I'd say to the detective each time I got the figures for months after arriving on the beat. I'd thank him and head for a telephone to report the generally upbeat comparison.

There was a feeling that we were lucky, that while New York, Los Angeles, and Detroit erupted, Chicago, in the wholesome Midwest, was more sane, more under control. That despite its reputation as one of the more segregated cities in the country, and despite the recent death of Harold Washington, its first black mayor, Chicago had inadvertently found the way to an acceptable level of losses. Six hundred sixty. Not bad.

The cops congratulated themselves for outstanding work. The press humored them. The public for the most part was content.

Walking around the grimy corridors of police headquarters, where violence counted only in bulk, it was easy to believe luck was eternal.

O N E

• • •

THE

COP SHOP

Police accidentally shot a man Monday while accompanying him to an apartment at 5266 S. State St.

May 3, 1988

T he crime beat was in the gutter.

Sixty years after Al Capone, it had become a lowly assignment for reporters just starting out or those about to retire, the night school and United Nations of Chicago journalism.

As it had been for decades, police headquarters at Eleventh and State, or the Cop Shop, as it was known, served as the beat's gritty Pantheon, the press room on the seventh floor its altar.

The raw ugliness of the building was inescapable, and the press room was no exception. The prison yellow walls; the thrift store brown drapes clotting like an unchanged oil filter; the fearless roaches; the fungus hanging from the air vents; the mounds of black flakes piling up in the light fixtures. I didn't know what the flakes were until one day when a janitor climbed a ladder, unhinged the plastic covers, and shook out a jug's worth of dead fly parts. On quiet afternoons I'd stare at the ceiling, trying to solve the mystery of how they got inside.

In the corner of the L-shaped room was a bathroom lit by a dim bulb, which was best for everyone.

The press room was rarely visited by choice. Had I not been obliged to, I wouldn't have set foot inside either. The trajectory of my career, which seemed to be moving sideways, or slightly downward, led me there.

My first job at the paper was reviewing B movies when the lead critic, Gene Siskel (the tall one), couldn't or wouldn't watch them. Screenings were held in a private, living room–size theater with cushy first-class seats and a thundering sound system. Even after watching a mind-dissolving film about, say, female mannequins coming alive or weekend sex binges, I felt lucky to be getting paid for it. I wrote features about old blues singers who hovered around Chicago, and about first-time movie makers. At low point, I reviewed the Ice Capades.

Then I went to the suburbs, where I covered a recurring disappearing act: disappearing farms, disappearing drive-ins, disappearing quiet. Although there was a lot of good material—greed, corruption, bad politics—the standard conflict thrashed out at countless village board meetings involved the location of shopping malls and traffic lights.

I was still waiting to become a hard-boiled city reporter, and the Cop Shop, I thought, would effect that change. I walked in on a bright morning, hoping to write some good stories, learn to cover a beat, collect material for the great American screenplay, and move on.

My predecessor stood before me.

For twelve years, Phil Wattley had dutifully worked the day shift, cooped up in the press room with fire bells, Teletypes, and police scanners channeling news of catastrophe to the rest of the world. On this morning the radios were almost quiet, hissing every few minutes with the location of a squad car or a calm "Ten-four."

I approached Wattley's desk, introduced myself, and shook his hand. The air around him smelled like Father's Day cologne.

In his mid-forties, he looked the part of police reporter, dressed in a fitted gray suit and crisp white shirt, his face aglow with a close shave. He spoke quietly, in short sentences that breezed out the side of his mouth; I had been told he drove a big black Cadillac with optional spotlight.

Although I had never met him, I had read his byline on dozens of stories. They were formulaic—who, what, where—and easy to criticize for their lack of feeling. I was sure I could do better. But I was also petrified of entering this foreign world with its weird vocabulary of "perps" and "vics," perpetrators and victims, that he had mastered. In the weeks before I was to start, I'd drive by at night to stare at the cobalt blue letters that spelled CHICAGO POLICE HEADQUAR-TERS, wondering how I would figure it all out.

For Wattley it was home. He was of the old school, having spent many days striding between his favorite lunchtime haunts and the soothing familiarity of the press room, tumbling into the leatherette embrace of its sunken ship of a couch. Like many of the old-timers who had preceded him, most of his friends were cops. By the end, he was one of them. His friends called him "The Commish."

Around Eleventh and State he had come to be known as the official namer of pattern rapists. There were the screen-door rapist, three or four North Side rapists, the dreadlock rapist, the shaver rapist, the pizza delivery rapist, the Tarzan rapist.

He would have lived out his career there if they had let him. Instead, in a decision made just a few weeks earlier, the editors replaced him with me, an outsider who didn't know a .45 caliber from a five-alarm fire, someone endowed with what they called "a fresh perspective." In this, as in most everything Wattley covered as a reporter, he saw no justice.

Wattley's new assignment was overnight editor. Between 10:00 P.M. and 5:00 A.M. he would man the city desk in the Tribune Tower and wait for plane crashes and earthquakes, neither of which had occurred in Chicago in a long time. But he preferred that to going to the suburbs, from which I was trying to escape.

When my boss asked me if I was interested in taking over the beat, I told her, "Cops. Sure."

■ ■ ■

I was no Green Beret.

I was a short Jewish guy from New York. I had never been mugged. I knew little about death firsthand, having attended a funeral only once, of an uncle who was buried in the Bronx. The first time I went fishing in the Catskill Mountains, I stared at the groaning mouth of a twitching pickerel and threw it back. The only cops I knew were from TV.

These were "Miami Vice" days, but my own telehistory went as far back as my fishing expedition—"Baretta," "Columbo," "Kojak," "The Rookies." The previous month I had spent a few days reporting on the filming of "Crime Story." Set in the early 1960s, the television series featured an elite band of Chicago detectives who chased safecrackers, thieves, and hit men from the Loop to Las Vegas.

One night on location, with excess only Hollywood could achieve, the director re-created a shoot-out on the front lawn of a ranch-style house on the Northwest Side. Shotguns blazed. Cars crashed through living rooms.

I thought the Cop Shop would be like that.

■ ■ ■

Wattley wasn't thrilled to be showing me around, not even for a day. We stood by his desk saying little to each other.

He was on the phone when another *Tribune* reporter, John "CrimeFighter" O'Brien, walked in unexpectedly. He carried a box of doughnuts as a gesture to the changing of the guard. I was happy to see him.

O'Brien, a tall, slender, nearly bald man in his fifties, had a knack for working through tense moments, finding some clever way to deride the bosses and to make job switches sound not-so-bad—life went on. He had survived a dozen different editors in the newsroom, never losing his enthusiasm for the job. He was an ex-marine, a family man. With an optimistic smile, he extended his hand to congratulate Wattley on what he called his promotion.

Wattley, driven on the beat to expect the worst of human nature, was startled. Holding an oversized jelly doughnut at his side as if it was a free weight, he dripped cherry jam down his starched cuffs and onto the dirty brown carpet.

"I just do what they tell me," Wattley said, sounding almost cheerful.

"I see they still do the civil service shuffle in this place," O'Brien joked as he imitated the tired, oblivious gait of the city workers trudging through the hallways.

"Some things never change," Wattley said, then took a bite of his doughnut.

A few minutes later O'Brien said goodbye, wishing me good luck and slapping me on the back. He left to cover his beat, loosely defined as Organized Crime, which was still a big topic in Chicago, and way up the career ladder from Eleventh and State.

Wattley looked me over quickly, coldly. Reluctantly, the official namer of pattern rapists peeled his suit jacket from the back of his chair to begin what would be his last walk through the old building.

Under his jacket he looked as though he was wearing White-Out. I later learned that he had come up with a nickname for me that same day: Mighty Mouse.

"Okay," he said, "let's go."

■ ■ ■

Completed in 1929, the year of the St. Valentine's Day Massacre, and renovated in the early 1960s when a giant revolving blue light was hoisted atop the roof, police headquarters was once state of the art. Now it was dangerously decrepit.

There was virtually no security beyond the front door, so that once you were inside the building for an appearance in gun court, for example, you could roam the halls at will. On a typical day the building was full of young gangsters, prostitutes, and convicted felons. Riding the elevator was like taking a short trip to jail, and getting stuck, Wattley warned, could be perilous.

A metal detector had been installed a few years earlier after a shooting in the Cook County building, but visitors still tried to sneak guns and other contraband inside. Once the guards thought they had caught a woman red-handed when something in her purse set off the alarm. At the bottom was a foot-long vibrator. Five years later they were still laughing about it.

We worked our way up from the lobby, Wattley introducing me as "the new guy" whenever we ran into someone he recognized, which seemed to be about every five steps. His sources among the cops were upset about the switch; they stood to lose a reporter who had earned their trust and become, more or less, an ally. I didn't even try to remember their names because I assumed they wouldn't have much to say to me.

The second and third floors were the heart of Chicago's outmoded 911 system, which looked like something left over from the 1965 World's Fair. Showcased behind large glass windows, Plexiglas boards lit by green and red bulbs tracked the location of police cars in the districts. Overstuffed dispatchers in blue uniforms logged emergency calls on computer cards and barked instructions into the tube-like mouthpieces of their headsets, creating the never-ending banter heard over the twenty frequencies of the police radio.

The communications system was nearly thirty years old and desperately in need of updating. It took dispatchers al-most forty seconds to answer some calls. And unlike in other large cities, uniformed police in Chicago responded to more than two-thirds of the emergency calls they received, even those involving cats stuck in trees and neighbors playing the Psychedelic Furs too loud.

A plaque on the wall said the system had been installed early in the 1960s under O. W. Wilson, a respected superin-tendent who believed that police should respond quickly when summoned by the public, simultaneously providing se-curity and fostering community relations. Though the vol-ume of calls had grown too large to make such a philosophy practical, it was still favored by the current superintendent of police, LeRoy Martin, whose glass-doored office was on the fourth floor.

On the fifth was the flag-draped auditorium, where press conferences were held. The Sheet, the police report-er's friend, was on the sixth.

"Think of it as a tip sheet," Wattley instructed as we walked into the first deputy's office, where the chronologi-cal log of all major crimes was kept.

Most everything that happened to cops was listed on the Sheet. It worked like this: An officer at the scene would call the first deputy's office, where a description of the crime was pecked out on a green IBM Selectric and kept in the type-writer so that reporters (let 'em herniate) would have to double over to read it upside down. When the page in the typewriter was full, the officers, two bottom-heavy cops per shift who spent most of their time trying to solve word jum-bles, added it to a clipboard that sat on a Formica-covered counter in front of them.

They were Big Mac–eating men, and it showed. Their brains were glued to the only responsibility they could handle.

"Anything doing?" Wattley asked, leaning against the counter. On the paneled wall behind him were photographs of Martin and Mayor Eugene Sawyer, who had been voted into office by Chicago's aldermen after Harold Washington died the previous November of a heart attack.

"Nah. Nothing but crap," one of the cops answered, which was the usual reply. From the police perspective, there was never anything worth looking into on the Sheet. It was all cheap. It had all become the same story, the same stupid shootings. Over what? Nothing quality.

Most of the time the media agreed, out of necessity. There wasn't enough space in newspapers or airtime on television to cover half the daily mayhem, so only the sexiest crimes were reported, those involving household names, football coaches, athletes, the well-to-do, the residents of fine, quiet neighborhoods, the very young. That much was evident from just looking at what made the news.

Of course, until that morning I had been unfamiliar with how much this process of elimination left behind. It was all on the Sheet. As I glanced over several pages, each sorry paragraph seemed as though it could sustain a story, if only a short one.

Wattley pulled the clipboard toward him, studying the most recent entries on the top page of a pile going back a month or two. He expertly scanned for key words—"murder," "kidnaping"—his eyes and fingers combing for patterns, secrets, brand names, anecdotes on the order of "man bites dog," and coming up empty, as was often the case, though never wasting an ounce of energy or emotion.

"There's a lot of crap on here," he confirmed.

So he used a crappy case, a rape, to teach me the system.

"Now, this here on the left side is the district where it happened, and under that the time, the time it was phoned in, not the time of occurrence. You got to check that. . . . Here's the beat number. If it ends in a zero, it's a supervisor."

Often the Sheet was dead wrong. Never trust it, Wattley instructed. Always check spellings. And never—even though it appeared on the Sheet—never give the name of a rape victim.

"You've got to judge for yourself just by looking at it whether there's a story there. Like this one," he said, pointing to the middle of a page. "Some guy shot by the cops, 5266 South State, Robert Taylor Homes, tenth floor, 3:03 A.M. . . . We'll check that out later."

It was the least cheap item he could find.

■ ■ ■

Back in the press room, "The Oprah Winfrey Show" played on a black-and-white television, a piece of stolen merchandise that had never been claimed. A white inventory tag was still fastened to one of the antennas; on the other, for extended range, a triangular piece of aluminum foil was hinged.

Peanuts and popcorn spilled off one of the desks and onto the carpet. A window banged in and out like an old screen door, fanning the smell of spent cigarettes and thick dust that goaded the back of the nostrils. Barrels of clouds rolled across the West Side sky like a tornado about to strike.

The view from Wattley's desk, soon to be my own, looked directly across the hall at the locked glass doors of the gun lab, a museum of armaments. Nearly every type of gun was displayed on one of the walls, from Saturday Night Specials to submachine guns going back to Al Capone. A radio inside played oldies like "Georgia on My Mind." The technicians who walked around in lab coats seemed to have a sense of history about them, surrounded as they were by the raw ingredients that gave Chicago its tough reputation. They looked more alert than most of the people in the building, which, I assumed, was a result of working with objects, not personalities.

The ballistics mavens knew that gun models came and went in cyclic progression, from Thompson submachine guns to cheap, single-shot, sometimes homemade weapons, back to submachine guns. Spraying street corners with semi-automatic pistols like AK-47s or Uzis had once again become fashionable.

The press room had not displayed a similar pattern; its onetime status never returned. The press corps that trudged into the Cop Shop each morning was a small, disparate group linked by a mere thread to the fading spirit of its lineage, most notably the reporters and leg men who romped through Ben Hecht and Charles MacArthur's newspaper farce *The Front Page*. The actual room where Hecht had worked was a mile to the north in a massive gray county court building that had been renovated into tony law and advertising offices. Within its ornate quarters, Hecht and a band of reporters spent their days playing cards, trading lines of poetry, occasionally covering a trial, and making up stories which they filed on deadline. Once, Hecht and a colleague dug a ditch in Lincoln Park, citing it as proof that a major earthquake had struck Chicago.

Unlike the *Front Page* press room and some of its later incarnations at Eleventh and State, the Cop Shop I first entered in 1988 hosted no poker games; no empty bottles of bourbon were strewn on the floor, no one was laid out on the couch.

Camping out behind the tan metal desks that morning were reporters from the *Chicago Defender,* which covered news of importance to the black community, and from the City News Bureau, whose automatic dialing machines chased cadavers in every ambulance. *Sun-Times* veteran Jim Casey, who had covered cops for nearly three decades, was the *Tribune*'s, and Wattley's, main competition. Now he was mine.

Casey was an elder statesman. After shaking my hand, he resumed the truly important business of smoking, his silver lighter firing with a distinct click, followed by the rush of butane. He'd been smoking longer than he'd been reporting; each of his cherished Larks was a lucky charm between him and cancer of the lungs.

He was slim, almost bony. He looked a little like the actor Harry Dean Stanton. He favored polyester and a spit shine. He called his wife every day to find out what was for dinner and to tell her that he loved her. A gentleman in many ways.

Everyone else in attendance was friendly that day, but under the surface, because the press room was so small and its procedures so set, there was considerable apprehension about Wattley's departure.

As we sat, Wattley reviewed general principles.

Privacy. Phone calls in the press room were never private. If you wanted to keep a secret, make your calls elsewhere.

Cooperation. If everyone was working on the same story, it was okay to share basic facts. If there was to be a press conference, make sure to tell everyone.

The toilet was exclusive. About this Wattley was adamant. I could do whatever I chose, but he would never let a stranger use the press room bathroom; too many hookers were cruising the building.

And then the specific ones.

Wattley took out a rumpled copy of a police directory and in a low voice began going through it in alphabetical order.

Areas. There were six detective areas in the city, divided geographically, that investigated major crimes. Each had a commander. I should get to know them.

Auto theft. Auto pound. Bomb and arson. Central detention, for mass arrests downtown. . . . Cook County Jail. Detectives. The chief of detectives was Ed Wodnicki. I should get to know him. Districts. There were twenty-five scattered throughout the city. The Marquette district handled the paperwork on jail escapes, but you had to get to the review officer, who kept all the reports, before he went home at three in the afternoon.

We went through the whole book: gambling, gangs, internal affairs, hostage barricades, mug shots, narcotics, the control tower at O'Hare.

"You should know about standbys at the airports," Wattley said.

A standby was called when a plane was coming in with only one engine or some other problem. This drew scores of emergency vehicles to the runway.

"Don't worry. You'll know if there's a crash."

I imagined the police radios exploding with the clipped, excited phrasing of rocket launches: "Tell Fire we need a washdown. We've got a mess here."

A fire ticker, an antique that might have telegraphed the panic of the Chicago Fire, sat on a small wooden table by the door. Amazingly, it still worked, punching out in a braille-like code the location of the sounding fire alarm. The code was deciphered by consulting a card catalogue kept in six narrow drawers beneath the ticker. No one used it anymore, since just about everything came over the radio.

Wattley handed me a slip of paper on which he had scribbled a set of numbers. It would unlock the cabinet that contained the police and fire radios. The night side reporter, Henry Wood, whom I had yet to meet, had taken care to program them so they scanned every inch of the city. "Don't mess with them," Wattley warned. "It upsets him."

Phone numbers were everywhere. The top of the desk, covered with a large sheet of see-through plastic, was crammed with numbers: police districts, hospitals, ambulances, fire battalions. A number for every emergency: the morgue; the office of natural disaster relief.

I had three phones; Casey had four.

Staircase journalism, Jimmy Breslin's term for covering a story by getting out on the street and into people's faces, was not Chicago's old masters' idea of police reporting. For the most part, Wattley and Casey had worked for years without visiting the scene of a crime or the home of a victim. Phones were their feet. And once they called, they never had to call back. Every conceivable question had been asked, every angle covered—the caliber of the bullet, the escape route, the time, the address, the spelling of names.

Lifting the receiver of a smudged black rotary telephone on his desk, Wattley squinted and for the first time that morning asserted himself.

"Most people don't know why they call it a PAX line, but I do and you're about to find out." He was almost shouting.

The police auxiliary line, an internal phone line used only by police in police stations, was the ticket to knowledge. If you called on the PAX, whoever was on the other end instantly knew you were calling from within the department. While not exactly guaranteeing trust, it helped. With cops, every bit of near trust helped.

Wattley explained about IR numbers. An identification record helped locate police reports and rap sheets, which were hard to come by unless you had friends. Talking to a suspect in the lockup upstairs was also nearly impossible unless you had friends. Information in general was in short supply unless you had friends.

Finding these friends was my own problem.

■ ■ ■

If Wattley had any regrets about leaving the job, they were lessened by my first story, a brief about the police shooting he had plucked from the Sheet. The police had merely been doing a good deed, helping a man named Gilchrist recover his stolen VCR. Unfortunately, Gilchrist was shot in the butt when the police opened fire at another man who had unexpectedly pulled a gun.

Wattley stood beside me, grinning, as I turned on the old computer beside the desk. Its fan produced a loud, obnoxious hum as it transmitted the story to the city desk in the Tribune Tower, about a mile to the north.

He had seen the last of the great police reporters, the performers, actors, and gabbers who conversed with dial tones and cooked up false leads just to throw each other off.

And he had watched crime reach its current brainless state. Instead of brains, guns. He and Casey had learned the ropes from the veterans, and when they took over the press room the city belonged to them. No one would fill their shoes. Of that Wattley seemed delightedly certain.

At four-thirty, as we watched the early television news on the unclaimed set, my night shift replacement, Henry Wood, strode through the doorway in a charcoal-colored suit, his gray hair shiny, his back straight, his tie tight at the collar. He leaned over me and, in a great sledgehammer arc, slammed two worn leather-covered address books onto the desk.

"This is all I need to do the job," he said, mocking any reliance on computers, tape recorders, maps, and public documents.

I had once spoken to him when I was an intern at the paper. He had called to dictate a short story about a raid at an adult bookstore. Six or seven people were arrested when they were caught flipping through the dirty magazines, he told me. Obscenity charges. Got that? Then he hung up. Despite his having been stationed at Eleventh and State for so many years, virtually no one in the newsroom knew what Henry Wood looked like or what he did to pass the hours between roughly 5:00 P.M. and 1:00 A.M. every day.

Whereas Wattley was younger than I had imagined, Henry, who was known universally by his first name, was older. He had large hands, as if he'd pushed something other than a pencil all these years. He was a stubborn mule, that was clear, and he was battling a cancer that had already claimed a good yard of his intestines.

Henry wanted his seat early, to settle into its orange cushion, lock in near the phone. He wouldn't come out and say it. Instead he greeted me with "First day and you're working overtime already." Then he waved a copy of his profit-sharing statement like a magic wand, which showed that, at eighteen months from retirement, he had more than $200,000 in the bank.

Casey greeted him with the closing *Tribune* stock quote. Sometimes Henry would calculate how much his three and a half decades of service was worth at that moment.

"My biggest problem is going to be figuring out what to do with it when I'm out of here, my lad," Henry would say.

Wattley and Casey and Henry had the system figured out. They could sort out the stories from the non-stories, the good from the bad, the cheap kill from the quality one. The *Tribune* reporters had even made a good penny doing it. The company's stock had done well since it went public in 1983, a windfall for veterans like Henry. Retiring with hundreds of thousands of dollars in the bank would have been unthinkable for journeyman reporters even a decade earlier.

I wondered how long it would be before I too could walk away from the crime beat every night as they did, drive home, forget about it, be calmed by an expanding pension.

■ ■ ■

I spent the next few days trying to ignore my surroundings.

I'd arrive at headquarters at about nine in the morning, flash my press card to get past the guard at the entrance, and buy the day's papers from a blind man who ran a concession stand in the lobby. With his spindly tool-and-dye fingers he'd grab my change, ring up the sale, and drop the coins into the cash register. Glancing at the *Sun-Times*, to keep an eye on the competition, I'd rush upstairs.

The smell of grilled onions emanated from the walls of the press room. A police dispatcher Henry had warned me about, more than three hundred pounds of roly-poly flesh, must have spent his nights downing yards of Italian sausage in long, tensed-neck swallows. By morning the only evidence of his bliss was a curling sheet of greasy waxed paper on the couch.

Unlocking the cabinet beside my desk, I'd yank open the metal drawers and turn on the radios, waiting for the scanner to hone in on the nearest signal. Red digital numbers flashed wildly until a voice came in clearly.

I'd drape my jacket over the back of my chair, just as I had seen Wattley do it. In the desk he had left behind a police reporter's survival kit—a few telephone directories, a bottle of aspirin. On a bulletin board were pictures of Harold Washington, Mike Ditka, and Prince Norodom Sihanouk, doctored so that each gestured with his middle finger.

Complicated events were taking shape outside, but I was happy just to be settling in.

In other cities, crack and violence dominated public debate; in Chicago, with the murder rate at just under two a day, the biggest local stories were still political. That first week an aide to Mayor Sawyer apologized for having claimed that Jewish doctors were infecting black babies with the AIDS virus. A few days later a group of aldermen, accompanied by police, stormed into the Art Institute to remove a painting of Harold Washington depicting him in women's underwear.

Across the street from my perch at Eleventh and State was a private swimming pool, an object of envy and lust surpassing the gloss of the Snap-On tool calendar and the "Charlie's Angels" poster, circa 1976, that hung on the wall.

Beyond the pool were the rail lines, spires, and chimneys of the West Side. There, in three-flats and alleys, in the projects and restaurants, was the raw material that filled the Sheet—gang shootings, rapes, drug overdoses, robberies.

I filed a six-inch story about a group of schoolgirls who had been raped in a South Side neighborhood. The rapist had collected the gloves and mittens of his victims, which police later found stacked in a fruit bowl he left behind in an abandoned apartment. A few school bus collisions sounded over the radios, a fire, a cop killed in a car accident after she had suffered a heart attack. Otherwise it seemed quiet. At his desk a foot away from mine, Casey studied the papers and talked on the phone. Oprah, in her fat, dashiki phase, cajoled wives who had been beaten by their husbands but who wanted them back anyway.

I was glad not to have to face a major disaster right away; mastering the basics, the computer sign-on and the combination locks seemed like significant accomplishments. It was easy to imagine that this would be the relaxed pace of the job.

Then on a Friday morning when I bought the papers in the lobby, at the center of the *Sun-Times'* front page was a story with the headline HERO CABDRIVER CHASES, DISARMS HIT-RUN SUBJECT. I checked the byline. Casey. I hadn't covered the story.

Getting beaten like that gave me more respect for Wattley. I envisioned crime after crime that Casey would have reported on while I ignored them.

Humiliated, I went to check the Sheet. It listed a few more shootings than the day before. A few more of everything.

The cop behind the counter smoked a cigar, oblivious to the names, addresses, and ages he had just typed out. I could understand his lack of concern. There was an abstract quality to the violence of those days, as though it marched on silently a few miles away, seemingly without consequence.

T W O

...

DEAD PEOPLE'S RELATIVES

Police have classified the boy's death as gang-related.

May 9, 1988

A s a police reporter, the first sound I heard in the morning was that of a tinny clock radio that I hadn't listened to since the Beatles. My AM days started with the chilling staccato of simply arranged facts. The president; the deficit, fire on the West Side, no reports of injuries as yet; the ups and downs of bran muffins; the requisite sexual innuendo, the newscasters cooing at each other from behind their big padded microphones.

Then, on most mornings, came the sparse rendering of a terrible crime, starting with "Chicago police are investigating . . ."

"Other stories we're covering: A fourteen-year-old boy faces murder charges for the gang-related slaying of a sixteen-year-old gunned down last night in a West Side schoolyard."

The news report shocked me into work mode. I jumped up, showered, and said goodbye to my girlfriend, who would stay in bed debating which act to book for her next cabaret show—the straitjacketed break-dancer or the Cher impersonator? We shared an apartment in Ukrainian Village, a predominantly Polish neighborhood about a mile west of the Loop. It wasn't the prettiest area, but it was convenient. The drive to Eleventh and State took less than ten minutes.

By the time I walked into the first deputy's office the name of the dead boy, Leonard Santiago, had been typed out along with a brief description of his demise. Male, Hispanic; multiple gunshot wounds to head and abdomen; address 1400 Francisco. Offender in custody. I stared at the official farewell, taking down the time, address, and district as Wattley had instructed. The officer behind the desk chewed on a fat cigar and read a magazine.

A few police districts on the South and West sides of Chicago—Englewood, Wentworth, Shakespeare, Wood— contributed most of the casualties, dozens each month. Typically, such murders were reduced to three or four paragraphs, a brief, and tossed into a column with other briefs about drownings, traffic accidents, lesser court rulings, and rewritten press releases. Most of the victims were young blacks and Hispanics, but it wasn't racism that resulted in the scant attention these deaths received; rather, it was a wearing down of the spirit that seemed to affect black, white, and Hispanic reporters and editors equally. Nearly everyone was tiring of cheap crime, crime that happened daily, in the places it always did.

At the same time, the police blotter, as it had been traditionally constructed, full of careful but heartless language, was no longer a staple of the modern newspaper. Tales of murder and mayhem, unless they had a twist, were supplanted by stories about dead alewives stinking up the shores of Lake Michigan.

It was with equal parts of curiosity and of desperation to file my first real article from the beat that I set out that day to figure out what had happened to Leonard Santiago. Not an epic—just something that took notice, fifteen inches maybe. Anything but a brief.

■ ■ ■

Although cops were under order to share basic information with the press, they rarely had the patience for it, especially when they didn't know a reporter personally. Wattley had been right about that, I quickly found. I stumbled through my first frantic week of calls, trying for the right mix of force-fulness and supplication that would squeeze facts out of onions. With what I thought was great resourcefulness, I tried different accents—Italian, Polish, South Side Chicago. I tried dirty jokes. I tried wheezing, as though I was about to have a heart attack. I even tried earnestness: "Hello, I'm the new police reporter for the *Tribune*"—which, to my chagrin, was met with "So you're the guy who replaced Wattley."

These calls were the key to getting the job done. I psyched myself before dialing the four-digit PAX number to Grand-Central detective headquarters, which was investigating Santiago's murder.

To my surprise, the sergeant who answered the phone sketched out the basic facts without much prodding. In the background I could hear the reassuring sound of papers shuffling.

"Let's see. At approximately twenty-one hundred hours, the victim was playing softball in a schoolyard on Francisco Avenue. The suspect rode up on a bicycle, pulled a small-caliber handgun from his waistband, and fired three shots at the victim." The bullet, said the sergeant, went "through and through" Santiago's skull, then skittered across Francisco Avenue, never to be found.

"Anyone charged?"

"Charged with murder, last name Ortiz, first name, Luis. Age fourteen."

Ortiz was a "gang banger," as gang members were commonly referred to by the cops and the media in Chicago. The sergeant said this with certainty, in the same tone in which he disclosed Ortiz's astrological sign: "Ah, what a shame—a Leo."

"What gang was he in?"

"We don't give out that information."

Cops didn't like naming gangs because it could be misconstrued as recognition. Gang bangers would go to the newsstand in the morning, read about themselves, feel proud, and kill again. For the most part the media complied, rarely publicizing whether the suspect or victim belonged to the Cobra Stones, Vice Lords, Disciples, Latin Kings, or any of the more than forty other major gangs and hundreds of offshoots in Chicago. We abided this self-censorship, even though its hypothesis was not tested in any precise way. Were these kids really encouraged by reading about themselves? No one knew. But withholding the names of gangs seemed the more responsible course to take, and the etiquette was rarely challenged.

The only exception to this rule was made for El Rukn, the most notorious Chicago street gang that in two decades had grown from a band of scrawny street thugs into a semi-organized criminal empire on the South Side of the city. The Rukns had earned seeing their name in print.

■ ■ ■

Ortiz had proclaimed his loyalties as he pulled the trigger.

"Kings rule," a witness heard him shout in a tribute to his boys, the Latin Kings.

In a sparse interrogation room, Ortiz explained his actions with simple, halting logic to detectives who had heard the same story many times before. Santiago, he said, had lived on one side of Humboldt Boulevard, while he lived on the other side. Therefore, Santiago was an enemy. That was the only reason he gave for killing a young man whom he had never met.

Lacking any admission on the suspect's part, police had their own questionable methods of determining whether someone was affiliated with a gang. Sometimes there were gang symbols tattooed on a suspect's arms. Sometimes the circumstances of the crime—teenagers on the street in the middle of the night—suggested gang involvement. Sometimes the name was on file in one of the districts, where police kept index cards of every suspected gang member they came into contact with, even when no crime was committed. It wasn't a fair system, or a reliable one. But it was the only data base the cops or anyone else had on citywide gang membership, which was estimated to be at least fifteen thousand.

"As far as we could tell, the vic wasn't in it," the sergeant said. Santiago had not been a gang member.

This news improved the chances of getting the story into print. Many cops, and many editors, shared the conviction that young people who died in gang shootings often deserved to. There was no longer any sympathy for gang members willing to kill for the color of their clothes, or the right to sell dime bags of cocaine on a street corner.

Santiago had been an innocent bystander—or at least, a bystander. The paper would take fifteen inches on him.

■ ■ ■

Until that afternoon, "Cocho" Santiago had lived in a shingled bungalow on Francisco Avenue.

I had never been to the neighborhood, though it was no more than a mile from my apartment. That's how quickly the topography changed in Chicago, a city of ethnic diversity but limited ethnic interaction, except in a handful of restaurants.

The trees stretched over the street, shading its working-class homes and the three or four squad cars parked along the curb keeping vigil.

I climbed a few rickety steps to a gray porch and knocked. A woman finally came to the door.

"Good morning. I just heard about Leonard. I know this is a difficult time for you, but I also think this is an important story."

I blurted the words out in a near fit without expecting them to register. Wearing a loose-fitting shirt that exposed her fleshy stomach, the heavyset woman unlocked the door, looked me over, and walked outside. Through the basement window I could hear barking and the wild patter of a large dog.

The woman said her name was Diane Ortiz.

"I'm Cocho's aunt," she said, lighting a cigarette.

There were rules I tried to follow when talking to dead people's relatives. They had no good reason to answer my questions.

I had done some interrogations like this before I got to the Cop Shop, when I worked the city desk on weekends and crime was the only news happening. And before that, at home, with parents who had survived the Holocaust. The only way to hear their stories was to ask in the bluntest way. Once, to my father: "What happened to your parents?"

He was sitting at the dinner table, three or four cigarettes ground into an ashtray in front of him, a long day over his shoulder.

"When we got to the camp, we got in line with everybody else, and my mother told me to go to the other line. I saw them walk away, and I didn't see them after that. Three days later a man said to me: 'See that smoke? That smoke is your parents.' "

He squeezed the seltzer bottle into his glass, drank it, and belched halfway down.

I just got used to asking.

The rules were:

Walk to the front door slowly but confidently.

Be firm but polite.

Be sure there are no large dogs.

In the beginning, pretend you are a cop. Walk like a cop, hips weighted down as though slinging a gun. Keep your notebook hidden. This, ideally, will get you an introduction.

Then stop being a cop. Be curious about everything.

"He was a good kid, a normal kid," Diane Ortiz said.

How come they were always decent kids, the cops would mock, always pictured in their graduation caps, tassels falling into their eyes?

"Cocho and his brother, Gus, lived here since the fall," Ortiz explained, her voice cracking from tears and nicotine. "They came from the Bronx to get away from New York. I would yell at them, 'You have to tell us where you're going. You have to tell us when you're coming back.' They didn't like it at first, but they listened. Mainly they stayed on the block."

The door swung open again. Gus stepped onto the porch, gripping its wooden railing. He stood in a T-shirt and jeans, his hard eyes staring down the block toward the barren schoolyard where his brother fell bleeding.

They had been playing softball that night, the seventeen-year-old said. Another kid rode up on his bicycle, started calling them names.

"When we were over at the courts, the kid came over and took out a piece."

In Cocho's room, a mound of clothes was piled up on one end of his bed. The dresser drawers were pulled out. Standing there was like listening to one of those tapes with subliminal messages, a badgering voice repeating the obvious, that he had been flesh and blood and was killed for no good reason. And when the echo stopped, I was silent.

You keep your posture straight. You look for telling detail. You try not to let it get to you.

There was a baseball bat leaning on the wall. And on the dresser some letters from a private school, the Blair Academy in New Jersey, where Cocho had been a fine student.

You get used to long pauses.

■ ■ ■

It felt good to get back outside.

Ortiz held cigarette smoke in her lungs until the angry words blurted out. "I want out. I want out of here."

The next stop for her was going to be the suburbs, she promised.

"It seemed okay here for a while. And then this. Oh, I hate it."

Gus too was making promises.

He planned to join a gang. "To do what they did."

■ ■ ■

After he was convicted of Santiago's murder, Luis Ortiz called me from Menard Correctional Center in southern Illinois, where he was serving part of his twenty-five-year sentence. At the time he was in solitary confinement, "the hole," as punishment for fighting with other prisoners.

Shooting Santiago, he said, "was, like, an act of revenge" for all the times he had ridden on his bike and gotten beaten up near that same schoolyard.

"It was, like, a reaction," he said. "I wasn't intending to kill anyone. I just wanted to scare him."

The gun he used cost "not even $80," a fraction of the $500 he said he had been making every two or three days from selling coke and reefer in Humboldt Park during the glory days of a fourteen-year-old gangster.

"It was exciting," he said, the shouts of inmates and prison guards in the background, nagging at him to get off the phone. "Fun with the fast crowd."

"I've learned a lot about life and how I messed up. If I had the chance to apologize to his family, I would."

Then, abruptly, he hung up.

■ ■ ■

The afternoon Cocho was killed, Superintendent LeRoy Martin named the new head of the gang crimes unit: Sollie Vincent, a fast-talking captain who wore a beret and carried a mahogany walking stick.

The announcement was made in a short written statement distributed in the press room. Henry kept a stack of these promotion announcements pinned to the wall, the older yellowed pages going back a decade.

Head of the gang crimes unit was considered an extremely important job since it entailed gritty street work—"enforcement" was the euphemism—and community relations. The carrot and stick.

I went up to the twelfth floor to introduce myself to the new commander.

Sitting behind a long metal desk, Vincent hardly looked like a public relations specialist. He scooped a pack of cigarettes from atop a pile of papers, rapped one against his hard palm, and lit it with a gold-plated lighter. He leaned back in his chair, blowing perfect smoke rings at the ceiling, his big arm across the desk, reaching again for the cigarettes out of habit and need. His tobacco-stained fingers were adorned with diamond rings. He spoke in a slow, deep voice. King Sollie. Commandant.

"Gangs are complex things," Vincent said, the first line of an onslaught of rhetoric he was cooking up as he sat there. Then, sotto voce, "Know what I'm saying?"

From the minute he took over the gang crimes office, King Sollie talked a game that no one understood. Though I never heard him speak at the daily briefings held each morning in the superintendent's office, I could imagine the surprises he pulled out of his power vocabulary.

He was one of those cops who, furnished with an office with a window and a title, felt obliged to dish out half-baked social commentary.

"How do you define a gang? Is some kid hanging out on the corner because he's got nothing better to do considered a gang member? If that is true, then I myself might have once been considered a member of a gang. Generally, gang bangers are a bunch of unfortunates, and one must never stop viewing them from that particular perspective. I began asking myself, What are the options? What are the alternatives? Generally I have to concern myself with suppression methods. It's a matter of keeping your finger pushed in the dike."

King Sollie's problem, and the city's, was that the dike was bursting.

A map on the wall in his office was pocked with red and black dots—red for shootings, black for killings—densely clustered in a dozen or so neighborhoods. By the official count there had been only forty or so gang-related (the phrase just rolled off the tongue after a while) murders that year. Everyone knew the official tally was a joke, and whenever we referred to it in the newspaper we'd run a qualifier: "The actual number of gang-related murders is considered to be dramatically higher. . . ."

The Chicago Police Department was able to keep the official number of gang murders low by refusing to classify a homicide as gang-related unless it resulted from "organized gang activity." Although Cocho's murder was considered gang-related, many others like it were not.

Most of the hundreds of young killers in Chicago were affiliated with gangs, however. Some were official members who were tattooed with upside-down pitchforks or Stars of

David, and who kept guns in their pants and eagerly looked for rivals to fire them at. Others were former members never fully out of the gang's orbit, caught on the fringes as wise old consultants to a new generation of apprentices.

And no one, not the cops, nor the politicians, nor the press, knew what to do to slow down the rise in the number of killings.

King Sollie smiled a broad, confident smile, as though between his teeth he hid a secret plan. He looked as if he was about to say "We'll incinerate them," which would at least have been decipherable. Instead he gassed on.

"There are more kids out there with guns than there are police officers. We've got to develop some tactics to implement at this stage of the game. My people are on the case. We got to come up with something. We will. Oh yes, we will."

■ ■ ■

Chicago had been a gang town since the 1920s, when its tough reputation was forged by Alphonse Capone and a thousand hoods of lesser note.

Capone won control of the bootleg liquor market by pumping lead and breaking heads. At the height of his power, every two-cent beer tap in the city either belonged to him or was run at his behest. He owned cops, judges, jailers, politicians, and of course a newspaper reporter or two.

Jake Lingle, a *Tribune* police reporter, wore a diamond-studded belt buckle Capone had given to him as a gift. Lingle was gunned down in an underpass at Randolph Street and Michigan Avenue because, some historians have argued, of either unpaid gambling debts or an attempt to use his clout within the police department to strongarm factions of the mob.

These days the gang wars were fought over drugs. And both the soldiers and the victims were the underclass. There were still traces of fifties-style basement-IQ gang bravado in Chicago. But even the dumbest cops could recite what was becoming a sociological cliché: "How can we expect them to stay away from making $500 a day selling dope when they can only make $3.50 an hour washing dishes?" No one had an answer.

The Rukns, who made more money than any of the others, had started as a politically active black youth club in the Woodlawn neighborhood, just south of the placid University of Chicago campus. Members served free lunches to the poor and won government backing for community programs. But under the leadership of Jeff Fort, a charismatic Mississippi-born, South Side–bred hustler, the youth club was transformed into a crime syndicate that financed itself through extortion and drug dealing.

The Rukns, who killed primarily over drugs, and members of hundreds of other gangs, who were learning to, were all climbing the peak first scaled by Capone. Shooters called themselves Nitti, after Frank Nitti, Capone's loyal assassin, or Bugsy, after Benjamin "Bugsy" Siegal, or Tony Montana. And running with them were kids like Luis Ortiz with guns in their pants.

■ ■ ■

That first week, a cop from the weapons lab across the hall handed me an envelope for Wattley. Inside were copies of an old photograph of the St. Valentine's Day Massacre, an epic composition of seven men in wool trench coats spread out like dead seals in gabardine on the floor of a North Side garage. A sea of inky blood covered the cement floor.

Another photo showed a hooded man strapped into an electric chair.

I placed the pictures in the desk drawer, planning to turn them over to Wattley when he visited. They lay there as silent testimony to a truism held by cops, especially those on the gang beat: In the end, if the state doesn't get you, your enemies will. And the cops would only applaud; they knew how elusive the state's justice was.

The cops considered themselves protectors, hard workers, and occasionally noble ones. They had endured a public relations setback in 1968 at the Democratic National Convention, when, under the orders of Mayor Richard J. Daley, they launched a riot of their own to bust up a Yippie protest in Lincoln Park. Heads were cracked open with batons and ax handles. For years, even law-and-order hardliners found it difficult to be enthusiastic about the Chicago police and their tactics.

Yet by the time I first walked into police headquarters at Eleventh and State, the tide had turned again. Cops were in. The digressions and ugliness of 1968 were all but forgotten. Exactly two decades later, police had become made-for-television movie heroes, portrayed in prime time as fearless soldiers fighting a war in which they were clearly the underdogs.

■ ■ ■

King Sollie granted my request to spend a Friday night with two gang crimes officers named John Howe and Clyde Raymond during their rounds in Humboldt Park.

The three of us climbed into an unmarked navy blue Crown Victoria whose long seats had ripped upholstery. I stretched out in the back.

Raymond, a powerfully built black man in his thirties, drove. Howe was slimmer, a halfback compared to Raymond, about forty years old, with deliberate eyes that had led him through the jungles of Vietnam and now through dark intersections on the West Side.

They were quiet cops who earned their pay. They knew their enemies, remembered their names and the names of their brothers and sisters. They watched Hectors and Julios grow up in Humboldt Park or West Town, drop out of school, get initiated into stealing and killing, go to jail, come out, die or rot on the street. They said little to each other, except for occasional meditations about good hamburgers and days off spent on fishing trips in Wisconsin. A lot of cops had a thing for fishing.

The first stop that evening was a Laundromat that had just been robbed. By the time we pulled up, half a dozen cops were already there looking for the suspect, a Cuban named Lario.

We were on our way to a fleabag motel to find Lario when, at about six, a call of "shots fired" on Wolcott Avenue was broadcast over the police radio.

We sped toward the address through an increasingly gentrified neighborhood about half a mile from my apartment. At intersections Howe scanned the cross streets without twisting his neck more than an inch, whispering "clear" before we charged through, the big engine of the Crown Victoria making that determined carbureted *whoosh*. The headlights flashed on and off in the manner unmarked cars announced themselves.

As we turned onto Wolcott, the commotion was just ahead of us. Raymond rammed the car up onto the sidewalk.

The body of the young man was face down, a patch of jeans and a sheet of skin flapping over the back of his thigh. A pool of fresh blood spread beneath him, another victim of an act of vengeance.

None of the cops cheered, but none of them looked very worried either.

I walked to where the victim was lying, his torso on the grass, his lower half slumped over the curb and into the gutter. I had thought the blood would be Swiss-army-knife red, but it was much darker, an arterial purple.

Around me, the cops jotted down names on small pads of paper, looked around for people they recognized, and shopped for witnesses. "Yo, homey, come here a second. There's something I got to ask you. Yeah, you. Come here. You in it?"

The pillars of journalism—who, what, when, where— calmed me as the paramedics lifted the man's limp body onto a long inflatable tube so the blood wouldn't pour out.

In a swift motion, they loaded him into the back of an ambulance.

Raymond walked to the ambulance door. Reaching into the victim's pants pocket and using his thumb and index fingers like a delicate tong, he removed a driver's license. When Raymond looked at his hand, there was blood on his fingers.

"If you get that blood on you, it dries quick," Raymond shouted in disgust. "But if you got a cut, you got a problem."

For the moment, AIDS worried him more than bullets.

Neighbors crowded on rickety porches to see the familiar scene: the unmarked cars pulling onto the sidewalks, the slamming of doors, one, then another, the unfastening of holsters, big metal cop flashlights poised for home-run swings.

Racing around in blue windbreakers, walkie-talkies close to their mouths, were city employees of the Chicago Intervention Network, whose job it was to make friends with gang members and intercede with tough love and advice. It was no secret in police circles that some of these counselors had kept their gang ties.

The witnesses and witnesses-to-be talked about the shooting as though it was a scene from a kung fu movie.

". . . shot him in the ass. *Pow pow pow* . . ."

"Hey, go talk about it somewhere else," Howe yelled at a group of people gathered around the ambulance. It was important not to let them congregate and get their stories worked out. Before you knew it there would be a dozen witnesses describing the same Jaguar that was never there.

The cops sifted through the crowd, asking questions and getting some answers.

The victim had been shot by two or three people as he walked toward a gold Buick they were hiding behind. They opened fire when he got within a few feet, leaving the victim and the car bullet-riddled heaps.

Howe and Raymond studied the constellation of nickel-size holes curled along the car door like the Big Dipper.

Only automatics made such picturesque designs; here one had forged a connect-the-dots pattern on the driver's side. The license plate was registered to someone at Cabrini-Green.

For my benefit, they repeated the obvious. Another Friday night, another gang shooting. This guy was lucky because he just got his rear blown off. What had he done? What they all do. They point three fingers up to the heavens or two down to the ground, outlining a pitchfork or some other gang sign, or scream "Kings suck" or "D's die." Then the guns come out.

The cops didn't come up with the names of any suspects, but from the crowd, they had learned that the victim was a Vice Lord, the suspects Disciples.

There were dozens of gangs in the city that called themselves Vice Lords. On the West Side they controlled a good portion of the dope trade. And where they didn't, they fought for it against Disciples, Latin Kings, Spanish Cobras, Rukns, and half a dozen other gangs. That summer they were fighting with the guns they had stolen from a railroad car.

The logical place to look for the suspects was at Cabrini-Green, the sprawling public housing project just a few blocks from some of the priciest real estate in the city. The Disciples ruled about half the buildings in the project.

"They don't get caught in five minutes and they think they've committed the perfect crime," Howe said.

We got back into the Crown Victoria and headed for Cabrini, about two miles directly east. Raymond stopped the car in front of a grocery on Division Street. He ran inside and stood at a metal sink in the back room, washing his hands with fierce determination.

■ ■ ■

Cabrini, "the Green," was cut off from everything around it. On its western border was a highway ramp that swept past the high rises. On the east were culs-de-sac that impeded the flow of foot traffic from Cabrini into the Gold Coast and toward Lake Michigan, whose shores were just half a mile away.

To the south were the remains of Chicago's heavy industry, salt plants and steel forgers, along the grimy north branch of the Chicago River. And just to the north of Cabrini was Yuppie City, the windowless rear walls of its upscale condominiums nearly backing up to the project.

When it was built in the 1950s, Cabrini, like a dozen other public housing complexes in Chicago, held the promise of decent, affordable living. The buildings, each as tall as fourteen stories, were Spartan but clean. They were separated by green lawns and playgrounds. Families gathered outside at night during the warm months. The residents were working-class people of many races and colors. They managed to get along.

But those who could afford to soon moved out, leaving behind the very poor, and a fractured dream that took only a few more years to come apart completely. By the mid-1960s, poverty and despair had filled the high rises to capacity. There was no effective security in the buildings, and gangs and violence flourished. In 1971, two police officers were killed by snipers as they crossed an open field between the buildings. The cops who came to retrieve their bodies were pinned down by gunfire.

After that, the city took its revenge through neglect. The housing project deteriorated further, until 1981, when Mayor Jane Byrne, in a desperate attempt to salvage her political fortunes, moved into an apartment there, accompanied by hundreds of Chicago policemen. She stayed on and off for a few weeks. In her diary she kept a count of the number of cockroaches she and her husband squashed. She talked with residents, taking down their complaints, promising to help. Spirits were momentarily renewed. But when Byrne gave up and moved back to her plush apartment, less than a mile away, the killing continued.

The victims were almost exclusively Cabrini residents:

the elderly on the way home from the store, the young on the way to school. And that was fine with the rest of the city, as long as it didn't spill into neighborhoods like Mayor Byrne's. By and large, it didn't.

By the late 1980s, the Green was only half occupied. The Chicago Housing Authority sealed off apartments as they were vacated, seemingly preparing for the day when the project could be torn down to make room for the expansion of Yuppie City. But often gangs would break through the walls, taking over the closed-off apartments and converting them into safe houses and drug warehouses.

The gangs controlled most everything at Cabrini. Some buildings were ruled by Disciples, almost all the rest by Vice Lords and Cobra Stones. Residents put up with this arrangement because they had no choice. Shootings were a nightly event. Children slept on the floor to stay out of the line of fire. Drugs were sold openly in the unguarded breezeways. In this environment, the tenants of Cabrini endured more than forty violent crimes per thousand residents per year, nearly twice the city average.

■ ■ ■

As we approached the project, the only light came from its perimeter, where yellow sodium bulbs glared hazily in the humid night. There were no streets leading to the buildings and parking lots inside, only alleys, and short cuts known to drug runners and police.

Raymond jumped a curb, cut toward an alley, and drove into the heart of the Green, rolling to a stop in a parking lot. A fire burned in a trash can. Mothers held their kids close by. And teenagers in gang colors stepped fast. It looked like a township in South Africa, only without the open, dusty space.

"Hey, homey. Where you get that jacket?" Howe summoned a kid wearing a black and purple windbreaker. Disciple colors.

36

"It was the last one left in the store," he answered softly.

"You may not be a D, but you're going to get shot wearing that," Howe lectured him.

Another group of cops drove into the project, led by a lieutenant they called Crazy Eddie. He was a tall guy, over six feet, with a stern marine haircut.

With a vague description of the getaway car, two or three Crown Victorias drove around the parking lots checking license plates on a computer, checking inside the cars, carefully looking over anyone in black and purple clothing.

Some of the residents recognized the cops and said hello. For the moment, no one had anything to say about the shooting.

There was no panic visible in any of the cops or any of the people they questioned. It was routine for everyone involved, except me.

After about an hour we left. Crazy Eddie and his crew stayed, stopping cars, asking more questions. The shooters were nowhere to be found that night, or any other.

Driving out of Cabrini, we crossed the north branch of the river on a steel bridge about a hundred yards to the west of the housing project. Just like that, we escaped its oppressive heat and sadness and were speeding toward the West Side.

The gold Buick was still in the middle of Wolcott Avenue, only now it was ablaze—a gang ritual, as Howe explained. "They do it every time."

Though I hadn't noticed it earlier, down the block was another car, this one already burned to a blackened shell.

From Wolcott we went directly to Humboldt Park, where the air was alive with salsa music and the smell of burritos.

Humboldt Park was very different from Cabrini-Green, but the problems were similar. There were some beautiful homes near the park itself, but for the most part the Puerto Rican neighborhood was racked by unemployment, drugs, broken lives. No block seemed untouched by the violence that Howe and Raymond knew inside out.

"Mario lived there," Howe said, pointing out a dilapidated house. "He was killed, and so was his brother. Bought it. There were thirty people watching." There was a touch of compassion in his voice that lasted for a moment. Then it was gone.

"Bruno got killed right here. His brother, Jose, killed two people by the driveway. . . . They mark the day every year. May 18 . . . Over there, in the park, a kid named Ortiz was talking, calling signs. Two guys go past the baseball backstop and pop him twice. Then they go around and shoot him again. That was retaliation for a Cobra killed. There's one on every block here." And so it went, murder for retaliation, murder for fun, murder for nothing.

Lookouts whistled as we drove past, making sure everyone knew the cops had arrived. Dealers quickly hid their dope in lead pipes and soda cans, then took off, running.

Howe looked out the window at a scene he had witnessed so many nights that the memories blended together, the years, like his compassion, evaporating before his eyes. The dark streets invited trouble. That would be a good place to start to change things—light. But that wasn't his job. His job was shoring up the dike. That was the best he could do.

His eyes skipped around the street, looking for action. His gaze was met by the glares of budding experts, some younger than ten and on bicycles, who were learning to outwit him, outrun him, lie to him, get one over on him. But in the end, they were trading on stolen time.

"They'll all be dead soon," he said.

T H R E E

...

BARRICADE

A member of a specially trained Chicago police unit was shot in the head and critically wounded Thursday. . . .
July 15, 1988

O n a clear, hot day, the sheriff came calling on Tommie Lee Hudson.

Hudson hadn't paid his mortgage in four years, and now a Cook County sheriff's deputy, along with a few burly movers, were going to force the ex-cop out of his two-story brick house on Stony Island Avenue, a wide, neon-lit boulevard that cut through the South Side.

But Hudson felt strongly about the house, had an attachment to it that went beyond the deputy's hard logic. He had been evicted before, in 1986, but he moved back in. And that's where he stayed, assembling an eclectic arsenal—a .22 Magnum Derringer, a Sheridan air rifle, a replica of an Italian cap-and-ball revolver, a hunting bow and arrows, and three homemade bombs.

When the deputies burst through the front door with a sledgehammer, Hudson steadily raised the Derringer in their direction and let go with three loud blasts. The would-be evictors scurried down the front stairs to a crawl space beneath the rotting porch, where they frantically radioed for help. One of them had been grazed by a bullet.

The faint wail of sirens grew louder and clearer, and by the time the squad cars pulled up, Hudson had decided he was going nowhere.

The siege of Stony Island had begun.

■ ■ ■

Dispatchers spoke a vocabulary of "situations." There were racial situations, drug-related situations, domestic situations, and implication-type situations. By 11:00 A.M., what we had going on Stony Island Avenue, in the dispatcher's inimitable cadence, was a "barricade situation."

"Forty-nine Edward, go ahead." Forty-nine Edward was the heavy weapons van.

"Forty-nine Edward to the barricade."

A barricade sparked a fixed police response. Members of the hostage barricade team, which included about fifty cops assigned to various unrelated units all over the city, were summoned to Stony Island over the police radio. They trained at the Great Lakes Naval Academy in "containment and assault" every month or so for situations like this one. At the scene, they would establish a perimeter so there could be no escape, choose surveillance sites, and set up a control center. Most of the time, waiting resolved the problem, and the barricade simply fizzled out.

In case it didn't, Forty-nine Edward had everything needed to wage a small-scale war: grenades, bullets, body armor, tear gas, bullhorns, and a couple of cheap, hand-built periscopes with which to peek around corners.

When the barricade dispatch sounded in the press room, the automatic dialers swung into action, calling the Gresham police district every sixty seconds or so to repeat the same questions. "Are there any hostages? . . . Is anyone wounded? . . . Does he have a gun?"

Breaking news stories had this effect on young reporters, quickly transforming them into gorillas who communicated in wild, simplistic news-speak. The City News system of police reporting, which espoused the maxim "If your mother tells you she loves you, check it out," relied on the sheer volume of questions. Its employees, typically fresh college graduates anywhere from curious to mad about journalism, were even lower on the career ladder than I was, most overtly in their paychecks. As a reporter for a large metropolitan daily, I earned a decent salary, at the time in the forties. City News reporters earned half that, and they never saw their bylines in print. If I ever felt sorry for myself, I had to look no farther than the next desk for consolation. They filed copy by phone to a rewrite person in the central office, who then sent it by computer to a list of subscribers that included every major news organization in the city. Their stories often were recited verbatim on the evening news and appeared in print beneath other reporters' bylines.

To a large extent, they were the unheralded backbone of Chicago journalism. City News was every editor's tip sheet, without which many would have no idea what stories to assign. With City News, stories rolled by on computer screens all day. The most basic police stories were usually slugged "Jonesdead" or "Simsdead," "Threeshot," and the like. An editor would glance at the screen's contents and, because it cost nothing to cover himself just in case news broke out, instantly call the beat reporter to check it.

As long as I was in the press room sitting next to the City News reporter, I knew exactly which copy was moving from Eleventh and State. He consulted the Sheet on the sixth floor just as I did. He listened to the same police radio. So when an editor called I could say, "I know all about it."

If you wanted to appear competent and in control, you called the home office while the City News reporter was still gathering information, preempting his dispatch by at least fifteen or twenty minutes, which was my strategy that morning. In the old days, fifteen or twenty minutes could be the difference between making a deadline and blowing it. Now it was simply a matter of image.

"Listen, there's a barricade on Stony Island. I'm looking into it. Call you back."

Casey, of course, was annoyed by the distraction. Unless someone had been killed, a barricade was of minor significance. Usually it resulted from a domestic disturbance, a husband angry at his wife, or vice versa, yet it was only another cheap crime, one of the cheapest. That was the calm assessment of an elder statesman three decades into the business.

If Chicago were a tabloid town, like New York, a barricade would have been big news no matter what the outcome: cops in riot gear, tense standoff, weary neighbors. But Chicago was not New York. For the two surviving newspapers, a sense of decorum unknown in New York guided how and when crime was reported. This was the product more of the operation of basic market forces than of sensitivity training.

Although Rupert Murdoch and his protégés had given Chicago a taste of *New York Post*-style screaming headlines— HEADLESS NUN SHOOTS PRIEST, that type of eye-grabber—tabloid journalism never quite caught on. A restrained tone guided news coverage in Chicago for fear of alienating readers with countless stories of heinous crimes.

By the time I started at the Cop Shop, the crime stories that attracted the most attention occurred beyond the city's borders. When a seven-year-old girl from the suburb of Midlothian disappeared and then turned up murdered, the crime stayed in the news for months.

A man barricading himself in an inner-city house was not a story unless someone was wounded. Rapes were not stories unless there were at least ten rapists, or half a dozen victims, or the victim had been out with her husband, quietly fishing for perch in the Lincoln Park lagoon, or the assault took place in a crowded train station during rush hour. Even then a rape story got as much play in the papers as, say, a non-playoff high school baseball game.

Fires were not stories unless there were at least three people killed. Then you could expect about five column inches per victim. Murders were noteworthy if the victim lived in a nice part of town, had escaped the housing projects only to be offed in the wild crossfire of drug dealers, had gone to a prestigious prep school, was an ex-marine back in the South Side for a visit, was shot by police, or maybe was dunked in hot water by his mother's boyfriend. Otherwise they were condensed to briefs and forgotten.

Stories bigger than box scores paid homage to the innocent because innocence upbraided, rooted out, burned in hot water, or shot up by mistake made better copy. This was no secret. We took down names, sketched life stories, re-created the moment of impact.

The old-time newsmen recited stories from Eleventh and State by rote, without emotion, dictating into the phone and punctuating with worn-out humor. Their spirits were occasionally renewed when either crooks or law enforcers got their comeuppance—like the time a burglar got stuck in an air shaft and froze to death, or a prison escape was carried out with a gun carved from soap, like Dillinger's 1934 breakout from an Indiana jail. Also, lost or injured sex organs gave them a jolt. Otherwise they were bricks. If you weren't careful, the same sour fate beckoned.

■ ■ ■

When word came from Stony Island, Casey shifted the metal police radio on his desk, making sure the antennas were pulled all the way out, then lit up a cigarette and waited for the barricade to go away.

The word "dinosaur," which Casey had cut out of a paper, was glued to his desk. But the word didn't describe him at all—it wasn't even close. He was still capable of deconstructing a police story with the precision of a surgeon, until he understood exactly what had happened. When he was interested in a case, his mind zeroed in, methodically questioning detectives, witnesses, victims until the facts emerged with clarity and truth. Casey bagged every relevant piece of information on the first try. If an editor called him, wanting to fill in some gap in the story, Casey usually had the answer right there in his head. He could do the job with his eyes closed.

But he needed a lot to get interested. The case couldn't be straight-ahead and simple. Almost every story I chased my first couple of months he considered cheap. Drug dealers deserved what they got. And gangsters. And teenagers who were out on the street too late. Even cops when they were dirty or crazy.

On this blazing afternoon, Stony Island Avenue showed hardly any potential.

■ ■ ■

By noon, the SWAT-style barricade team had surrounded the house. Negotiators were attempting to talk Hudson out of what had become a serious predicament.

Their objective, as almost always in these negotiations, was to leave him enough dignity to walk out the door without thinking it necessary to kill anyone, including himself. The strategy was similar to Henry Kissinger's approach to diplomacy; if no one feels like a mule, the chances for compromise are dramatically improved.

Cops assured Hudson over scratchy bullhorns that they understood the horrible forces that led men to desperate acts like this. Everything would be all right if he came out with his hands up; no one would get hurt.

But Hudson did not respond. His apartment remained quiet and dark. The shades on the windows, two poster-size ones in front and three in the rear, were drawn. The electricity inside had been turned off that day. He had no phone.

There wasn't much to do in the press room. The criss-cross directory, a thick book that listed telephone numbers by address, was of little help. Hudson's neighbors were all outside, watching. The cops were all at the scene. The only way to get information was to go there.

I switched off the police radios and shut the drawers, twirling the locks clockwise two or three times. Casey heard me packing up and asked where I was going. When I told him, he laughed and said to have a good time.

■ ■ ■

Having a press card at a crime scene makes you feel anointed. Mine got me through the sawhorses and yellow tape strung across the street like velvet rope about two blocks from Hudson's house.

I parked my car along Stony Island. I could see Hudson's house, its brown wooden porch hidden behind a healthy-looking tree, and wondered how close I could get. The street was closed off directly in front of the house. The best vantage point appeared to be just beyond it, so I walked around the block to get there.

Marksmen paced the rooftops of the houses next to Hudson's and of the modern glass and steel Volkswagen dealership across the street. Forty-nine Edward sat in a parking lot at the corner. A few yards away, in the shiny waiting area of a Midas muffler shop, a group of reporters milled around a pay phone, each apprising his office of the precarious quiet.

There was no yelling, no hysteria, no extraneous movement; just the occasional hiss and click of police radios. Cops tossed pebbles at Hudson's windows to attract his attention, but he didn't respond. They waited quietly for him to surrender. They had spent the entire morning waiting. That was the strategy. Nine times out of ten it worked.

■ ■ ■

By noon it was 98 degrees, and Hudson was deciding how to handle all the attention he was now getting. He certainly hadn't gotten much before.

Shortly after leaving the police department in 1971 he had had a breakdown. An ex-girlfriend contacted by police said he had not been "in his right mind."

He collected guns. But all the guns were registered, and when relatives told his fellow cops about the collection, the police said there was no legal recourse unless Hudson hurt someone. Sure, he had killed a couple of dogs, and the cops knew about it; but that wasn't enough to put him away.

Now Hudson was doing his best to prove that he was certifiably dangerous.

I phoned the *Tribune*'s city desk. The Grump answered.

Although only in his mid-thirties, the Grump was thoroughly old school.

"Who told you to go there?" he asked.

"The morning crew."

"For your information, we are not in the habit of covering barricades." He said this in a low drawl of a voice. "If I were you, I'd head back to Eleventh and State."

He gave off a little snort and hung up without another word, one of his charming trademarks. A police reporter's place was in the bureau, at the desk, talking to cops about what the cops had seen. That the news flowing back to police headquarters from cops at the scene was one-dimensional, misleading, and in most cases out of synch with what actually occurred didn't matter to the Grump. I was to go back there, he had ordered. Although I had a two-way radio, a portable police scanner, and a pager, my mobility was expected to be limited. The police reporter's job was primarily to babysit the nonportable radios. Angry, I surrendered to higher authority and drove back to headquarters.

On these summer days the press room, about the size of a second-grade classroom, was a torture chamber. The air conditioner was broken, and with the sun beating hard on the eastern wall of the building, the temperature inside would soar to over 110 degrees. A lone swimmer was splashing in the pool across State Street.

The heat never seemed to bother Casey. When I took my seat, he just looked at me. He wiped his forehead with a white handkerchief that was still neatly folded.

"You're back," he said. Then he made a sound, *"Yuuuu-huuh,"* a noise beyond clearing his throat, and closer to a yelp of superior wisdom. He was still more interested in his toy soldier collection than in Tommie Lee Hudson.

"What are you spinning your wheels on now?" he asked, as he did almost every day when I started.

■ ■ ■

Barbara Gooley, Hudson's sister, turned on the afternoon news. Her brother was the lead story. Half in shock, she called her father, then rushed to Stony Island.

At the scene, she stopped a few police officers and told them why she was there. "He's my brother," she said quietly. They instructed her to wait in a squad car. As a precaution they locked her inside, just in case she tried to run toward the barricade, which sometimes happened.

Gooley hadn't realized how far gone her brother was. He had been telling her the IRS was after the family, that agents were tapping the phones and would soon come to get Gooley at her job in the post office.

Staring out the squad car windows, watching the frantic coming and going of police officers, Gooley remembered that her brother had been one of them. He had walked the

47

beat in the Filmore district on the West Side. When he left the department he was suffering from dizziness and nose bleeds. Hudson told his family the condition started after a bullet fired by his partner at a wild dog ricocheted and grazed his head. He moved to Arizona, then Colorado, to live with relatives, but the pain would not go away. He returned to Chicago, where his sister tried to get him help, but he wasn't interested. Finally, she said, the family gave up.

■ ■ ■

In the alley behind the house, members of the hostage barricade team kept a close eye on Hudson's rear windows, but they hadn't seen him all day.

One of the cops assigned to the rear of the house was a seven-year veteran, Bernard Domagala. He had been eating sausage and eggs that morning at a diner on Archer and Pulaski when the call for the hostage barricade team was broadcast. When he got to the scene, Domagala staked out a spot behind a garage so he could poke his head out every few minutes to look for Hudson.

Domagala had spent the afternoon on Stony Island baking in the hot sun a few yards from his partner, who took a position inside the garage. The only break in the day came when Domagala commandeered a juice jar from his supervisor and filled it with lemonade at a Salvation Army truck. He shared it with his partner.

Earlier in the day, Domagala had requested one of the makeshift periscopes kept in Forty-nine Edward so he could peer around the corner of the garage without sticking his head out. The periscope never made it to the alley. So Domagala scanned the porch with his eyes, first sticking the barrel of his pump-action shotgun past the garage wall and following it with a quick protrusion of his head. Barrel, head. Barrel, head. Barrel, head.

At about 4:00 P.M., the moment his gun protruded a fourth time, witnesses said, a loud crack echoed through the alley.

In the press room, the police radio picked up again, the dispatcher's voice lifting from the drone, this time more ominously. Four floors beneath us, a veteran dispatcher who worked at a control panel, McGreevey, I thought, was desperately seeking information instead of belting it out over the radio. His authoritative brogue instantly turned the press room into a drama I was starting to recognize, in which we all had parts out of the movies and stories moved along a perfect bell curve, beginning, middle, end. He was the first line of defense, trumpeting the march of the doughnut army as its soldiers tore ass into the many horrible endings they had dreamt.

"We've got an officer down," McGreevey said.

The phrase "officer down" was a Condition Red that sent the press room into unparalleled frenzy. It busted the routine. This was true not only in the press room but also in the street, where you could feel the heightened state of affairs, the cops unleashed, their standards shifting to meet the affront, even in the minds and fists of the smart, restrained ones.

We cast off for facts. The automatic dialing machine went into convulsions.

Hudson, who had spent the better part of the day running up and down the stairs of his house, finally communicated by firing a single gunshot from his cap-and-ball revolver. The marble-size lead ball hit Domagala near the middle of his forehead, close to his right eye. The lead stretched on impact into a dart-shaped piece of shrapnel, ricocheted off the right side of his skull, and traveled around the inner circumference, taking with it shards of brain tissue, until it lodged in the base of his skull.

An ambulance backed into the alley to get him. On the way to the hospital he talked about the color of his shoes (black) and his socks (black) and his clothes and his family and everything but getting shot.

As this was communicated over the radios I thought, yes, it was time to call the Grump. In the most controlled voice I could muster, I told him the news.

"Oh, shit. You better get back down there," he said.

When I left, Casey was hunched over the phone talking politely but intensely to police friends who would quickly bring him up to speed on the events of the afternoon.

■ ■ ■

The mood on Stony Island Avenue had changed. I parked on a residential street a few blocks away and ran toward the barricaded house.

By this time the press had gathered at a Bureau of Sanitation office on Seventy-third Street, just off the avenue. I stood at the top of a brick staircase that led to the office, looking into the mouth of an alley choked off by squad cars.

Hudson, police said, had been setting up on Domagala; his shot was perfectly timed with the officer's movements. It wouldn't have been hard. Inside the apartment, Hudson had turned a kitchen table on its side and wedged it against the door, covering its edge with a bath towel. He steadied his arm on the table as he shot through a tear in the window shade. All Hudson had to do was watch for the shotgun barrel; Domagala was sure to follow an instant later.

Barbara Gooley never made it out of the squad car. She sat there, locked inside, when her brother fired the shot. An officer came by a few minutes later. "The officer who was shot was my friend," he told her.

The police brass pulled into the alley, churning up a cloud of dust. They climbed out of their cars and stood in a semicircle about a hundred feet away from us.

Superintendent Martin was in civilian dress, his shirt collar jutting over the wide lapels of a sport jacket bought from the same West Side tailor he had been going to for thirty years.

He walked toward the reporters, stood behind a saw horse, and said to a group of advisers, "I want to get this thing done by nightfall."

Then he walked back to the circle of boss warriors conferring near the alley. They all appeared remarkably calm.

"What's doing, Bobby?" the chief of detectives, Ed Wodnicki, said as he lumbered toward me in his Neanderthal gait.

Wodnicki reminded me of a teacher in my high school, Rabbi Meir, a short man, maybe five-six, with a prominent gold tooth, who, in a feat of strength and balance, could squat all the way to the floor on one leg while the other pointed forward like a ballerina's. Born in Romania, Rabbi Meir had seen his father shot in the town square during World War II. Because of this, no doubt, he had a tough exterior, crazed at times, even with his students. It was not beyond him to grab a kid who wasn't paying attention to his lectures on the Old Testament by the neck, call him a donkey, and toss him out of the classroom. But on the inside, the rabbi was more cunning. He knew he couldn't rely on brute strength alone; he understood that there would always be someone tougher than he.

It was the same with Wodnicki. On the surface, he was the toughest cop. His arms pushed outward from his swollen lats. He had a round face and a big Grabowski head. But there was something human about him that evening, some pity showing that you wouldn't under the circumstances expect.

"We think the motherfucker may have a gas mask," Wodnicki told me.

Years ago, a tip like that could make a reporter's night. Jimmy Olson calls the city desk and dictates a new lead for the next edition: POLICE SUSPECT CRAZED GUNMAN HAS GAS MASK. But now, deadlines popped up only once, at about 9:30 P.M., and information had to be squirreled away for the big picture.

Standing near Wodnicki was King Sollie, wearing his beret. Domagala was assigned to King Sollie's gang unit. His regular job was taking guns away from Disciples in Englewood. He liked his work, considered it fun, and did a lot of chasing and laughing with his partner.

That Hudson had once been a cop no longer mattered to any of the police on the scene. The main thing was getting it over with; the superintendent himself had said that.

Blood had been spilled. The sun was setting. Fraternity was no longer an issue, if it ever was. The cops with the bullhorns turned them off and placed them on the ground.

A police officer in a suit walked up to the boss warriors carrying a pile of white bulletproof vests as though they were freshly washed towels. A few assistants helped the men into the body armor, the bosses lifting their arms as for a fitting and squeezing into the vests. Prepared for battle, they waddled toward it down the alley.

■ ■ ■

The first volley went off like fireworks an hour after the superintendent had spoken. Dozens of canisters of tear gas shot into Hudson's house for at least fifteen minutes straight. A white mist poured into the alley. And they kept on blasting, the canisters leaving soft white trails in their wake.

Hudson fired out of the apartment with his cap and ball but hit no one.

After twenty-five rounds of tear gas, Hudson still hadn't emerged. Had he killed himself? No one knew. So the police kept on firing.

A few minutes later, at 6:55 P.M., the front door opened on Stony Island. Hudson, a strapping man dressed in an extra large white T-shirt, hobbled onto his front porch waving a white flag. He was immediately sacked by two cops, who laid him on the ground and stuck their shotguns into the back of his neck. Then he was shoved into a police wagon and carted to the Wentworth detective area, a few miles north.

With the stinging smell of tear gas in the air, the reporters gathered around the superintendent, a public relations master who shot from the hip with astounding accuracy. He was especially convincing in breaking stories like this one, when he appeared composed but not above expressing emotion.

Martin called for better handgun control laws. He said he was "shocked and . . . dismayed," that a former police officer would shoot another member of the force. And he said that barricades should be resolved peaceably. He put it this way: "I've got a man with a bullet in his head, and the offender is in the wagon in one piece."

Domagala's partner put it another way: "The little coward motherfucker gave up."

The boss warriors got back into their cars and drove away. Only a few crime lab technicians and reporters remained, combing the alley for anything that might have been missed, perhaps another bullet shell. There was a red splotch where Bernard Domagala had fallen, forty-three feet from Hudson's rear door.

I had expected it would take longer to pack up, that someone would keep vigil. But there was no question as to what had happened, who had fired the shot. Television reporters loaded their equipment into their news vans and sped away with time to spare before the ten o'clock lead-ins. They would have riveting footage.

Martin headed for Michael Reese Hospital, where Domagala had been taken. He had been talking the whole time, saying he was okay, until they sedated him. Surgery lasted seven and a half hours, six of them to remove the lead from inside Domagala's skull. The pellet was placed in a glass medicine jar to be saved as evidence.

Meanwhile, Hudson was questioned in a small room at the Wentworth police station. Relatives waited quietly for charges to be announced, which came a few hours later: attempted murder of a police officer.

Gooley later insisted that the incident could have been avoided if only the sheriff had included a friend of Hudson's in the eviction team. She said the battle in her brother's mind was over the china and silverware left to him by his grandparents, who had raised him. They died in a car accident, and the items were all he had of theirs.

I called in the ending to the rewrite man. He wanted

to know times and addresses and how many police had been at the scene, and whether it was true that the officers threw a sledgehammer at the door. Not true, I said.

I dumped everything I had, knowing that only the barest facts would make it into the paper.

Returning to my car on the street where I had left it, I drove north on Stony Island Avenue, stopping at a nearby candy store for a cold drink. Then I took the side streets toward the expressway, in a part of town I had never seen before. It seemed almost countrified, with large trees, handsome churches, and small rib joints, greasy and inviting.

A certain powerlessness had been laid bare on Stony Island. The cops had Forty-nine Edward. They had bullhorns and bulletproof vests. They had camaraderie, and they were in the right. But by nightfall, there had still been bloodshed.

There was also anger. As a reporter, you had to try to understand it thoroughly, as though the tragedy had befallen your partner. You had thought it was going to be another typical barricade. Instead, there was a gunshot. You found out it struck your friend. You thought he was going to die. You felt your heart breaking. Again, you feared there was no justice, that Hudson would plead insanity and get off, avoid trial, stay out of jail. You swore you would kill him if you saw his face. And you cursed the bosses for not gassing the house four hours earlier, before everyone was drained by the heat.

And there was the sadness.

When Domagala awoke two days later, his head was swollen to almost twice its size, his face black and blue. When he left the hospital, he wasn't able to hold his twin babies for fear he would have a seizure and drop them. Two years later, his friends said, Domagala battled an infection caused by his wound.

Four years later, Hudson had yet to stand trial.

The story played for two days and then died. The public lost interest, and so did we.

F O U R

∎ ∎ ∎

FIRE

Fire is one thing you never forget.
Witness to a Southeast Side blaze, July 14, 1988

Hardly a week went by at the Cop Shop without a fire. Fires were tougher to get into the paper than murders, even if they were arsons that had resulted in murder. Two or three fatalities were the minimum for anything more than a brief, and the cutoff point seemed to keep getting higher. Seven was big. Two was borderline. A fire with no deaths, unless it incinerated a few city blocks, barely got mentioned.

There were big fires that vaporized warehouses, melted bicycles, sent babies out the windows; there were small ones that left families homeless. There were accidental fires caused by electrical short circuits, faulty space heaters, careless smoking, children playing with matches. There were assorted arsons, and there were fires that couldn't be explained. Fires were part of the beat, the scanners sounding all day with their locations and progress.

An editor we called the Doctor offered simple advice for when you sat down to write a fire story: "Make 'em laugh, make 'em cry." This didn't mean you had to write prose worthy of Flaubert, or even Dreiser. It meant to showcase the facts that awakened readers' greatest fears ("What if something like that happened to me?") but also gave them a glimmer of hope. A story might end, "The owner of the house looked at the rubble and said, 'Got to start all over again. But I've done that before.' "

It was ancient advice. The city editor of the *Washington Post* during the Watergate scandal once visited my college in upstate New York. At the time I was enraptured with the New Journalism and argued that there must be some way to enliven certain stories, like fire stories, which seemed to have been written according to the same formula since the beginning of time. One might tell the story from the fireman's point of view. Or from a survivor's point of view, or the ambulance driver's. The *Post* editor scowled at me, let out a disgusted sigh, and went to the next question.

There was no new way to cover a fire. There were the raw facts: the address, the time, the unpredictable route a fire traveled, the destruction, the lost lives, and in some cases, the heroism. Through decades of fire stories, the only difference was that now there was one deadline, which meant you had more time than in the past to write decent sentences.

My first was a seven. Three of the victims were children.

By the time I got there the three-story building was a husk; it now resembled the blight of the rest of the block, which had been badly burned a few times before. This was Lawndale, where fire was as common as nighttime.

The trees were blackened. Bicycles and baby carriages, braided from the heat, were piled in the backyard. The street number was scrawled in spray paint over the front door.

Neighbors who saw the building go in the early morning hours continued to watch over the rubble. Some of the people who had lived in it were still at the scene, picking through piles of clothing and kitchen appliances scattered outside and praising a neighbor, an unemployed handyman, for kicking in doors and saving their lives.

He stood there too, waiting to tell his story.

"People call me a hero, but I'd rather they give me a job," he said.

He had returned to the scene wearing a baseball cap and a sports jacket. Like most people who live through fire, he had a glazed look on his face, his eyes seriously bloodshot, as though he had been sitting beside a barbecue pit all night.

"I could hear the children hollering up on the third floor. I went back in, but I couldn't make it up there. There was too much smoke. I tried. I really did. There was just too much fire." He repeated the story countless times for reporters from television stations, radio stations, newspapers.

An old man with skinny, striated arms sat on the hood of a white station wagon parked in the lot beside his former home. A small leather suitcase and a duffel bag that held a few T-shirts lay at his feet. He looked prepared for a short road trip. He didn't say anything but kept staring at the house and smoking a cigarette.

I walked up to him and started to ask what had happened, where he had been, how he got out, whether there had been smoke detectors. But he was busy sorting out his life and planning his future, and he didn't want to hear me. He let me know it by the way he put out his cigarette. I walked away.

"Every vacant lot you see was a fire," an overweight woman who lived down the block explained, pointing to the barren patches of land. Her voice rose with anger and bitterness because this was one of the few times the public would hear from her. "That one across the street was set. . . . The church that was down there burned. That one fenced in, that was a fire.

"This was once a very beautiful neighborhood," she added, memories getting the best of her. "The buildings were clean, kept up. You could sleep on the porch and look at the stars."

Detectives with clipboards stumbled around the building, looking for clues they hardly ever found. The fire department said arson, the cops, that it was undetermined. They disagreed often. When the cops ruled arson, it meant they would have to count the deaths as homicides, to be reflected in their statistics, so they were cautious about reaching such a conclusion.

That morning investigators found an empty gas can, a clue, but there were other cans too. The detectives said samples would be sent to the lab, but the samples always seemed to come back negative—no accelerant. So much of the evidence was destroyed in cases of arson. Which was part of the reason why no more than 10 to 12 percent of such cases led to arrests or indictments.

Walking through the rubble was like walking on a blasted-out patch of the moon. Fire had transformed the elements into an unrecognizable black mass. Soot got on my skin, and the smell of smoke wouldn't leave my clothes for days. Only scraps and remnants survived: a quarter of a mattress, half a kitchen table—a cross-section of everyday life. Relics caught my eye. A smashed flower vase. A baby shoe. A writer could always use one of those.

Fires were among the few news events whose coverage was still dominated by newspapers. Television could show the flames, but after a while, one fire looked just like the next. By contrast, the still shots published in newspapers, taken in moments when people were too dazed to protest and everything showed on their faces, captured the pathos best. Photographs that ended up winning prizes often depicted fire scenes. The *Tribune*'s photo for this fire showed the mother of several of the victims wearing a blue nightgown, her mouth in a wide, painful frown as she leaned on a friend's shoulder for comfort.

■ ■ ■

A lot of the time in covering fires you got to the scene after the flames were out, meeting up with boarding services, insurance agents, fire department employees handing out fire prevention leaflets, and of course the familiar bunch of fellow reporters on the tragedy beat.

There was something comforting about running into the same people, knowing that nobody wanted to be there, knocking on doors, watching the body bags come out, shaking down crying mothers for interviews. Reporters at fire scenes were very decent to each other. Radio reporters had the toughest job, filing urgent-sounding dispatches every half hour. Almost everyone else, television reporters included, had time to figure things out. Since competition was not much of a factor at most fires, the line of what was considered acceptable and humane behavior by reporters was much more clearly drawn.

The day after I covered my first fire, a woman named Ramona threw her fourteen-month-old baby out a second-floor window when flames engulfed the room.

This blaze, investigators said, had been caused by careless smoking. You could see the way the burn marks spread from the living room couch, where Ramona liked to smoke, outward toward the walls. In the front yard was a pile of metal springs.

Ramona's house was in a neighborhood that originally had had a suburban feel but that had gone bad. Abandoned apartment buildings on city blocks were unnoticeable after a while. But along culs-de-sac and curving streets, boarded-up ranch-style houses, each shaded by one tall oak, had an eerie effect. The neighborhood looked as though a disease had struck and sent everyone packing.

Ramona's baby fell into the arms of a neighbor waiting

below. He had heard a deathly scream at about five in the morning and came running in his too-tight undershirt. He tried to douse the flames with a garden hose.

"She didn't see me," said the neighbor, who had played in the outfield when growing up in Missouri. "She just dropped it."

The skin on the baby's hands was rolled up from being burned. She cried a little.

Ramona was dead. The baby's grandmother was too.

The neighbor wrapped the baby in a towel and rushed her to a hospital.

Later, when the excitement was over, he stood outside the brick house, spent and confused, but still willing to recount the events of that morning.

"Fire," he said, "is one thing you never forget."

■ ■ ■

Fire fighters' enemy was obvious. The goal was to bring the blaze under control, and if they acted right, with both brains and axes, they could do so without getting killed. The cops were losing that sense, that they were up against an enemy they could defeat. They were losing in general.

Fire fighters passed on their secrets from one generation to the next. They taught each other how to eat smoke so they didn't panic and choke when it clogged their throats; how to clean the truck, check the saw blades; how to polish the fire poles so they could slide half asleep from their narrow cots to the hook and ladder that idled below.

They learned how to find the right spot for ventilation, cutting through the roof so smoke could escape. The quicker they got through the roof, the easier it would be to search for survivors and extinguish the flames. They mastered reading buildings, knowing where the different rooms might be and how to find them in the dark and smoke. Where to look for people: in beds, under beds, in closets, even in dresser drawers. How to feel the way along walls while crawling on their bellies, because lifting their heads into the smoke could choke them. How to endure being cut by nails, hypodermic needles, broken glass. How to sense the heat with their ears, since they could not feel it with their gloved hands.

In celebration, they learned how to cook and eat mounds of brisket and banana cream pie; how to slice carrots and celery in time, their big gum-soled shoes tapping on the musty floor as the Temptations sang on a scratchy cassette player in the background.

All this for $40,000 a year. Max. And a few finger paintings from the local kindergarten.

Firemen and police.

You could see them side by side at arson investigations. Firemen hauled water lines and axes. Cops held clipboards, and wore ties knotted at their navels.

Society had messed with the resolve and honesty of police by expecting too much from them. The simple, well-defined role they had played for generations—Stop, thief!—was no longer enough.

Unlike fire, the criminal had become a more complex enemy, one that led them down dark alleyways, into abandoned buildings that were customized fortresses, and around in circles.

HEART ATTACK

On vacation when he died, Mr. Wattley's final message to his fellow staff members, left on the newspaper's computer bulletin board, was "Gone Sailing."
August 24, 1988

O ne morning in August, Phil Wattley died.
   Earlier that week, his friends remarked, the wildly inflated numbers on the gauge measuring his blood pressure read somewhere in the neighborhood of 200 over 150. But Wattley paid no attention.

Casey was stunned. He passed the news on respectfully from the press room, repeating it dozens of times to cops and reporters. There was a touch of shock in his voice, unlike anything he expressed when relaying his stories to the rewrite man at the *Sun-Times*. As always, I heard only one side of the conversation. "Listen, you're not going to believe this . . ."

To the obituary writers, Casey intoned that Wattley had

been like a younger brother, that although they had been in competition, there was a closeness between them. "Often he'd get one on me, and then I'd get one on him, and then we'd go out and have a cocktail."

The funeral was out near Wattley's home on the Northwest Side. I didn't want to go, not out of disrespect or laziness, but because I wasn't sure I'd be welcome.

When I took over the police beat from Wattley, word traveled that I had instigated the change—that I had demanded to be assigned to Eleventh and State, while harping on the outmodedness of the old school. Now that Wattley was dead, resentment intensified, and I became a prime suspect in his undoing. No one ever said anything outright, but I could sense it, especially from a few veteran cops, fire fighters, and reporters.

I walked into the service near its conclusion. Police officials who had been Wattley's friends for years sat along the back row wiping tears from their eyes and coughing to cover up. They acted with the decorum and sadness reserved for a fallen comrade. They inhabited the same world, shared to a large extent the same values, and hoped for the same happy endings.

Traditionally there had been an element of boosterism to the boilerplate police stories that originated in the press room at Eleventh and State. Hero cops were immortalized and any mistakes or excess minimized. To a degree, that was a catch built into the beat system, one that carried the potential to threaten journalistic integrity. Sources were "friends." And you couldn't burn friends, lest you lose your sources. At the Cop Shop, the agreement was especially binding because the degree of empathy was greater. Exposed to the daily routine, the reporter could not help but feel some compassion for those in the blue uniforms. Their transgressions, anything from drunken driving to beating a prisoner to insulting one with a racial epithet, were generally viewed by the press as minor lapses in what was considered the larger responsibility of fighting urban crime. The question was, where did you draw the line?

Just a few months into the job, I felt I was being drawn into a forgiving mindset. Sometimes when I drove through a bad neighborhood, I would reach for the handset of the two-way radio and hold it near my mouth in imitation of an undercover cop—a positively stupid gesture, yet one I felt gave me some added security. If you were willing to impersonate a cop, you didn't distrust them enough.

It was a dubious complicity that had worked both ways. In the past, it wasn't unusual for the cop reporter to make a few calls on behalf of an editor who, for instance, had collected too many traffic tickets. The records could be purged. Just like that. Or if someone in the newsroom was having troubles, say his house had been broken into, it was the police reporter who ensured the case got attention it might not have normally had. The press may have been the enemy, but not the police reporter.

■ ■ ■

Approximately a hundred mourners filed into the hallway of the funeral home, where they shook hands and consoled each other. After a while they drove to Wattley's house to eat and drink. He had lived on a tranquil street lined with aging maples and rosebushes; the drive home from Eleventh and State must have been pretty schizophrenic. A cop made enough money, starting at $30,000, to move away from the inner city. Most lived in quasi-suburban outposts on the Far South or North sides, on quiet streets just like this one, or perhaps not quite as nice, and segregated by color. A municipal law made it illegal for city workers to live beyond the city's borders, and so thousands of cops, fire fighters, and others crowded into white ethnic enclaves.

Wattley's shiny black Cadillac was parked near the garage, its massive hood reflecting trees and rooftops. Outside the driver's window was the high-beam lamp.

He also left behind his wife, his daughter, and a twenty-nine-foot sailboat aboard which he had worked off the daily atrocities.

It was a beautiful summer day late in August, and people milled about the kitchen talking quietly about his death, balancing paper plates in one hand, drinks in the other, as words about premature heart attacks stuck in their throats like chicken bones.

There was panic, of course, because Wattley was in the prime of life, and because the diets of so many reporters and editors in the newsroom were still paced by potato chips, cigarettes, and diet Cokes. And there was anger because of the way his career had been uprooted. The *Tribune* had taken an old pro who knew the city, and who could get the job done without a stutter, and replaced him with me, a New Yorker, who could not.

His death, some said, was the latest evidence of the breakdown of the old *Tribune,* and of the insensitivity of the new corporate way. Among some of the old hands this was a frequent complaint, but one invariably quelled by fatter paychecks and job security within a contracting industry. All over the country, newspapers with dwindling circulation were shutting down, but in the *Tribune*'s newsroom there was not even a suggestion of layoffs or pay cuts.

As we stood in Wattley's kitchen a journeyman reporter said to me, "You must feel pretty weird." His eyes were glassy and sad. "I mean, people see you as partially responsible."

I paid my respects quickly, then drove back to Eleventh and State.

Turning my car over to John, the ever-cheerful Syrian attendant, improved my mood.

The parking space cost $70 a month, which the *Tribune* paid. I could have parked in the police lot for free, but I didn't want to ask for a favor from the glazed-over chief of the news affairs office, which controlled who got which spaces.

The press room was quiet that afternoon. A City News reporter sat at his desk eating lunch. I looked over at the pool. A bikinied woman was sunbathing. Small pleasure.

Even though I had rarely seen Wattley or spoken to him,

his death and the reporter's remark left me feeling slightly besieged. I had assumed that at some point Wattley and I would meet again, maybe over a beer, to compare notes. But that would never be. The last time I had spoken with him was the night I went out with Howe and Raymond. I called the newsroom from Humboldt Park to tell him about the gang shooting, which didn't interest him in the least—nor, I had already learned, should it have. It was a shooting without significance. Inconsequential. Cheap.

On my desk were souvenirs he didn't bother to take with him: a stack of daily bulletins featuring officers killed in the line of duty; a rumpled guide to police headquarters; a loosely bound book of district maps; a list of the number of murder victims by year going back to 1930 (344); a couple of police radios.

Although the evidence didn't suggest it, Wattley had had fun in this room. It was an imperative of the job. I realized that the photos of the hooded man in the electric chair and of the St. Valentine's Day Massacre had been passed along to him for entertainment more than anything else. Trench humor.

Once on Rush Street I watched a plainclothes cop stand in front of a beer-soaked singles bar, talking excitedly as he handed a bouncer one Polaroid and then another until they were spilling out of the bouncer's beefy hands.

"This one was on the Dan Ryan. This one was along the Stevenson. Here's a good one."

"What are those?" I asked.

The cop handed me a few photos. They had been taken by police photographers moments after major car accidents. Bodies were split into two or three pieces. One man's head had landed fifty feet from his wrecked car, wedged into the steel traffic divider.

The cop and the bouncer snorted with maniacal laughter.

By the time Wattley died, no one in the press room was

having much fun anymore. We took care to clean the tiny refrigerator in the Teletype room once every two weeks, since
if we didn't Casey would throw a fit. We no longer won stories through impersonation or journalism-as-performance-
art. We no longer faked heart attacks to see how well
paramedics did their jobs, or checked into mental hospitals
to see what kinds of pills were dispensed.

My other colleague at the Cop Shop, Henry Wood, was
one of the few surviving reporters whose memory went back
to those times. Once he actually said, "Those were the days,
lad."

Henry too had been dying, gradually, piece by piece. I
think the cancer started in his lungs and worked toward his
colon, but it could have been the reverse. Either way, by the
time Wattley died the doctors were opening Henry up regularly to remove infected organs and tumors, until now only
half of him was left. The cancer had grown like grapes
around his disposition. The grapes grew into peaches, and
the peaches into cantaloupes. Incredibly, he looked okay.
He'd roll into the press room wearing dark-colored polyester suits, throw his phone books down, and announce he
was fine; we shouldn't even think he was finished. He didn't
inspire sympathy because it didn't seem he wanted or
needed any.

At dusk, when he came in to start his shift, he was pure
bile. He might have been an angel at home, a loving husband, a volunteer for worthy causes, and I have no reason
to doubt he was any of those things. But at the times I saw
him, the hate would run through his fingertips, wrapping
around the black rotary phone he held close to his mouth
(and disinfected regularly). It was as though he was a living,
walking experiment demonstrating the fatal effects of toxic
thoughts. A case study.

He watched the television news at five, a litany of one-
liners brewing in his hollowed gut.

"The bastards, they deserve what they get. I don't see
why we have to run obituaries for these people, let alone

five-column stories with a head shot. How many of these queers have dropped at the paper? Five? Six? It's getting to the point where some of my police friends are asking whether the only people we hire these days are queers. I'll tell you one thing, the Colonel would never have stood for it."

The Colonel was Colonel Robert McCormick, the late publisher of the *Tribune,* who had run the paper through the early days of Henry's career. The paper was the Colonel's outlet for a blend of protectionist advocacy and paternal sermonizing. The Colonel was Father Tribune.

The *Tribune* I worked for staffed its editorial board with progressives, blacks, and women; its political expression was solidly in the middle of the road. Its reporters were college educated and, for the most part, sensitive and vigilant humanists. Few issues sparked raging ideological splits among the rank and file.

Henry grumbled on the night shift as though none of these changes were for the better. He saw no need for them. He cursed under his breath because they had imperiled his station.

Even most cops occasionally exposed the raw bottom line of their emotions, usually by repeating some story that showed they were still human. But Henry seemed impenetrable.

■ ■ ■

Sergeant Leroy Levy walked into the press room rolling a fat cigar between his teeth, even though he had given up smoking years before.

"That's terrible about Wattley," he said.

Levy had been a cop for twenty-five years and was an expert on organized crime in Chicago. It was his hobby. He was not just your average armchair mob-ologist but, as he said, a "mafiologist." We talked often about the Chicago syndicate whenever he came by to eat a sandwich.

Without any introduction, Levy launched into a personal story about being a cop, how the job lent you swagger and arrogance, which hopefully went into abeyance when it was a question of keeping the conscience alive.

Back in 1964, Levy was checking liquor licenses near Milwaukee and Western in the Shakespeare district when he strolled into a dark bar under the El tracks. A man in a short-sleeved T-shirt stood stoically behind the counter, fixing his eyes as though caught in a trance. Seeing the police officer adorned with three sergeant's chevrons and a blue hat, the bartender stiffened.

"You'd think he'd say, 'Hi, how ya doing?'" Levy said as he ate.

Levy looked at the bartender and on his forearm saw faded blue-green numbers.

"Are you Jewish?" Levy asked, which was at once the right and the wrong question.

In Yiddish, Levy said, *"Gibt a kook auf min nomen."* Look at my name.

This calmed the bartender.

When Levy asked him for a pack of cigarettes, the bartender refused to take his money.

A woman walked to the front of the bar—the bartender's second wife; the first had been gassed during the war.

In America they had adopted a son. But the son was embarrassed by his parents because they were short and spoke with thick accents.

Levy, the bartender, and the bartender's wife became friends. The bartender would ask Levy to help him with his son, who had become a junkie. He stole. He lied.

The son survived; his father didn't. Haunted by the past and fearful of his own son, he hanged himself in the basement of his home.

"I really liked him," Levy said. "He made me cry when I saw how scared he was of me."

Levy looked toward the ceiling, grinding the cigar between his teeth. In three decades as a cop, he had seen a lot. But this story was different. He was choking back tears.

■ ■ ■

At about four-fifteen I drove to the Tower.

It was a quick ride from the Cop Shop. You could park in the parking lot after four-thirty or so, which made it easy to stop by and file a story or talk to friends.

The Tower itself was one of those marvels of American architecture, a skyscraper fashioned from Indiana limestone and crowned with a Gothic peak. When it was completed in 1925 it dominated Michigan Avenue. Boats on the lake would use it as a beacon to return to shore. It was an extraordinary achievement back then, and it remained so. Outside, its walls were studded with chunks of famous tourist destinations—the Alamo, Westminster Abbey, Mark Twain's house.

The newsroom, which occupied most of the fourth floor, had shed much of its original character, though there was a black-and-white photo pinned to one of the columns in the center of the room that served as a reminder of how things used to be thirty years earlier. In it you could see heavy wooden desks, a wood floor, stiff chairs and typewriters everywhere, behind which men, almost exclusively, composed their lines. The picture was full of motion and excitement. It was the city room back then, because it was the city that made the news: politics and crime, and crime and politics.

Now the newsroom was quiet. The clacking of old-time typewriters was stilled, and carpeting muted the shuffling of feet, the hollering of wild-eyed editors, and the mean-spirited defensiveness of reporters, myself included. Each reporter had his or her own cubicle, the vast open space of the old city room having been partitioned off. At the center was a cluster of computer terminals around which metropolitan editors like the Grump sat, directing coverage and editing copy, some of which needed to be rewritten from top to bottom only minutes before deadline.

The vast newsroom woke up on three occasions during my time there. The first was when a plane crashed at Dallas–Fort Worth Airport. The second was when the *Challenger* exploded. The third was when Harold Washington died.

At these times there was an instinctive migration to the metropolitan desk at the center of the room, where the editors kept a small color television set. Dozens of reporters would gather silently, hoping to grab a piece of the story for themselves. There was no better place to be when those events unfolded, as pure adrenaline and enthusiasm took over.

But I was glad for the quiet just then, the funeral service having strapped my desire to do any more work that week.

An editor called me over. The wires were reporting that police had made an arrest in an arson fire that had killed five people a few weeks earlier. Could I look into it?

The fire on Campbell Avenue had consumed the bodies of two women and three children, ages two and three. Before the fire was set the women had been beaten to death, the children smothered with pillows.

Brighton Park detectives had just arrested two men for the slayings. The suspects had gone to the house to collect on a drug debt owed them by one of the women. When she refused to pay, they allegedly killed everyone in sight.

Together with another reporter, I spent a couple of hours pinning down the story. We were promised a decent amount of space, even though it was a Saturday paper, which was significantly smaller than a weekday issue.

I was able to find the father of one of the victims. He was a Chicago police officer.

S I X

∙ ∙ ∙

EL RUKN

POLICE SAY SHOOTING MAY HAVE BEEN ORDERED BY RUKNS
September 23, 1988

S hortly after midnight, Eugene Hairston told his roommate he was going out to buy some ice cream.

He pulled on a frayed denim jacket, slammed the door
behind him, and began walking deliberately along Thirty-
eighth Street, about a car's length from the curb.

He had been smoking the rock in the first-floor apartment, and the cool air stunned him when he stepped
outside.

In the playground across the street the shadows came
alive, swings lurking like wild boars and rats scurrying across
the cracked pavement. Fear was a dulled reflex, a faint warning whose call he had stopped noticing in his youth, maybe
sooner, so that fear no longer existed for him. Enemies had

tried to kill him at least twice, but they never got close enough, and he assured himself they wouldn't now.

His whole life had been an ugly little march to nowhere. There was a time, two decades earlier, when he had felt some enthusiasm, had won some respect—had told people what to do and when to do it. And they listened. It was a crazy time on the South Side, money and friends to be made if you had the guts, which he did. Just by getting arrested, it seemed, you could make friends—white lawyers and their wives, and rich liberals with trust funds who thought there was something beyond the extortion and drug dealing, something socially meaningful. But those days were over. No more unexpected friends. No more money. No nothing.

Again Hairston saw something move. Then a flash and a loud pop, which he instantly recognized from the rapid-fire soundtrack of his life. Before he could take another step, bullets tore through him, first his right calf, then his left thigh, another ripping open his gut so that his stomach burst forth and his back burned, and another to his head, along his forehead, which sent him falling to the ground. From inside came a voice he didn't know. It was begging for help.

■ ■ ■

A block away, two weary police officers were approaching the end of an unremarkable shift. They heard the gunfire, saw the flashes, and ran toward the violence.

One of the cops, veteran Bob Skahill, looked down at the victim's bloodied face. The man on the ground said, "Help me. You know me." But Skahill didn't recognize him because of all the damage that had been done and the washes of blood soaking through his clothes.

Skahill and his partner took off after the shooters. Entering the Ida B. Wells housing project, a labyrinth of low-rise apartment buildings, they felt the drive and adrenaline that had eluded them that night, and for the first time in hours felt they were earning their salaries, sweating and running and not letting fear get the best of them. Pale blue television light flickered behind the bed sheets and cheap shades that covered the windows; for those inside, the craziness was always just beyond the paper-thin fabric. No one even bothered to push away the curtains to look.

The shooters got away.

Winded, Skahill returned to the victim, whose voice was gurgling with blood as he pleaded, "You know me. . . . Help me. Help me."

Only then did Skahill realize that Eugene Hairston was dying right in front of him.

■ ■ ■

Skahill had met Eugene "Bull" Hairston two years before, when Bull took over a drug operation at the corner of Forty-seventh and Indiana.

"So you're Bull Hairston," Skahill had said.

"So you're Skahill."

"Heard a lot of stories."

"They're all true," Hairston had responded.

Dozens of cops and criminals had forged relationships on the streets, trading on past reputations, meeting on common ground with grudging respect. Skahill had what he called a "good-natured rivalry" with Hairston. They saw each other almost daily, meeting by chance in the neighborhood or once in Hairston's "office" in a drug house on Forty-seventh Street, where he had carefully arranged a couch and a desk. They talked about everything—politics, murder, women; Skahill frankly found Hairston easy to talk to, easier than some of the boobs in the department whose idea of law enforcement was saddling the cop on the street with bureaucratic nonsense like the point system. If you arrested a dope dealer you got a point, but if you arrested a theft suspect you got two points. Some incentive to go after the drugs.

One afternoon, Hairston was in the mood to be candid.

"I've been a crook all my life," he told Skahill. "But you've got to catch me."

Skahill tried. But other than a few minor drug arrests, he didn't succeed. Hairston rarely carried any dope, and people in the neighborhood were too afraid to tell the cops much about him.

Hairston ran a drug business—of that Skahill was certain. He just couldn't prove it. So he went about his own business, staking out Hairston's runners, arresting them, keeping the heat on. And in the course of doing so, he once saved Hairston from his own bully tactics.

Hairston had driven a woman to Lake Michigan, pushed her in, and left her there. He had wanted the murky water to be a lesson to her not to sell dope on his corner. The woman crawled out of the lake and came looking for revenge, a pistol in her hand. She found Hairston sitting in a friend's car at Forty-sixth and Calumet Avenue. Shouting "You dirty bastard," she pressed the gun against his temple.

Skahill, who happened to be on duty when he saw the assault unfold, rushed over and told everyone to calm down. Even on Forty-sixth Street you didn't go shooting people up in front of a cop. The woman walked away, cursing. That was the kind of relationship Skahill had with Hairston. He wanted to catch him, but he didn't want to see anyone blow his head off.

Eventually the cops prevailed. Hairston lost the drug operation when dozens of arrests finally made it unprofitable.

The word on the street was that Hairston's new vocation was sticking up dope dealers. By then even the cops had lost interest in him—nobody wanted to spend tax dollars arresting former drug dealers who were robbing the current ones.

Now here he was lying on the ground, gasping for air.

Skahill remembered whispering to Hairston that the ambulance was on its way. He felt sick he hadn't caught the guys who had shot him. And he felt embarrassed that he was so rattled. If circumstances had been different he might have called Hairston a friend.

Maybe in another lifetime. Hairston, his body split open and draining of blood, died on the way to the hospital.

Skahill and the detectives searched the playground across the street for evidence. In the bushes they found a 9mm Hungarian semiautomatic and a Taurus .357 with six exploded rounds. A few feet away were a black jacket and cap and a gray hat with the letter *M*. Maybe there would be a print, Skahill thought. Maybe this time something would turn up on the ballistic tests.

■ ■ ■

On the Sheet, Hairston was accorded the usual honors: "Male / black / 44 / multiple gunshots to head, chest, abdomen and right leg / 38th and Vincennes on the street / no suspects."

It was a slow morning four months into my tour at the Cop Shop. For the moment, Hairston's death was the focal point of the reporters on duty in the press room, if for no other reason than the deliberate nature of the crime.

I was growing accustomed to scanning gray descriptions of drive-bys—"shots fired from passing vehicle, possibly a late model Buick or Oldsmobile"—accounts of vague, hastily carried out, cowardly acts, bullets missing their mark or killing by accident. But even from the terse language of the Sheet, it was clear that Hairston had been singled out as he walked along the dark street, killed with enthusiasm and from close up.

I picked up the PAX line and dialed the Wentworth detectives on the South Side.

"You calling about Bull?" the sergeant asked before I could finish a sentence.

"Bull?"

"Bull Hairston . . . Eugene Hairston."

"Right."

"Yeah. You and everyone else. What do you need?"

All morning the sergeant had been fielding questions about Hairston from the big shots downtown, from Eleventh and State, from the FBI and the U.S. attorney's office.

"What's the big deal about this one?" I asked. The question was complicated because the answer required a short history lesson.

"Come on. . . . How long you been on the job? He and Jeff Fort started the whole thing," the sergeant said.

Eugene Hairston was not just another shooting victim on a Wednesday night but a link to one of the bloodiest and most enigmatic criminal outfits in Chicago's history, El Rukn.

Over the years so many layers of police lore had built up about the Rukns that at times they seemed to be not a gang but a theory that had been dreamed up, deconstructed, and fitted back together by the dozens of law enforcement officials who had devoted their careers to dismantling the organization. Fort was the Rukns' stern-eyed ayatollah, the city's public enemy number one, a killer who communicated with underlings by code and wore a Chinese coolie's hat. For more than twenty years Fort had made headlines each time he was arrested, acquitted, and chased anew by an expanding army of investigators.

Hairston's murder was simply the latest episode in the Rukn saga.

■ ■ ■

I had first heard of the gang shortly after I started at the paper as an intern in 1985. A front page story detailed the testimony given to a Cook County grand jury by a Rukn "general," a thirty-two-year-old high school dropout who had reported directly to Fort. Breaking ranks with the secretive organization, the general, Anthony Sumners, spoke of at least nine murders and a massive Rukn-run narcotics operation.

At about the same time the Rukns unsuccessfully sought recognition as a religious group, the Moorish Science Temple of America, El Rukn Tribe, which would have allowed gang members the right to hold private meetings while in prison. Despite the setback, they continued to wrap themselves in the rhetoric and robes of Islam.

And then came a long series of raids, arrests, and prosecutions. The Rukns were implicated in double murders, triple murders, extortion cases, armed robberies, narcotics trafficking.

A raid in August 1986 on a Rukn-controlled building on the South Side led to the recovery of thirty-seven firearms, including three submachine guns and a U.S. Army antitank rocket launcher sold to the gang by an undercover FBI agent. The rocket launcher became the central exhibit in the government's prosecution of Fort and the Rukns for preparing to launch terrorist attacks in the United States on behalf of Libyan leader Muammar Qaddafi. Fort was convicted and sentenced to eighty years in prison.

The gang's origins went back two decades, when Hairston, I learned from reading the files in the Tower library, had been Fort's partner and soul mate.

In 1965 the two of them founded the Blackstone Rangers, a Woodlawn gang based at Sixty-seventh and Blackstone Avenue in a onetime Jewish neighborhood on the city's South Side. Bull was the Chief and Fort, because he was shorter, the Little Chief.

At the time there was no shortage of young black men on the South Side prepared for revolution, confrontation, or some combination of the two. But while revolutionaries like the Black Panthers were cultivating a political ideology, Fort's Rangers gravitated to crime. They were driven, like Ivan Boesky, to every manner of hustling a buck.

Hairston had a way of talking to people, of convincing

them to get mad, to sign up, to rob and steal and deal. A police informant I once spoke to, a former Rukn, described Hairston as a clear-headed, nearly polite gangster. Hairston, he said, would talk to you before he split open your head with a baseball bat. There was a component of logic in the techniques of extortion with which he stalked the South Shore, with its synagogues and spiritual baths. "You know you're the only Jew in a neighborhood of blacks," he would warn certain shopkeepers. "You're going to have some trouble sooner or later." When they agreed to pay, Hairston sent over the peewees, the youngest gang members, to mop their floors.

For his part, Fort was portrayed by cops and assistant U.S. attorneys as a terrorist, pure and simple. The informant I met remembered Fort saying, for example, "Pay me or I'll kill your grandmother." He had more fire and violence than Hairston. He was a megalomaniac and a schemer who wanted people to bow down to him. Hairston's small-minded larcenies did not mesh with his ambitions.

Chief and Little Chief were imprisoned in 1972, Hairston for soliciting an ambush murder for a fee of a dollar, Fort for defrauding a million-dollar antipoverty education program. Control of the gang was maintained by the pair through a handpicked council of leaders known as the Main Twenty-one. Allies turned up in the most unlikely places. A Denver millionaire, Charles Kettering II, supported a quarter-million-dollar legal defense fund for the Rangers, who had the potential, he said, for "great social impact."

But when Hairston was released from prison in 1975, he found the gang splintering. Some of the members of the Main Twenty-one had started their own drug operations. When Fort was freed the following year he immediately held a meeting of the Black P Stone Nation, a confederation of South Side gangs dominated by the Rangers, in its headquarters at Forty-third and Indiana. According to documents filed in court, the Little Chief took Hairston into a side room, held a gun to his head, and told him his part in the gang was over. The Main Twenty-one was abolished, and Fort announced that the gang would henceforth be known as El Rukn.

Hairston left the gang in disgrace. He worked in construction for a while, then started dealing marijuana and pills, heroin substitutes known as T's and Blues. He made a decent buck, working several street corners. He rented a cheap room in a flophouse and bought a green 1971 Chevrolet Impala. He told friends, "I'm not getting what I want, but I'm doing all right."

And the Rukns grew. Boasting between five hundred and a thousand members during its peak in the late 1970s and early 1980s, the gang had come to symbolize the feared conclusion of urban despair and lawlessness. The Rukn style of guerrilla warfare was being copied by scores of gangs in Chicago. The week of Hairston's murder, for instance, the shooting was worst in Cabrini-Green, where snipers allied with the Disciples and Vice Lords fired at each other from high-rise apartments. These were not cataclysmic battles to determine control of vast drug markets but skirmishes over control of a single building in the project, or sometimes just a playground. In their struggle for a South Side neighborhood, the Rukns fought for one corner at a time, eventually winning control of dozens of blocks in a profitable mile-long swath. In the process, according to investigators, six hundred people had died, including one cop.

Separating the Rukns from any other dime-bag outfit was Fort, who was born in Aberdeen, Mississippi, in 1947, and who stopped going to school sometime during the fourth grade. According to an IQ test administered in Chicago when he was a teenager living in Woodlawn, Fort was retarded. Hardly. Even his enemies acknowledged that he was a gifted organizer and con man who thought very big. It was Fort who concocted the Rukns' religious guise, its welfare messianism, and the hierarchy of generals, ambassadors, and foot soldiers. Imprisonment did not stop him from controlling every aspect of the gang.

Now Fort faced another trial for the comparatively glitz-less crime of ordering the murder of a drug dealer named Willie "Dollar Bill" Bibbs. Jury selection was scheduled to be-gin under tight security in Cook County Criminal Court just a few hours after Hairston was killed.

At the time of his murder, police said, Hairston was any-thing but an active member of the Rukns. He was barely making enough money on the street to eat. He shared an apartment with a paraplegic. Friends said he spent after-noons in a treeless park drinking beer out of a bottle hid-den in a brown paper bag, babbling about one day buying an abandoned city building and opening a candy store there.

Yet the timing of his murder, coming just before the opening of Fort's trial, smacked of the orchestrated violence the Rukns were known for, and encouraged the ongoing mythicizing of the gang. As for the motive of the killing, de-tectives offered the nebulous hypothesis that Hairston might have disobeyed a final order from Fort, although they couldn't say what that order was. Even though the police viewed the Rukns as "a bunch of thugs, not Bonnie and Clyde," they couldn't stop believing that Rukn tentacles reached all over the city, striking at will to enforce the gang's own law.

Hairston had died a bum. But that morning the possi-bility took shape that he was somehow more, a piece in the Rukn puzzle that had to be snapped in, or no one would get any sleep.

■ ■ ■

Ed Wodnicki sat in his fifth-floor office, a color portrait of Mayor Sawyer staring down at his desk as a small testament to how far he'd come.

He had just returned from the morning meeting of the police brass, a snake pit of top officials like himself pretend-ing to be corporate executives. They discussed crime statis-tics and strategies in the superintendent's paneled office, but they kept a lot to themselves because the most important strategy for each was the advancement of his career, and one never knew who the enemy was or where he might be hiding.

Hairston's slaying was mentioned at the beginning of the meeting, causing ripples of nostalgia among the police officials, many of whom had wrestled with the Blackstone Rangers during their early years in the department. The ambush murder of a South Side gang cop in 1970 had set the course of their mutually contemptuous relationship.

In the neat picture he prepared in his mind, Wodnicki stuck a pin into the intersection of Thirty-eighth and Vincennes, where Hairston was gunned down. Hairston's joined a growing list of gang executions that dotted Chicago's South and West sides.

Wodnicki saw the approach of a wave of terror. There were people getting machine-gunned in telephone booths, for chrissake.

Like his boss, Police Superintendent Martin, Wodnicki was a street cop who understood the percussion of force that gave him authority. Also like Martin, he was relaxing some of his air of authority in order to become a diplomat, because only a diplomat could run a zoo like the Chicago Police Department.

So it came to pass that Wodnicki, who was used to employing profanity as punctuation, also learned to fortify his sentences with it, lifting tautology to a fine art, as in "The fucking motherfucker should be fucked."

And his career soared.

That morning, sitting in his yellow office, he felt good. He had a theory about the executions. The Rukns were "like a dog let loose."

A month earlier another former high-ranking Rukn had been killed with ten shotgun blasts as he exited his Mercedes in front of his South Side home. The good guys finally had the Rukns on the run, Wodnicki surmised. Therefore informants had to be killed.

What might Bull Hairston have said about the Rukns?

It was possible that, alone and desperate, he might have been willing to say quite a bit. There was no statute of limitations on murder, and Bull Hairston had been around for more than one.

But as soon as Wodnicki's theory took shape, it had to be pushed aside.

"We got a problem on the West Side, Boss," shouted an assistant as he charged into Wodnicki's office. A man had opened fire inside a West Side elementary school.

The call to arms rearranged Wodnicki's priorities, his glimpse of a new worldview. He grabbed his coat, called for his car, and rushed to the scene.

■ ■ ■

In the press room the quiet, contemplative, history-laden morning was shattered by police radios echoing a lone dispatcher's frantic calls for help.

Clem Henderson, a Vietnam veteran who liked to stand in the middle of the street doing karate and speaking what he called Hebrew, told a friend, "I'm going to kill everyone I see."

At about nine-fifteen, he began.

"How many officers are down?" the dispatcher asked.

Some voices said two, others more.

A dead cop made crime a simple matter again. I called the desk to deliver the bad news.

Clem Henderson had wanted a job, needed one, but all he got was grief and laughter. His "Hebrew" was about that, the bitterness of having stretched his big frame along the sweaty floor of the Vietnamese jungle only to be denied a decent life. While the Rukns were busy fighting the police, he had been fighting the Vietcong. And for what?

Now it was time to return to the moist earth, prepare for the Lord, be baptized.

Before leaving his apartment that morning, Henderson had strapped an ammunition belt around his waist and slid a .38-caliber handgun into his pants. For one last time he went looking for work, armed like a one-man Rukn army.

After the lumberyard on Ashland Avenue said no and the car wash the same, he walked to the auto parts store down the street and started firing, killing the owner and a clerk. Then he slouched toward the Montefiore School, where there were hundreds of children, problem children, children who beat up each other more than they studied science or math.

Henderson barged through the heavy steel doors that swung back toward the street as though they were hinged with rubber bands.

He saw a janitor and killed him with a single shot to the head.

Then he saw two cops, Irma Ruiz and her partner, Gregory Jaglowski, who happened to be at the school to pick up a student. Henderson picked off Ruiz first, cleanly, a shot through her heart. He fired at Jaglowski, wounding him in both legs, but leaving him mobile enough to reach for his own gun.

From the ground, Jaglowski fired a shot into Henderson's upper abdomen, spinning him around and setting him up for a final round. Henderson collapsed a few feet from where Ruiz lay. Shell casings littered the ground beneath them.

I knew the neighborhood. Ashland Avenue ran nearly the length of the city, changing color and accents as it passed through Mexico, Poland, Lithuania, Italy, and Africa. At Thirteenth Street it was mainly commercial, a cut-rate strip mall for auto supplies and hair curlers.

In the press room we chased numbers. The number of dead and wounded; the number of years Ruiz, the second female officer in Chicago shot in the line of duty, had been in the department; the number of commendations, awards, complimentary letters she had received; the number of children she had given birth to.

Then word arrived that the Rukns would be holding a

press conference at 2:00 P.M. at the Fort, their longtime South Side headquarters. They did this every now and then to counter an image problem that got worse with each passing year. Today's topic: Bull Hairston.

■ ■ ■

Guns and money. The words would have looked just right on the marquee of the old Oakland Theater. Instead there was only a handwritten sign nailed above the main entrance: SAY NO TO DRUGS. This was the Fort, imposing, laughable, sealed tight.

A sentry holding a walkie-talkie to his ear stood guard over the entrance gate on Drexel Boulevard. He wore jeans and aviator sunglasses, and his face bore the numbed look of newfound discipline, like a Moonie on crack.

From the outside, the Fort still looked like a fancy movie house, the regal kind that was getting torn down every six months or so in Chicago. The Oakland had been a burlesque hall. Now it stood alone, a relic surrounded by empty lots and earth-colored high rises, its white terra cotta aging gracefully, its walls reinforced on the inside with guns and thick piles of cash.

Bought by the gang in 1976, the Fort was its nerve center. The Rukns buried drugs and ammunition beneath the basement floor, hid more than $3 million in drain pipes and sewers, and shuttered the windows with steel to stop up the government's electronic ears.

It was from the Fort that the Rukns tried to enlist Qaddafi. A group of thirty gang members dressed up in three-piece suits got a few video cameras rolling and identified themselves as representatives of Rukn cells from all over the country. They pledged they would bomb government buildings and airplanes in exchange for Qaddafi's financial backing. The attacks, they said, would be carried out by mobile five-man Rukn units. Of course, no such units existed.

On more routine nights in the Fort, the Rukns held classes on Islam and hosted dances for poor neighborhood teenagers, introducing them to the gang. They punished violators—dealers who didn't sell enough dope, kids who skimmed from their bags of cocaine—by bringing them back to the Fort and putting them in a "circle for drums," a ritual of harsh beatings.

The Rukns mapped out their future there, taking detailed orders by telephone from their imprisoned leader. The Little Chief had plenty of time to scheme. From the federal penitentiary in Bastop, Texas, where he had been incarcerated on drug charges since 1983, Fort communicated over the telephone with his soldiers in an elaborate code that turned out to be a mixture of street jive, Swahili, and Arabic.

Fort believed the code was indecipherable. But with the aid of what would become a horde of Rukn informants and thousands of hours of court-ordered wiretaps, the government broke it.

The tapes revealed a leader obsessed with maintaining complete control of his organization and driven by boundless greed. Fort would call gang headquarters as often as ten times a day to harp on matters as trivial as outstanding $20 drug debts and the cost of car rentals.

"Love, truth, peace, freedom, four grapes and a half grape," Fort was told by a Rukn general in one conversation. Translation: Airfare from Chicago to Texas had cost $450.

A painting in a meeting room on the second floor, the Khabar Room, showed a man on a horse wearing a black mask and carrying a sword dripping with blood. When Fort wanted a murder committed he told his generals, "Put on the hood of the rider."

■ ■ ■

It was hard not to be caught up in the giddy high of getting inside the Fort.

I leaned on a dirty car with the handful of reporters waiting to be admitted. After about half an hour the heavy metal gate swung open and the sentry motioned for us to enter.

Guards led us up a stairwell, past a turret that looked onto the street.

We walked into a dark ballroom, where chorus girls once danced to Broadway show tunes. A mirrored disco globe dangled from the ceiling. A jukebox lit up a corner of the ballroom with Juicy Fruit colors.

In the center of the room, seated at a wooden lunchroom table, was Abdul Mumeet, spokesman and commander. I placed a tape recorder in front of his folded hands.

That afternoon the Rukns were not interested in discussing Fort, or the FBI, or the spiritual power of Islam. They wanted to talk about Bull Hairston. They wanted to remember him, to bless him, to deny that in this time of mounting troubles they had anything to do with his passing.

"We want it to be known that although Bull Hairston, Ibriheem, was not a member of the tribe, we mourn his death."

As Mumeet spoke, his white turban tilted toward a row of microphones and tape recorders.

"He was in good standing with the Rukn tribe. He was not a foe. He had his own ideas of what he wanted to do."

Then Mumeet walked away, dodging a few questions about Fort and his trial.

As the other reporters and I were escorted out of the building, we exchanged glances with a certain embarrassment that we were even there. We got into our cars and drove away.

■ ■ ■

One month later, a Cook County jury convicted Fort and four other Rukns for the murder of Dollar Bill Bibbs.

Fort was sentenced to seventy-five years on top of an eighty-year prison term for the charges of plotting terrorism. At best, he would become a championship weight lifter in prison.

Prosecutors geared up to finish the job, to move through the organizational hierarchy like termites, starting at the top with the generals, then the ambassadors, and finally the soldiers—the next generation.

Late one afternoon two weeks after Fort's conviction, a bright acetylene torch burned into the front gate of El Rukn Grand Major Mosque, lighting up Drexel Boulevard with a sunset orange glow. The cops looked like a construction crew in the autumn cold, digging with shovels, swinging sledgehammers, searing and picking their way into the Fort, the holy of holies. It was a fine day to be a cop, to be putting the Rukns away.

Fort's son, Anthony, who had been named in a freshly printed murder warrant, gave the raiders the excuse they needed to charge into the mosque.

Among the first to break into the Fort that fall afternoon was a group of Chicago police officers who had been assigned to the Bureau of Alcohol, Tobacco, and Firearms for the sole purpose of collecting evidence against the Rukns. One of the cops, Dan Brannigan, was known as Blondie by the Rukns. In a government wiretap, a Rukn general was overheard saying he planned to test the rocket launcher the gang had just obtained on Blondie. It had become a personal vendetta on both sides. A few other Irish cops assigned to the Rukn squad had gone to Mount Carmel High School at the same time Jeff Fort was organizing the Blackstone Rangers a few blocks away. Each of them had a story to tell about his teenage years, when the Mount Carmel kids had fought with the Rangers or watched from a bus as gang members threw stones at them. They had taken to writing Christmas cards to Fort in prison: MERRY CHRISTMAS, LOVE BLONDIE.

The Irish cops weren't the only ones on the Rukn detail, but their personal involvement was highest. They had seen the gang develop into the menace it had become al-

most in front of their eyes, and they yearned for the satis-
faction of finally beating it. It wasn't a racial thing, they
insisted, even though nearly everyone in the special Rukn
detail was white. Destroying the Rukns would benefit the
black community as much as whites.

They were envied by their peers. They had carved a
niche with what was considered a glamour assignment, and
they were making the most of it, having spent on average
five years on the Rukn beat, which kept them out of the daily
crud. They would scout for new informants, constantly
searching for missing pieces of the puzzle. They could mum-
ble the gang hierarchy in their sleep. And they were invalu-
able to the press over the years, becoming the front line of
a major federal investigation, yet without the pretensions of
their counterparts in the U.S. attorney's office, who communicated by press release when they bothered to at all.

Once I got a call in the middle of the night from Brannigan when he and his colleagues were in Mississippi arresting a Rukn fugitive. I couldn't have gotten anything into the
next day's paper, but it was the thought that counted. To
return favors, we published a short story with the mug shots
of a dozen or so at-large Rukn fugitives. Tips poured in to a
police phone line whose number was provided, and all of
the fugitives were eventually apprehended. That was the
kind of back scratching done to keep open the channels of
communication, a tactic perfected in the Cop Shop decades
before I arrived.

On this afternoon the job was less subtle. At about three
o'clock the cops punched through the side of the building
and piled in like commandos. Anthony Fort was not there,
but on their first pass they found thirty grams of cocaine,
three hundred grams of marijuana, and two handguns hidden in a secret panel. Based on the contraband, a federal
judge issued another warrant at five o'clock, allowing a more
thorough search of the old theater.

The cops had been there before, but on those occasions
they could only pull out a few drawers and rifle the closets.

This time walls were coming down, the floor was coming off, the ceiling out, and the front gate permanently removed.

Following the windbreaker-clad cops were burly gas and electric workers eager to cut utilities to the Fort; the gang had not paid bills in months. More than $700 was owed the phone company, so the telephones were removed. Ten feet of the building's facade had been blown out, and passersby could stare inside.

Following the detailed instructions of an informant, the cops found three more guns, thirty-nine grams of coke, three or four gallons of codeine hidden in a basement tunnel, and hundreds of documents. The search stretched well into the night and continued the following morning. Although the police had hoped to find an arsenal in the basement, it wasn't there.

Victories over local gangs had been few and far between. But the cops were going to make an example of the Rukns. No mistakes. No excuses. Even with Fort imprisoned, the prosecution of the gang was far from over; the raid proved that. In some ways it was just beginning.

The federal government, in an effort to eliminate any traces of the gang hierarchy, set into motion an unprecedented legal offensive that would take two more years to complete. A grand jury began hearing evidence in what would be the most extensive prosecution of the gang ever. Everyone was talking about a final blow.

■ ■ ■

In the meantime, the Chicago police had every other gang to worry about.

"With the Rukns down, it created a void, and we want to take preventive steps to prevent anyone from filling it," Wodnicki said at the outset of what I assumed would be one of our bull sessions.

"I'm gonna tell you something," he added in a more serious tone, his eyes widening and his steel jaw flexing so that his features looked as though they might freeze. "Over the last two or three years there have been twenty-five to thirty homicides, all narcotics-related, by factions opposing the Rukns. Nineteen of the offenders are known. It's a domino theory. A lot of people are trying to position themselves for the Rukns' spots—'Let's jump in and see what we can do for ourselves'—that type of thinking."

I considered the gist of what Wodnicki liked to call his "ver-bij."

"Let me understand what you're saying. All of these murders are linked in some way. Right?" Sometimes I couldn't help but sound just like him.

"That's what we're looking into."

Like a deranged Frugal Gourmet, Wodnicki began reciting a list of murders on the South and West sides, each notable for its brutality. One man was shot twelve times, six with a .38 and six with a .32, then burned over 90 percent of his body. One was machine-gunned in a phone booth. Another was bound and gagged in his closet and shot twice through his mouth.

In earlier theories, Bull Hairston and Tremain Banks had been shot up like rabbits, targeted because of what they knew and what they might tell in court. But that phase was over. Now began the fight for succession. And that promised to be just as bloody.

I wondered why Wodnicki was unveiling his hypothesis, going beyond his almost jovial summations of homicide investigations or his expositions of human nature as he saw it. Perhaps he actually wanted an article about the killings. Perhaps he wanted a task force under his command to do nothing but investigate them. Every boss wanted a task force. It conferred status and generated publicity, and made police detectives feel more like FBI agents, whom they envied. Whatever Wodnicki's motives, the murders themselves were ingredients of a very good article, an old-fashioned crime story reminiscent of the city's bootlegging past.

Ironically, neither I nor any other reporter at the time

had written much about drugs or drug murders in Chicago; they were not considered as big a problem here as in other cities. The Chicago police didn't even keep track of narcotics-related murders until the year I came to the Cop Shop. When I pressed the detective who kept the Book of Death to tell me how many homicides were drug-related he glanced at the book, scribbled a few numbers, and said, "Ten percent. And that's including the cheap stuff."

Other than Wodnicki's contention that the brutal execution slayings were part of a semiorganized power grab, there wasn't much to distinguish them from the cheap stuff. The victims came with the usual résumés: young black men under the age of forty, no known employment. Still, from about a dozen graphic cases I wrote a story for the Sunday paper that outlined the police scenario and the violence ravaging the South and West sides. I sat with an editor who, deleting all references to "execution-style" slayings, argued that there was no need for the piece to sound as though it had been written during Prohibition.

The theory that the murders were related was at once alluring and preposterous, relying on the word of a few high-ranking police officers. There was no hard evidence they were linked. But the story brought together many of the dealers and killers and theories I had been trying to keep track of for months and suggested, finally, that there was some logic behind all the bloodshed. It was satisfying to think I had at last begun to understand the constellations of hoodlums who worked the city, figuring out patterns like algebra problems and reeling off the principal characters as though they were on baseball cards. I'm getting closer to knowing the beat, I thought.

THIRTY KILLINGS TIED TO DRUG TURF BATTLES: The headline led the newspaper on page 1. It was an aggressive, tabloid-style story, and I felt good about it. But the insight, I would soon realize, was trivial if not illusory.

Months later a detective from the North Side asked me to meet him for breakfast. I had spoken to him once about a gun raid and figured he had something interesting to pass along when he whispered into the phone, "We need to talk."

We made small talk over coffee, until I asked him what he needed to discuss. Instead of guns or gangs, or anything related to police, he took a deep breath and started describing a new business he was involved in, one that could yield hundreds of thousands of dollars a year. On a piece of yellow legal paper he drew a diagram of this new business, which sounded a lot like Amway. "Just listen," he said. You get a supply of instructional cassettes for cheap and you sell them to your friends, and they sell them to their friends, and everyone makes money and saves money at the same time. When he was done drawing, the yellow paper looked as though a two-year-old had scribbled on it for an hour. A schematic of the police imagination would look about the same. Cops believed in patterns. They convinced them that their enemies could be as smart as they were. They justified the manpower and effort, and the drinking. But in the end, none of their diagrams and few of their theories made much sense.

■ ■ ■

The police worked on Hairston's murder, digging up a few interesting angles, the wildest being that Hairston had been killed because he was planning to resurrect the Blackstone Rangers.

But the tip never led anywhere, and the murder remained a mystery.

ONE GOOD COP

This street went for greed. The whole thing greed, money and greed.
Washington Park school crossing guard,
October 14, 1988

T he intersection of Fifty-eighth Street and Indiana Avenue, a mile south of the Fort, was the gateway to the Wentworth police district, home to more violent crime than anywhere else in the city.

That year there were sixty-seven homicides in the district, which included the Robert Taylor Homes, the largest public housing project in the country, and Stateway Gardens.

"Some of the folks around here, they live for death," a woman who had grown up in Stateway once told me. "Everyone wants to prove they're the baddest. Mainly you survive by minding your own business."

Even that was not easy. Residents of the projects would

rush home before sundown with milk and eggs, only to be shot at by snipers. There was no escape from the killing other than a closely held dream of moving to a better place. For most people that dream never materialized.

Cops liked to say you could drive a mile west along Fifty-eighth Street and buy drugs at every corner, which was essentially correct. This was the prized turf of many South Side dealers, past and present, whom detectives could list without hesitation, as though they had memorized their names for a quiz: Shorty, White Cloud, Cold Black, John the Baptist, and Flukey Stokes, who was buried in a Cadillac. Their spheres of influence were sketched by detectives on crude, grease-stained maps on which the cops drew lines between South Side dealers, West Side dealers, Mexican smugglers, and corrupt politicians. And every cop developed a unique version of the black market hierarchy, embellishing it with citations such as "the biggest dealer on the South Side, extremely bad guy."

Not a single court case had exposed the vast, far-reaching network that street cops claimed to know existed. When it came time to file charges, conspiracies turned out to be far less sensational, and far less organized.

In the Wentworth district the Rukns controlled some of the busiest corners, even though the Fort was just beyond the district's border. There was plenty of room for others: entrepreneurs with no affiliations who staked out their own spots, and held them sometimes for decades. There were ten-year-old dealers and seventy-year-old dealers. There was shooting every day. At the end of the year, when the numbers were in and the police department published its annual box score of major crimes, Wentworth was sadly and predictably first.

The whole district, with its high-rise projects and crumbling buildings, was a symbol of despair. Fifty-eighth and Indiana was its radiated core, its chamber of commerce.

What the cops didn't say is that they had a piece of the

action, that they got dirty all day and went home at night to enjoy the fruits of corruption.

Rumors had been circulating at the Cop Shop that as many as a dozen police officers were about to be indicted for taking bribes from dealers and gamblers in the Wentworth district. If true, it would be the most extensive police corruption scandal in Chicago in more than a decade. The indictments, to be handed down in federal court, would be covered by our reporter there. I would have to find my own way into the story.

In the second week of October, when the indictments became a certainty, I went to Fifty-eighth and Indiana. It was the type of neighborhood I told myself I wanted to write about, peopled by thugs and survivors largely forgotten by the police, the press, the rest of the city.

I drove south on Lake Shore Drive, which on this afternoon was like driving along the Riviera, only better. The lake was temperamental, its colors changing with the cast of clouds, the wind, the invisible pull of the moon. The eight-lane roadway hugged the shoreline, rolling out before me as the tide piled on along its edges.

Exiting at Fifty-seventh Street, I took a last look at the aqua blue sheen that stretched toward the horizon, then turned west.

Chicago is a city of neighborhoods, a patchwork of self-sufficient communities with their own ethnic bakeries, video stores, and restaurants. Crossing racial and cultural barriers was by choice only, and most Chicagoans chose not to. This led to a certain cultural myopia. In Chicago, a white person didn't have to deal with people of color, let alone the conditions that beset them in the Wentworth district. What happened there, save for the obvious urban decay, was a mystery even to me, though I did cross the line to do my job. I knew those other Chicagoans from the Sheet, from frantic phone calls, from grief-filled conversations about funeral arrangements. But I did not know much more. I never intended to add to racial typecasting, but that seemed to be the inevitable result of covering crime in the city. Most offenders were black or Hispanic; so were most victims. The best I was able to do was take down their words.

It was haunting to realize that along this bombed-out stretch of the city the cops were central to the problem. Every time I saw a squad car I wondered whether its occupants were on the take. Surely they had thought they could get away with anything here because it was so out of the way, so beyond scrutiny.

Buildings were spray-painted with cryptic slogans. CAIN AIN'T ABLE, said one, which neighborhood residents later told me was an advertisement for karachi, a mixture of brown heroin and barbiturates, the latest high-test drug. Abandoned buildings sat silently, as they had for years, bits of brick and concrete falling to the ground every now and then as they succumbed to snow, wind, and neglect. At night the buildings filled with squatters and junkies. Paper bags littered the sidewalks and alleys, some of them camouflaging clumps of dime bags. A group of men chased a dog around a vacant lot until they had to stop to catch their breath and take another drink.

A city transit department billboard said I was seventeen minutes from the Loop by train.

The action here was out in the open. I drove past barbecue joints, a few liquor stores, and small groups of young men standing around, waiting.

■ ■ ■

Until the turn of the century this part of the district, Washington Park, was economically anchored by a racetrack at Sixty-third and Cottage Grove Avenue. Its workers lived in small apartments east of Indiana Avenue, and wealthier residents occupied elegant homes along a road that would become Martin Luther King Drive. With the closing of the track in 1895, young clerical workers moved into the small but well-kept apartments. It was a diverse neighborhood through the 1920s, when blacks and Jews lived there. But in the 1940s the area underwent convulsive racial change as whites uprooted their families and moved a few blocks west, then picked up and moved again. By 1950 Washington Park was 99 percent black, and it remained that way as it went into deep and steady decline.

At the time of the Wentworth scandal, roughly half of the neighborhood's 20,000 residents lived below the poverty line, and fewer than 3 percent of them owned their own homes. The per capita income at Fifty-eighth and Indiana was slightly more than $4,400 a year. A third of the community's residents were under eighteen, and 70 percent of households were headed by women. Translated, the statistics meant the street belonged to the dealers, junkies, and gangsters.

It was in areas like this that drugs got their bad name. This wasn't some loud party-time neighborhood of bars and nightclubs where the bathroom stalls overflowed with shuffling feet and nasal drip. Fifty-eighth and Indiana was the other side of the rush. Here, on a long, broken street in a big city, you could only watch as cocaine and heroin worked toward the bone.

Here real reporting began. And already I was doing it all wrong. I hadn't arranged to meet anyone. I didn't know the neighborhood. As the only white person within a half mile wearing a suit and tie (though there were white cops, they wore standard-issue stone-washed jeans and sneakers), I stood out as much as if I had had a big cabbage for a head. "Here I am, come and tell me your life stories, tell me why you deal." It was like that. There's a chameleon-like malleability central to good reporting, some sixth sense that tells you what to say, even the cadence. But it was gone.

I parked on the sunny side of the street, the north side.

"People don't talk because of the drug dealers, you know. That's the way it is," said a man named Oscar, who had lived in the neighborhood for eighteen years. He was very thin, his bones forming sharp angles as he leaned against the charred shell of a store that had burned to the ground a few years before.

Oscar used to eat dinner across the street at the Rumpus Room. People would come from way down south to eat the crabs, the shrimp, the egg foo yung, and to mingle for hours downstairs at the bar. But the Rumpus Room had closed twelve years earlier. And the American and Chinese Cuisine Restaurant, its defunct neon sign advertising EXOTIC TROPICAL DRINKS, had closed five years earlier.

"It used to be a beautiful neighborhood, but dope took over," he said. And nothing replaced that.

Oscar's face showed no surprise, recognizing that buildings, like people, had limited life expectancies under these conditions. One day they were burned up, finished.

It was about three in the afternoon. A flock of children marched along Fifty-eighth Street on their way home from school. Some of them stopped in a candy store, yelling at each other about some little thing; others just kept walking.

The crossing guard, Robert Murry, waved them through the intersection. In a deep but scratchy voice she told me not to stay too long. Her lips closed over weakened teeth. Her resolve, though, was stronger than her gums, meaner. She was still willing to point fingers. Every day she watched closely as the schoolchildren crossed the street at her direction, knowing from looking closely at their faces that they didn't all have to turn out bad.

"There ain't nothing you can do about nothing, 'cept cross the kids. I protect them as best I can. They love me," she said, spelling out her formula.

"I lived here since sixty-one. But it's got so bad now, you can't call police to help," she went on. "There's nowhere to call. There's no help. Because they're in on it. I see it every day. What can I do about it? There's nobody to call. No more. They're all crooks."

Her words were stubborn and harsh, and could have been mistaken for ranting had the facts been even slightly different.

"A few weeks ago a cop pulled in front of the Moonglow and pulled away with a big pile of money," Murry said.

Could she prove it? No. But she knew it. She had seen it. And it wasn't the only time.

"This street went for greed. The whole thing greed, money and greed."

Eventually the fifty-eight-year-old crossing guard had resorted to packing a .22-caliber handgun inside her pants. "I want to live," she said.

The most she could hope for was to defend her small piece of the universe. Sure, a few good people wanted badly to do something about the neighborhood, to fix it, to exorcise its demons in church on Sunday and shotgun it on Monday, to reduce it to wipable soot and make life normal again. But they were powerless, and bitterness was all they had left.

Within half an hour it wasn't hard to understand why. After witnessing several quiet deals myself, the question was unavoidable and infuriating: If I could see it, if anyone who stopped at a red light could see it, how come the police couldn't?

The answer would soon be spelled out in federal court, although for the people who lived in Washington Park and other parts of the district it had been plain for years. The cops didn't notice because they were paid to be blind. Their betrayal was now a part of the equation, part of the lopsided battle between good and evil.

It took the feds years to catch on to the blatant fact that around Fifty-eighth Street, some of the greediest people were cops—at least a dozen of them, according to the indictment that was handed down on October 13. Two sergeants, ten patrol officers. Together they were accused of taking $160,000 in bribes from dealers, gamblers, and prostitutes. In exchange, the cops tipped them off to raids and stayed at arm's length as they conducted their dirty business.

...

Police corruption was nothing new in Chicago, especially on the South Side, where the vice of the Custom House Levee, a turn-of-the-century district of whorehouses and saloons, thrived on police "cooperation." In those days, prostitutes were forced to pay weekly stipends to police. One woman described the financial arrangement in the *Chicago Daily Journal* in 1914:

> The policeman had the habit of loafing 'round the entrance to the houses. When the owner saw them standing there, she knew what it meant, and then she would send down a dollar or two by the porter who would slip it into the policeman's hand. The coin would always lubricate the knee joints and make walking beat less irksome like.

By the 1920s, according to Richard Lindberg's colorful history of police corruption, *To Serve and Collect,* the Chicago chief of police, Charles Fitzmorris, admitted to the press that twenty-five hundred officers, roughly half the department, were "involved seriously in the illegal sale or transportation of liquor."

Police precincts had shared boundaries with political wards, and cops were the ward heeler's functionaries, protecting those who had paid, leaning on those who hadn't. Prospective officers often had to pay the ward alderman for the privilege of working in the department, where, once hired, they could find their own ample rewards. When Prohibition ended, gambling simply replaced bootlegging as the source of graft.

Attempts at reform were halfhearted and usually provided only a temporary balm in response to some public outcry. But in 1960, Mayor Richard J. Daley was forced to hire an outsider to clean up what had become one of the most corrupt law enforcement institutions in the country.

The outsider was O. W. Wilson, the only person in the then 123-year history of the city who effectively reformed the department. Wilson turned the entire system on its head, blasting the fiefdoms that were being managed by greedy police captains in many of the city's forty-one precincts.

Wilson had held an advantage; a Californian and an academic, he had few Chicago loyalties. Brought in by Daley to remedy the crisis of confidence that erupted in the wake of the Summerdale scandal, which exposed a band of crooked cops who were moonlighting as burglars, Wilson spit in the face of the old guard, promoted some minority cops, and finally managed to put a dent in rampant corruption.

Wilson's legacy was unique, almost mythic. Old Man Daley, though he resented having to recruit an independent thinker who would not cower in his political shadow, had acted wisely. In the neighborhoods, policing under Wilson became a responsibility to average citizens, even those who couldn't afford to pay for it. And surprisingly, he won the respect of cops too, who had been ready to lynch him when he first arrived.

But in the two decades since Wilson's administration, the department had once again stiffened. There were scandals, of course, more dirty cops, the most notorious being the Marquette Ten, a group of West Side officers convicted of taking bribes from drug dealers. There were the 1968 riots that, much like the Rodney King case, provided irrefutable, visual evidence of the brazen force and brutality implemented by the Chicago police.

And with the dissolution of federal poverty programs and the abandonment of the inner city by businesses, the middle class, and government, districts like Englewood and Wentworth were overrun by narcotics dealing and violence. Poverty and unemployment were once again acceptable so long as the fallout could be contained.

As I stood near the intersection of Fifty-eighth and Indiana, looking into the window of a dry cleaning store, I noticed a lanky teenager walking toward me from across the street. He wore a Detroit Pistons T-shirt and a baseball hat cocked to the right side of his head. He walked up to me, turned quickly, and said; "You get the fuck outta here 'fore I blow your fucking head off."

I walked over to Murry. She assured me it was time to go.

■ ■ ■

With the official announcement of the indictments at a press conference in the Dirksen Federal Building the following afternoon, the bosses counted their blessings and made headlines. Corruption, they declared, would not be tolerated.

Superintendent Martin clasped his hands behind his back, said something about the greed of Ivan Boesky and Wall Street, and ended his comments with the assurance that the cancer had been rooted out. "If it was more widespread, there would be people out there who would know," he said. He looked somber, admitting that the afternoon reminded him of "burying a relative."

The past week had exposed the duality of the police experience, which no doubt contributed to his dour mood. On the one hand, cops deserved recognition of their bravery, and just days before they had received it. In a ceremony at City Hall two days earlier, Martin had watched proudly as sixteen police officers received awards for performing "above and beyond" the call of duty. Two of the officers were honored for disarming a man who had booby-trapped his body with a grenade. And a few days before that, he stood stoically beside Gregory Jaglowski, who received the Blue Star Award for his courageous actions during the shootout at the Montefiore School. Posing for television cameras and photographers in the hospital where he was being treated,

Jaglowski, choking back tears, said of his slain partner; "Irma was the only hero."

Martin thought Mayor Sawyer said it just right as he pinned a medal to Jaglowski's orange hospital robe. "Today Jaglowski means bravery. Today Jaglowski means courage." That's what being a cop was all about.

On the other hand, two ongoing federal investigations portrayed the cops as thieves. In one, a former police sergeant admitted that he had accepted bribes to fix parking tickets. And in the other, eight licensing detectives stood accused of taking bribes from vending machine company owners to expedite their clients' liquor license applications.

On a secretly recorded tape played in a courtroom two floors above where Martin stood, one of the accused cops explained why he would never turn in his fellow officers: "I lived in the city all my life, a policeman . . . and there ain't no way . . . I am going to go out . . . [to be a] stool pigeon. . . . I'd rather do seven or eight years or whatever I'm gonna get and hope they leave me alone."

Martin understood both sides. He liked the fraternity. He liked the loyalty police had to one another. But as chief, he couldn't allow it to compromise the integrity of his department. So at the news conference, at least, he found the will to praise those who had broken the code of silence as heroes.

The cop he named a hero that afternoon was Cynthia White.

■ ■ ■

In late 1985, White's longtime boss, Mardren Johnson, asked her to meet with the department's internal affairs division as a favor.

In the cramped internal affairs office on the twelfth floor of police headquarters, White agreed to embark on a new career as an FBI informant.

That year internal affairs, aided by a sergeant on the South Side, had discovered an oddity in a series of gambling arrest reports from the Wentworth district: in each of several raids, only one person was arrested. A few weeks after the incongruity was detected, in a raid on a Wentworth gambling house, a wire-room employee brazenly declared to the cops, "The boss is going to want to talk to you." At a meeting at a tavern shortly after that, the sergeant who led the raid was offered $500 to lay off the numbers game.

Internal affairs approached the FBI and the U.S. attorney's office with the information. The time was ripe for a large-scale investigation of police corruption, and the Wentworth case was promising. That the district was an impoverished black area would prove that federal authorities had not forsaken the good people who lived there. Everybody knew that the Wentworth district police had been suspect for decades; now the government was finally going to do something about it.

There may have been another agenda.

The first gambling raid was executed against the numbers operation run by Richard Williams, who was the stepson of a Chicago alderman, William Beavers, a strong supporter of then-mayor Harold Washington and a former cop. The feds liked bad cops—almost as much as they liked crooked politicians. The link to Beavers, though it never surfaced, surely was an alluring entrée to City Hall, one of the most intensely corrupt institutions in the country. In the previous fifteen years, twelve aldermen had been convicted for misusing their office.

White's job was to act as the crafty bag woman for Johnson, who by FBI design had just been named commander of the Wentworth district. She spread the word that bribes could no longer be solicited by greedy free-lance cops; rather, they would be collected in a new streamlined system in which she would be the only authorized conduit to her boss. Anyone who did not pay her, who did not cooperate with the program, would be raided.

"I'd use the term 'under the bridge,' " White said in court, looking positively sweet and maternal in her corporate dress. "I'd ask for officers who previously took bribes. I said I wanted to know the officers wouldn't be flamboyant with regard to spending the money."

As part of the plan, another cop was recruited to distribute the bribe money to officers who were members of the "the club." White was relieved that at first she didn't have to hand out cash herself. She feared that word would certainly get back to her husband, a twenty-nine-year veteran of the department who, she decided, would not be told of her undercover role. But the officer who distributed the cash dropped out of the investigation after a dispute with his supervisors at internal affairs, and White was forced to undertake his responsibilities as well.

The FBI rented an apartment near the Wentworth district headquarters, planting a camera in a television set and microphones everywhere, including the closets. In the scantly furnished apartment, White invited the officers of the district to join the commander's club.

Sometimes she was so surprised by who showed up to cut a deal that she felt like crying. Like when the dynamic duo stopped by in December 1986. They were good cops, White thought, two of the hardest-working police in the district. They'd go regularly to Du Sable High School to talk about the drug problem. Now they wanted membership in the club, specializing in shaking down dealers.

"I mean, we all understand why we're here," said one of the cops on tape.

"You can speak, because neither of us are neophytes," the other cop barked at her.

So White spelled out the arrangement: "Once a month I receive certain funds from them gamblers. They have no problem with the boss."

At the trial she wept when she testified about the meeting.

The investigation would continue for two years as dealers, gamblers, cops, and thieves revealed themselves to White, a high school dropout who was proud of her work, who believed that what she was doing was good for the department and the city.

There were meetings with bookies who waited for payment out of their clients' social security checks; a cop who represented John the Baptist, a drug dealer who wanted to open a cut house to process drugs with the blessing of the district commander; a cop who had been lounging at a table in a restaurant when it was raided; a cop who wanted to introduce one of the most notorious dealers on the South Side, Flukey Stokes, to her boss.

And then the cops finally grew suspicious of her.

One searched her at a soul food restaurant on the South Side, but missed the wire that was tucked into her bra.

A different cop, worried by rumors about White's undercover role, demanded they meet at his apartment. Alarmed, she left the recorder home that day. He told her, "I'm not going to let anyone hurt me or my family. I would kill someone who tried to get me."

White quietly said she would do the same thing. The cop believed her and let her go.

The FBI pulled White in from the street in September 1987, when the rumors grew rampant. Until the indictments were handed down, she worked with prosecutors on the case, reviewing for them all she had said, heard, and witnessed.

When the case went to court in late 1989, the defense put White on trial. She was described by defense attorneys as "a perjurer and a viper." "She was a starlet who starred in and wrote her own Hollywood script," said one lawyer. "She did whatever she had to to get ahead," argued another.

But the jury believed Cynthia White, and ten of the officers were convicted.

Superintendent Martin presented her with the Award of Valor, which she accepted one afternoon in his office before the media. Around the same time, she was promoted to sergeant.

But there was yet another story, one that White wanted to tell but didn't for years. She shared it with me over a cup of coffee after she finally tired of the abuse she continued to get for having worked against police corruption. Some of that abuse, she said, came at her from the top of the department.

She wore oversized glasses, a flowered dress, and a cross that settled in her bosom. I could see the charm and the steel will that drew men in and kept them talking. I had watched the tapes from that barren apartment where she cut deals. She spoke a rough language. She moved like a longshoreman, yet there was something warm about her, seductive.

Her worst memory was of a meeting with Martin in his office a few months after the trial was over. She had pleaded with him to exempt her from having to attend sergeants' class at the Police Academy because she was afraid of having to confront the resentment of cops who felt she had violated the blue wall of silence and pride that shrouds police officers.

"The superintendent said, 'You're just paranoid,' " she recalled. Martin told her to attend the class. " 'Now you're going to learn the meaning of the word bravery,' " she remembered him saying.

She broke down in his office. He leaned over and offered her a brown paper towel to wipe her tears.

" 'Someone should have taught you the facts of life. You don't just do things like this.' "

She went to the academy, where, on the first day of class, an officer spit on her shoes. The course lasted a month. After graduation there was a short ceremony outside the superintendent's office honoring White's contribution. She was given a job in internal affairs, the only place within the department she felt safe.

The first week she was there, she said, another officer approached her and asked if they could talk.

He said he had been selected to explain to her the difference between good money and bad money. Good money was bribes you took for a job you were going to do anyway. Nothing wrong with that, the internal affairs officer said. Bad money was dope money, or remuneration for a job you wouldn't otherwise have done. Did she understand?

When we met she was working internal affairs cases, mostly by herself. She still burst with pride over what she had done in the Wentworth district, but she feared the day the department would put her back on the street, where the spitters ruled.

Martin never spoke with White after the ceremony. He denied he had anything but respect for her, denied he had treated her badly.

"She was a fine police officer," he told me. "I wish I had more of them."

E I G H T
...

THE BOSS

MARTIN BLAMES CRIME ON JAIL SQUEEZE
November 19, 1988

S ome days at Eleventh and State I would walk around
the building talking to people, looking for stories.

For Casey it was a reflex. That's how he had come to
own the building. He didn't have to beg anyone to glimpse
a report; people handed them to him. He had scoured the
building so many times, starting in the soul food cafeteria
on the Thirteenth floor and working his way down, that he
knew every filing cabinet.

I started at the top of the police hierarchy because I
felt I didn't have the time to start at the bottom. Instead of
taking secretaries out for happy hour, I took a few big shots
to lunch.

Much of the police brass liked to eat at Manny's, a deli

where the polyester count was almost as high as the cholesterol level and matzo balls swam in puddles of chicken soup like freshly boiled sixteen-inch Chicago softballs. Manny's brimmed at lunchtime with postal workers, cops, aldermen, cops, fire fighters, and more cops, fattifying for the afternoon ahead and saluting each other over mounds of corned beef.

The county medical examiner, Dr. Robert Stein, used to eat there after completing the morning's autopsies.

"Hi, Doc," I once greeted him.

"Hello," he answered, chewing what appeared to be lox and onions between old, yellow teeth and staring at me as though we had never met.

"You know what uniform I wear in Florida?" he suddenly shouted. "Shorts and a polo shirt. That's right!"

There were few places as thoroughly Chicago as Manny's. There everyone was equal, obediently gripping warm wet serving trays just out of the dishwasher in the long line before the meat carver. "Hey you, you're a surgeon. Give me an extra slice. You're beautiful." Power was defined not by restraint, but by an extra potato pancake. Dieting meant eating a bowl of cottage cheese with the stuffed veal shank. It was a bureaucratic Lutece, where everyone knew everyone else and a better pension was just a screaming Formica table away.

One of the big shots I occasionally lunched with was LeRoy Martin, who, I thought, deserved better than Manny's. The first restaurant I took him to was nouvelle Midwest, not far from police headquarters. When we sat down, he was fidgety and visibly perturbed. He said: "This table is okay as long as a car doesn't crash through the window." So we moved a few tables toward the center of the room. Everything was normal again, and his mood improved.

"How come a place like this doesn't have anchovies?" he asked the waitress. "I've got to buy you people a jar."

The job of disseminating the official police version of events belonged to the director of news affairs, a former newspaper reporter (it must have been in another lifetime) who now spent her days issuing press releases—"Police Participate in the Illinois Torch Run for Special Olympics"— and supervising a staff of yawning desk-bound servants. Once during an interview with a police official at which the director was present, I suddenly heard a low-grade snore. I looked across the table to see that she had fallen asleep— thankfully, as her altered state loosened up the conversation.

With sensitive cases, the news affairs office actively worked against the media, plugging up the flow of information with nonanswers and foot-dragging. Getting at the facts behind a police shooting was the true test of a reporter's ability. The policy was to withhold the name of the officer because a provision in the police union contract prohibited revealing it. With good sources, though, it was possible to get the name of the cop. It took me months to figure out how to untether the name from detectives, how to find the reports on these incidents, and even then it was never a sure thing.

The director of news affairs was also supposed to clear interviews with Martin, but it was easier and more fruitful to approach him directly. If he didn't have the facts, at least he had a heartbeat.

There was a refinement about Martin, an ease uncharacteristic of most of the cops I had to deal with, some of whom refused to give out their own names just to be difficult.

Sometimes, oblivious to the standard rules of daily journalism, they'd say "I better not see my name in the paper. Use my boss's, understand?" Commanders often intentionally assigned their nastiest, laziest, and dumbest officers to the phones to ward off the meek. Every time you heard their rough, spiteful voices, you knew you were in for a fight, and the fact that as a taxpayer you also supported their careers made little difference to them. You were nothing but a fly, a splinter, a nuisance.

Martin was a gabber, a gentleman, and a decent guy,

which, to a journalist, meant he took the time to talk to you. Not that he was incapable of distorting the facts. Not that he understood the city's streets. But he was the kind of person you'd like to watch a Bears game with, anchored by a six-pack of cold beer and a bucket of ribs.

If he had not been named superintendent, Martin would have been happy spending his days as an administrator in a dead-end job. He had attained a higher level than he thought possible as a black man who had joined the force when he did. He had been reasonably well paid, and was able to go straight home every day, except when there had been a plane crash, a cop shooting, or some other catastrophe. He would have retired to play endless games of golf with his wife. Instead, Martin won a prize he had never even dreamed of. And when he got over the wonderment of how far he had come, he fit right in.

■ ■ ■

Over lunch (poached salmon), Martin comfortably looked back on his roots. His parents were Mississippi cotton pickers who had never finished grade school. Arriving in Chicago at the Illinois Central train station, they settled in a tiny apartment on the city's West Side near Roosevelt Road and Ashland Avenue, a few blocks from Manny's.

They fed the kids pork and beans and oatmeal, and not much else. And they watched over them, smacking them when necessary. In that neighborhood, in the 1940s, cops were barely needed; law enforcement then, like nuclear armament, worked on the principle of deterrence.

"In those days if the police brought you home, there was no debate about whether you were wrong. It was just prima facie evidence," Martin explained over lunch. "When a policeman brought you home in my neighborhood, that was a disgrace. Because nobody in our neighborhood wanted that."

A pioneer of sorts, Martin joined the police department in 1955. There were then two hundred black officers, five black sergeants, and one black lieutenant. Promotions he didn't expect. He didn't even bother to learn the name of his precinct captain.

He started walking a beat at Ninety-first Street and Cottage Grove Avenue, a crowded stretch of dry cleaners, shoe stores, and beauty salons on the South Side, which Martin remembered as "a middle-class neighborhood, a very nice assignment for a rookie police officer." Old newspaper clips from the *Defender* and the *Tribune* which he kept in a folder documented his rise through the ranks. There he was, Officer Martin, calming a horde of white teenagers who nearly rioted when five Negroes wanted to swim alongside them at Rainbow Beach; Sergeant Martin arresting seven persons at a South Side betting parlor after a mother complained that her son was losing his weekly paycheck on horses; Lieutenant Martin heading the burglary unit in the Wentworth district; Commander Martin taking over the reins of the narcotics division.

A few months before being named superintendent, Martin made the news again for helping to solve a series of smash-and-grab burglaries on the West Side—a solid case, but hardly a calling card for the top job.

Martin was the dark horse on a short list of candidates that also included a Hispanic and a white police official, both of whom were savvier, more experienced police administrators. West Side politicians who had come to know Martin over the years threw their support behind his candidacy. But the decision ultimately rested in the hands of the city's mayor, Harold Washington, who would listen to his political allies, though he did not necessarily do what they wanted.

Martin met with Harold Washington twice to discuss serious police matters like staffing shortages and budgetary constraints. His third and final interview took place on a Friday night at the end of October 1987 in the mayor's South

Side apartment. A bodyguard had just delivered a bucket of fried chicken, and the mayor promptly offered some to his guest.

"Mr. Mayor, I didn't come here for dinner—I came here for a job," Martin recalled saying.

They both laughed.

" 'You know, if I appoint you superintendent, it won't be an easy job.' "

"What has ever been easy for a black man?" Martin responded.

This time, Martin remembered, they just looked at each other without saying anything.

Washington shook Martin's hand and told him that one of the three finalists would hear good news from his aide on Saturday morning.

Just eight hours later, Martin's appointment was emblazoned in bold headlines across the front page of the *Sun-Times,* which arrived at the new superintendent's doorstep before dawn. The exclusive was a source of embarrassment for us at the *Tribune,* and a shock to Martin, since the Washington administration had intentionally leaked the story to a terminally ill *Sun-Times* reporter before even telling the appointee.

Although I was still a suburban reporter, I happened to be working on the city desk that Saturday, months before I took on the police beat.

"I had all but given up," Martin said when I reached him at home in our first interview.

From the mayor's office came the highest praise. In the words of an aide to Washington, Martin "wasn't hampered by experience in the upper ranks." He was, Washington's people hoped, "somebody who could shake up the men a little and not be constrained by the police mentality."

Perhaps Washington saw himself in the veteran cop: a proud black man who from a lowly position had mastered the ropes, watching the Irish cops for years and learning to get along with them. His color, Martin liked to say, was blue, like the uniform.

"Even though I was black, I was one of them," he had said.

Washington needed Martin to carry out a reform agenda. There was a growing feeling among civic leaders that the police department needed to be coaxed into redefining itself. The mantra was economy, putting more uniforms on the street without spending more money on hiring. The 911 system needed to be revamped.

Martin appeared to be someone who could rise to the occasion, take a few bold steps that might even put him at odds with the rank and file, and massage the people with goodwill.

On that raw Saturday, Washington stood by Martin's side at a City Hall news conference, transforming a dull nugget of police brass into a success. Martin, enveloped by the mayor's aura, was instantly popular and, for the most part, untouchable. If he had been divinely chosen, he could not have been more secure in his job.

At the end of the press conference Martin's wife, Constance, pinned four golden stars on her husband's shoulders. She had tears in her eyes.

He offered a simple pledge: "I hope I can leave my term knowing that I've lowered crime in the city. Our youth are kind of running around without direction. I want to try and get a handle on that."

■ ■ ■

As they would with Washington, and largely because of him, people were willing to take a chance with Martin. Many whites felt that this black guy, like the mayor, could be trusted.

A week later Martin was speaking his mind. During a break in his confirmation hearing, he called the police department "the toughest gang in town," a throwback to the stormtrooper image many Chicagoans would have preferred to bury. But the worriers were in the minority. Most people loved Martin's battling rhetoric. He spoke the language of middle-class frustration, straight up. During the hearing he maintained that cops were basically honest people who were doing everything they could to keep the peace. He spoke of unemployment and the painful growth of the underclass, arguing these were conditions that needed to be addressed if crime was to be fought effectively.

He sounded as though his heart was in the right place, that he cared about the city and had a few ideas to save it from the hara-kiri taking place in New York, Los Angeles, and Detroit. His confirmation was uncontested.

■ ■ ■

Martin's first crisis arrived in just three weeks.

Harold Washington was sitting in his fifth-floor office in City Hall late that same November, looking forward to leading a dynasty. His last act was bending over to pick up a letter that had fallen from his desk. When he reached down he suffered a massive heart attack and died. Gone was Martin's chicken-dispensing rabbi, and with him the dream of rooted black political empowerment that many had believed would take hold.

Thousands of citizens, black and white, solemnly walked through the marble lobby of City Hall to pay tribute to Washington. On the day he was to be buried in Oak Woods Cemetery they lined the streets of the South Side to glimpse the funeral cortege. A large crowd pressed against the gates of the cemetery, clamoring to get in so they could trek to the grave site, an unmarked plot along a narrow footpath. The only obstacle was a line of police officers and their new boss, Martin.

Washington's casket, carried by a black hearse, rolled through the gates, followed by a procession of three hundred cars. As the motorcade swept by, the crowd of about ten thousand chanted, "Harold . . . Harold." Hawkers sold buttons, T-shirts, and posters with the mayor's picture. Politicians wept.

The crowd begged, shouted. But someone high up in the city bureaucracy had decided that this was not to be a public burial, that the late mayor, who had lain in state for a week in City Hall, ascending from mayor to Saint Harold, Perfect Harold, would last be seen by a gathering of dark suits, aldermen who had ridden his coattails and visiting dignitaries who could only marvel at his easy way of doing the city's business.

Martin stood in front of the wrought iron cemetery gates, his smooth white gloves cutting through the gray daylight, shouting "Don't give up the street—don't give up the street! We can't give up the street!" The gates closed and the crowd surged forward, pressing against the iron spikes, which flexed like rubber. A line of police horses kicked up dust as they danced along the sidewalk. "Don't give up the street!" Martin shouted as he directed a knot of decorated police officials around him. They followed the boss's orders, but their faces revealed a preoccupation with whether the crowd, and shortly after the city, would careen into prolonged riots as they had imagined dozens, maybe hundreds of times.

Somehow Martin's pleas prevailed, without beatings, without tear gas. The horses calmed, snorting in the November air like idling semis, and slowing their gait. Harold Washington was buried that frigid afternoon amid a lot of cursing and anger, but without violence.

Watching the scene unfold from ten yards away, I was convinced that Martin, just as the press release had said, was a "hands-on" administrator who was willing to get those hands dirty. It was a good debut.

Washington's death left Martin in charge of the second largest police department in the country, and beholden to no one but himself. In less than a month he had become the most powerful superintendent in the history of the department, with the ability to implement policies, procedures, and reforms without a long political ax hanging over him. Also gone was the impetus to change.

Of course, with Washington dead and the city beginning to slide backward, some cops were now calling him "nothing but a barnyard nigger," a development that initially left the new superintendent unfazed.

■ ■ ■

When I needed a source of last resort, someone to confirm the facts of an important story I hadn't yet pinned down, or to enliven one with some bluster, I'd walk into Martin's office on the fourth floor and wait for him in a paneled anteroom, perusing back issues of *Law Enforcement Bulletin* or *Crime Control Digest*.

The best time to do this was at the end of the day, shortly after the blue shirts began their journey home, charging past the candy stand in the lobby and through the revolving doors. The building emptied out in a few minutes, leaving behind just a few reporters, janitors, and police officials, including Martin.

The Deacon, a bony and slightly grizzled former West Side beat cop who was Martin's trusted aide, would greet me, then deliver a short sermon on the sins of the press.

"Now tell me this," he would say, calmly pumping his words until he speared the ones he was looking for. "You— you—you write about the El Rukns, but you don't write the truth."

"What's the truth?" I'd ask.

"Oh, you know what the truth is."

"No, tell me."

"Don't ask me. You know everything."

And that's how we'd end it, as the Deacon motioned me into Martin's spacious office.

Martin's suite was stocked with plaques and tributes,

souvenirs collected during his first year in office: police hats from Paris, Moscow, and Athens; accolades from law schools and community organizations; an engraving of his round, beefy face taken from the monthly police bulletin.

A nineteen-inch television set was tucked into an elaborate dining room–style shelf unit overflowing with mementos.

"You know who my hero is?" he once asked.

"Who?"

"Ariel Sharon," he announced.

The Israeli general was everything Martin fantasized being: a military leader, a modern-day Patton who was unencumbered by American-style liberalism.

"They have a spray they use to see if you fired a gun. We could use that here. . . ."

Beneath the refinements, Martin was a spit-and-polish law enforcement guy who felt inhibited by the Constitution. Though he was not an ardent crusader for civil liberties, he knew that tampering with them would be bad publicity. He would have liked to make massive roundups of gang members, sending them to boot camp for rehabilitation or pass out long, uncompromising jail sentences. When neighborhoods heated up and he sent in the troops to temporarily restore order, he liked to say, "Oh boy, Harvey Grossman and the ACLU are gonna be all over me on this one." He knew he couldn't just kick some ass. And so he became the next best thing—a celebrity promoter of law and order, armed with sound bites if no plan.

If he couldn't be Sharon he would at least, reveling in shoddy analogy, be Mike Ditka.

One night in late 1988, sitting behind his desk in an orange padded executive chair, Martin reveled away. The topic: his controversial transfer of two police officers who had ticketed his daughter for a traffic violation. The transfers had nothing at all to do with the ticket, he argued; he was simply exercising executive privilege.

"It's like this. If Ditka would just let everyone bid on

their positions, the Fridge would want to play wide receiver. They wouldn't win a game."

He argued that he would never intentionally kill traffic tickets because the press would embarrass him. He used the same logic to explain his aversion to bribe taking.

A few months later, when the police union filed a grievance on the grounds that the transfers were a form of harassment, Martin backpedaled and the officers were returned to their old jobs. He made the move quietly, after the story had faded.

■ ■ ■

I enjoyed the access. On another evening, when Martin had been superintendent for about a year, I walked the silent halls of headquarters to see him.

The Deacon waved me in to the inner sanctum, where Martin sat upright, leafing through a stack of papers.

"You know what this job has been?" he asked. "It's been a love feast."

He leaned forward, grabbed an asthma inhaler from the desk, and sprayed a soothing blast of medication into his lungs.

"Everything all right?" I inquired.

"Oh yeah. My health is good."

He had suffered a heart attack in 1984, continued to take blood thinners, but for the most part seemed to be in good physical condition. He hardly missed a day on the job.

"Here you go, Boss," offered the Deacon, handing over a starched white shirt.

Martin stood up and peeled off his button-down blue uniform shirt, which he wore over a white T-shirt. His thick arms bulged.

"Excuse me one second."

There was a dinner that night and Martin wanted to look like a civilian. He was a large man, very dark, with a little bit of Santa Claus across the middle. His uniform jacket was usually too tight, especially when its gold buttons were fastened to the top, so that it looked as though the circulation to his head might be cut off. In non-official clothes he was looser. On Fridays, when his schedule was light, he'd walk around police headquarters with his collar spread wide open, his little hat on top of his head as if he were a bus driver visiting the zoo. He didn't appear hemmed in by his responsibilities, his upbeat persona eclipsing the largeness of the job.

He loved his standard-issue blue police shirt and navy blue pants and wide patent leather shoes because they so clearly defined his life, symbolizing the unlikely rewards granted him. And he took umbrage at those cops who didn't share this veneration, even those directing traffic on the hottest summer days.

When a deputy chief from the South Side refused to suspend an officer caught not wearing his hat, Martin demoted the deputy on the spot. It was one of the most decisive actions Martin took as superintendent. But the new generation of police officers, a generation that had made fun of Cub Scout uniforms as kids, resented this brand of formality.

Martin stood up and stretched his arms forward to straighten the cuffs of his white shirt.

Suspended from the ceiling, above his desk, was a cluster of two-hundred-watt bulbs and reflectors installed by a previous superintendent to backlight press conferences. Martin had no use for them. He preferred to address reporters in the auditorium, beneath the greenish fluorescent lights, or outside on the city streets, or informally in his office. He was a natural on camera, appearing as though he had rehearsed his lines for hours. In the beginning he seemed to like calling the press together just so he could sound off.

Superintendent, what is your position on the Guardian Angels?

"My people are the only ones trained to handle the

thugs out there. What are the Guardian Angels trained for? To catch thirty-eights with their teeth?"

Superintendent, what do you think of the mass release of prisoners from Cook County Jail?

"It's affecting our quality of life. A few weeks ago, I observed more compassion for three whales than I have seen for people walking the streets of Chicago." If whales flown to the city from Canada could live luxuriously in a giant lakeside fishbowl, surely the city could find room to warehouse criminals. Let them sleep in three shifts. Even better, Martin proposed, convert the city's shuttered hospitals into jail space.

His message had two reactionary themes: that the rights of the criminal had under liberal administrations become a higher priority than the rights of the average citizen; and that everything was under control.

But by Martin's first anniversary on the job, in the fall of 1988, crime statistics suggested that the streets were hardly calm. Even though the murder rate was surprisingly low, the incidence of most every other crime was on the way up. Martin and his all-is-well antics were undaunted, but others in the city were worried about a new wave of violence. One of them was Jesse Jackson, the founder of Operation Push on the South Side. Jackson held his own press conference at police headquarters to call for the establishment of citizen patrols similar to the Guardian Angels. People were scared, Jackson said. It was time to act, to help the police, before Chicago erupted.

Although Martin stood by Jackson's side in the auditorium, back in his office he rolled his eyes at Jackson's suggestion, again insisting that there was no need for volunteers or vigilantes. There wasn't even a need for more cops, he said—only more jails.

It was true that the situation at the Cook County Jail was teetering on chaos. The inmate population was by court order not to exceed 5,559. But in late 1988 the population had swelled to more than 7,000. Thieves and rapists were sleeping on mattresses in the hallways, leading a federal judge to impose a $1,000 a day fine on prison officials. To keep the budget in line, the county freed about 120 prisoners daily, mostly drug suspects.

"I got something for you," Martin said as he rooted on the top of his desk for a sheet of paper. "This is it. I've got one guy in the Eighteenth District who's been arrested twenty-three times in the past year alone. Twenty-three times. My men are making arrests like crazy. We're doing our job. But we got no place to put them. If all of them were incarcerated, I could probably get the system working as smoothly as a Rolex watch."

He tossed the memo back onto his desk.

"What else can I do?"

Virtually no one, from the mayor on down, demanded that he find an answer.

During that winter he was so popular that some people in the news business considered him a viable mayoral candidate. At first thought the idea seemed to me odd, to say the least. Martin could point to no accomplishments in the last year, no innovative new programs to fight crime, no neighborhoods rescued. While community-based policing was the buzz all over the country, Martin aggressively opposed the strategy and continued to back old-fashioned, response-driven policing. Squad cars still maniacally cruised the streets, waiting to answer emergency calls. That's the way things had been done when he joined the department. That's the way it should be.

The stubbornness was apparent from the outset. Yet the brazen manner also revealed his potential strength as a public official. He was an improviser, unafraid and uninhibited as he stood before the television cameras and spoke, early on winning more supporters than detractors. That he wasn't doing much to improve the department mattered little. He was believable. That's what counted.

Martin had also shown that he could walk the city's racial tightrope with surprising ease. Only the second black to hold the position of police chief—which, at a salary of $100,000 a year, was the highest-paying city job—he had become an important representative of the city's black communities, and he acted without alienating whites. Within the police department he promoted both blacks and whites, mainly old-timers who, like Martin, had made their names as tough street cops.

One of them was Ed Wodnicki.

Martin and Wodnicki had known each other for years, meeting at police retirement parties and St. Jude parades honoring comrades who had died in the line of duty. When he became superintendent, Martin promoted Wodnicki to chief of detectives, and eventually made him the number-three man in the department, in charge of the organized crime and detective bureaus. Together they reminded me of the Honeymooners, Ralph and Ed; though one was black and the other white, both were bare-knuckled sons of the working class, hard-nosed cops doing apprenticeships in public relations. Together they set the tone and agenda for the entire department. If there was any question as to whether integration had penetrated the Chicago Police Department, one could just look at the top.

Or so it seemed.

Wodnicki's office, like Martin's, was a frequent stop in my rounds. Nearly every report generated on the street passed through it, and if there was a question I couldn't get answered by the area detectives, I could turn to Wodnicki. He was learning to be less contemptuous of the media, and he rarely minded being quoted by name.

"Treat me nice," he'd say, "or I'll come piss in your soup."

I thought Ralph and Ed had a chance. But right under their highly trained noses, the city was edging toward a new threshold of violence.

For me, the best example of how "youth were kind of

running around" came some months later, in a South Side high school.

The cops who typed the news out on the Sheet didn't think much of it. "Chester Dunbar / stabbed / Harper High."

I rushed down to Brighton Park, where the victim's classmates were being questioned by detectives. When they had finished describing the murder to the police, they lingered on the rotting sun-bleached stairway of the old stationhouse to retell their versions once more, this time to reporters. They were laughing and smiling as though they had been named teenagers of the year.

It happened like this, they offered, their voices rising as they vied with one another to tell the details of the story. The teacher had been collecting homework when two boys walked in and held Chester, and then one of them stabbed him in the chest with a butcher knife. Right in the middle of geometry class. No fooling.

"Chester said, 'My back.' And fell down," a girl named Arlyce recounted for the reporters.

"Were you scared?" I asked one of the students.

"I got to say that it didn't scare me because I've seen worse," he said, his eyes flitting. "My brother got shot in the head right next to me."

"The teacher was crying," came another voice. "She was in shock. They gave her a bunch of cold water and took her out of the room."

Then they bolted out of the station, screaming and walking on their toes, rushing home to catch themselves on television.

Two sixteen-year-old boys were charged with the murder. The cops said it was over a gang rivalry. But what exactly the rivalry was about, neither the cops nor anyone else could say.

N I N E

. . .

LE CRACQUE

RAIDERS BUST CITY CRACK OPERATION
December 4, 1988

T he poached beefcake dime-size hoop earring camou-
flage double-stubble flak-jacket ponytail parade of
narco-raiders jumped out of a blue van, maybe two vans.
Draped in blue windbreakers and crowned with baseball hats
and team letters (CPD for Chicago Police Department; DEA,
Drug Enforcement Administration—as though everyone
didn't already know), they burst through the front door of
an old red house at Forty-fourth Street and Greenwood Avenue in the first crack raid in Chicago's history. Code name:
Le Cracque.

Forty-fourth and Greenwood was to be the preemptive
strike against crack cocaine that Chicago police and the U.S.
attorney's office could point to as a symbol of their resolve.

There they set up an elaborate undercover operation, working the corner for about eight months. They hid a video camera on top of a utility pole to record drug transactions. They rented an apartment in a nearby high rise, watching through binoculars the people who came and went twenty-four hours a day. They recruited informants and bought a lot of crack, in dozens of hand-to-hand buys. They were so eager that they almost blew their cover initially when agents bought crack with hundred-dollar bills, which made the dealers suspicious because it was a business based on twenties.

Mistakes were made, but in the end they didn't matter much.

Linked to the ring was thirty-five-year-old Marlowe Cole, who once allegedly sold heroin to the Rukns. Cole's rap sheet overflowed with nearly fifty drug and weapons charges, but his most serious mistake was getting involved with crack dealers at a time when the government was hungry to break the business. From that moment on, he might as well have put a target on his back when he dressed in the morning. He had no legitimate source of income, but a Rolls Royce was parked in his front yard. He also had a few safe deposit boxes that he didn't tell the Internal Revenue Service about.

The operation at Forty-fourth and Greenwood wasn't IBM. It was a relatively unsophisticated curbside setup. But it was lucrative, and its success explained why dealing crack had become such big business.

Stanley Wright, twenty-one, who lived near Forty-fourth, first got rich on that corner.

He worked hard, and like most of the sellers on the street, spent nights running from one buyer to the next without worrying much about the law. The blinking red light of the video camera affixed to the utility pole didn't deter him or anyone else. The dealers just blew it to pieces with a shotgun and kept on working. A thousand dollars a day was hard to resist, no matter who was watching.

"It's not as easy as everyone thinks it is," Wright complained to a girlfriend in a telephone conversation tape-recorded by the government and replayed at his trial. "Because the money is good, but it's a big hassle because you got to set it up, you got to find the stuff, you got to cook it, you got to bag it, and then you have to find somebody to sell it. . . . You gotta keep up with what they come short and what they don't come short, and you got to worry about them getting caught and this and that and the other. You gotta worry about if they're gonna tell if they get caught, and if they have to do some time, and they're gonna tell on you to keep from having to do so much time."

Reasonable concerns.

In all, thirty-five people, including Wright, were indicted in Operation Le Cracque. The bust was announced at a press conference by the U.S. attorney, Anton Valukas. A cadre of police brass stood in a row behind him, their arms at ease, their faces glowing in triumph.

When the head of the Chicago DEA office, a veteran DEA administrator in Washington who had returned to the Midwest to retire, took the podium next, he publicly lent credence to a theory based on a combination of perverse hometown pride and principles culled from Econ 101 that had been gaining popularity in law enforcement circles.

There was so little crack in Chicago, the DEA chief said, because the street gangs were keeping it out. Gang leaders feared the easily manufactured drug would decentralize the dope business they controlled and overwhelm the market with free-lancers and ambitious young competitors. So, in a meeting of criminal minds—an updated version of the 1957 gangster summit in Apalachin, New York, that has never been documented or even detailed with any credibility—the big bad gangs of Chicago, the heirs of Al Capone, closed the city's borders to crack.

Thus began one of the great Chicago myths—perpetuated, I hate to admit, in some of my own stories as well as by university professors, criminal justice experts, and eventually the *New York Times*.

To his credit, Raymond Risley, the commander of the Chicago police narcotics unit, never bought the theory. But he arrived at an equally untenable conclusion about Forty-fourth and Greenwood. "As far as we know," he said, "this is the only crack operation in the city."

■ ■ ■

When I started at the Cop Shop, one of the first stories I tried to write was about crack dealing in Chicago. Big cities and small towns alike were being torn apart by the drug, yet it had never been discussed in the local media. For a reporter, the subject offered a valuable opportunity, based, as good stories always seemed to be, on the misery of others. But when I spoke to police and drug counselors, they insisted crack was not widely available, though they were dumbfounded as to why.

The news affairs office had proof.

Of the 5,105 seizures of cocaine made in the first half of 1988, 51 were of crack. Less than 1 percent.

I checked with each of the twenty-five police districts, staying on the PAX phone for hours at a time. They all said the same thing: No crack here.

Officials at the DEA, the swank, suit-heavy federal agency responsible for tracking the large-scale movements of drugs in the United States, were of the same mind, although they noted an ominous increase in the number of free-base cocaine users seeking treatment.

There was no better illustration of cops' simultaneous blindness and wild imagination than the official line on crack. But narcotics police were not the only ones engaged in denial. Even drug treatment facilities were perplexed. "Every conference we go to, we hear how terrible crack is," one program director said. "Then we come back here and it's not that bad."

Risley, a low-key man who after nearly thirty years in the department saw more utility in a computer than a police scanner, was adamant. Cupping his hands together with professorial grace, a scholar, at least by comparison with most of his peers, Risley argued that midwesterners had learned from the mistakes of others—that the media barrage about crackheads, crack murders, cracking up had settled into the vocabulary and the psyche, scaring Chicagoans into sticking with old and reliable drugs.

After hearing the refrain enough, I reported what the cops, drug counselors, and even some users believed: that crack had somehow sidestepped Chicago. That in itself was a pretty good story.

■ ■ ■

It wasn't good enough for my editor, Aloysius Brooklyn. The crack had to be out there.

If I had any doubts, Aloysius Brooklyn obliterated them with the uncompromising and occasionally misguided logic that was his trademark.

"Grow the fuck up," he'd tell me over and over, pulling his thick glasses forward with both hands, then pushing them back close to his eyes as though they were held by a tight elastic band.

You could see it coming from all directions, he'd shout as he sat at his computer terminal, from across Lake Michigan and down the Mississippi. It was exploding just beyond the city's border in smaller towns like Fort Wayne, Indiana, and Peoria. If it wasn't here yet, it would arrive soon. And when it did, no one in Chicago would be able to say the *Tribune* hadn't said so. His was a rambunctious approach to civic duty.

I had known Aloysius Brooklyn for years. The first thing he said to me was something like "You're ruining your career, writing movie reviews." He was always dispensing advice, especially when you hadn't asked for it. It was a reflex for him, being this authoritarian father figure.

In the hula hoop–size circle at the city desk he flailed

in, his thoughts were preeminent, all-important, sparked by television news, Russian novelists, and American realists. He had a graying goatee, spoke a few words of Yiddish and Spanish and more than a few of Russian, and dressed in regulation blue editor's shirts. Being edited by him could be as tormenting as getting a bad haircut. A little more here, and a little more there, so that when it was done the story was unrecognizable. But he was right more often than not, and for that many people would never forgive him.

His instructions were simple: Find the crack.

■ ■ ■

There was certainly plenty of everything else.

The dope arrived in the projects, in Cabrini, Henry Horner, Robert Taylor, Stateway, after 2:00 A.M., when most of the patrols went home for the night. It came to the city by train, by bus, by plane, but mainly in the door panels of cars or vans, which were customized by highly paid midnight mechanics.

Most of the time the drugs came via Mexico. Whether it was Colombian cocaine or brown heroin or potent reefer, it moved through Durango, a ramshackle town with long blocks of cheap motels, across a muddy stretch of the Rio Grande to El Paso, then north.

Every now and then the police would find some of it.

One morning a bulletin from the news affairs office arrived in the press room to announce the biggest drug raid in the history of the Chicago Police Department. A press conference was scheduled for eleven o'clock. These were days of cocaine-filled boats and warehouses, and seizures across the country were growing by the ton.

When we got downstairs to the auditorium the cocaine was laid out on a table, a smorgasbord of bricks of the white powder and bundles of cash. It had been seized by police from a garage on the South Side, where it had sat for several weeks. There were 117 pounds of cocaine and 1 ounce of brown heroin. Police always liked putting a dollar value on drugs seized in raids: Today's cache, for example, was worth "an estimated $13 million," a phrase an editor would wisely knock out because the figure was always meaningless.

Compared to the loads being recovered in New York and Miami, it was relatively small, though by Chicago standards it was significant. The haul was proof that the city, despite not being a main port of entry for narcotics, continued to be a distribution point for drugs bound for the Midwest. Chicago had always been a transportation hub; why should it not be in the narcotics trade? More disturbing, however, was the discovery of the brown heroin alongside the cocaine. This was a development authorities had not been prepared for, and they viewed the coupling as especially worrisome.

An eighteen-year-old man was arrested and charged with possession of the drugs. According to police, he was an operative of the Herrera family, the major supplier of brown heroin to Chicago for the past two decades. That the Herreras were now transporting cocaine supported the argument that a major change was taking place in drug smuggling in the United States. With police pressure mounting on known ports of entry such as Miami and San Diego, Colombian cocaine traffickers had contracted with established heroin traffickers like the Herreras to transport their product along the old pipeline and into America's midsection. If they achieved half as much success as with heroin, the Herreras, who had proved elusive targets for law enforcement in the past, would surely become significant players in the local cocaine market.

I had never heard of the Herreras until the press conference, primarily because their dealing in heroin made them passé. But in the back of the auditorium stood a cop who had made the family the focus of his career. His name was Tom West. Dressed in a camel hair trench coat and aviator sunglasses, he looked like Clint Eastwood, cleaned up after a shootout, a shot, and a beer.

West had spent more than half his life as a Chicago police officer. He joined the department when he was nineteen, starting out as an undercover recruit for the Red Squad, a police spy unit. His job: handing out leaflets for the Socialist Workers' Party on college campuses.

By the early 1970s, West was fighting the next big enemy, drugs. He learned how to chase the bag on Forty-seventh Street, a heroin supermarket, by watching from rooftops as dealers handed off glassine envelopes near the El station. He stumbled on the Herreras in October 1973, when he busted a sixteen-year-old boy who had pulled up to a hot dog stand on a shiny new Harley to sell some smack. During his interrogation, the kid described a drug house on the South Side where his suppliers were mixing Mexican heroin from five-gallon ice cream tubs. At first West thought the kid was lying to save himself. After all, any bust was big news at the time, so much so that when a kilo of the stuff came in as evidence, the cops would gather around to stare at it.

One afternoon, West and his crew raided the cut house and, to their amazement, found the teenage dealer had been telling the truth.

West spent the next decade chasing the Herreras and their operatives, arresting them and sometimes missing nickel bags in exchange for tips and clues, for the pager numbers of suppliers and the addresses of safe houses. Because of infighting, there was no shortage of informants. West owed his greatest successes to them, the best days of his career, long days, as he recalled, "that never started without a lot of fucking laughing."

Now he was a cop who laughed when anyone mentioned the war on drugs, because he knew that law enforcement could do no better than hold the line. Even that was getting to be nearly impossible. West remembered when you could name the top dealers in Chicago on one hand, a time when the cops felt they had a chance. But he had been to Durango and seen the army of profiteers packing, dealing, and hauling dope. It had gotten so big, so pervasive, that sometimes, when the adrenaline wore off, he felt entirely useless. Back home, the department was running around in circles, spending too much time getting nothing done. It all added up to chaos.

If the cops were waffling, the cocaine in the South Side garage was a sign of the Herreras' resolve. For years, brown tar heroin had been as plentiful as cough syrup in Chicago. But the family was forced to diversify in 1987, when Mexican authorities arrested the Herrera patriarch. Within months, the younger members of the family reached agreements with the Colombian cocaine cartels to transport their drugs into the United States.

The backbone of the pipeline was highly paid but scantly informed mules who drove the narcotics north from the Mexican border. The mules didn't know where the drugs were hidden or for whom they were working. They'd simply drive to Illinois, making very few stops, and ending their two-thousand-mile journey at a designated drop-off point in Chicago, usually a remote outdoor parking lot.

The 117-pound shipment spread out on the table had come up in three cars from Durango. The cops watched the load for weeks, hoping to ensnare any high-level dealer drawn to it. But only the eighteen-year-old visited the site, and they finally arrested him.

As the bosses took credit for the raid, West watched quietly from the back of the auditorium, seemingly content to be out of the spotlight. He had gone all these years without publicity; why start now?

A few weeks after the seizure, I went to meet him and his team in the back of a dark Italian restaurant a few blocks from the Cook County Criminal Court building. Seven of them sat around a table flanking one of their informants, a scrawny Guatemalan kid they called El Raton, "the Rat." Without disclosing many details, West said the Rat was saved by his crew after he had been kidnaped the week before by the Herreras and duct-taped to a bench press in the basement of a two-story house on the West Side. West told the story with a grin; pulling off these adventures was among the few remaining pleasures of the job.

The Rat left the restaurant shortly after I arrived, and I never was able to figure out exactly what had happened to him.

Informants were a strange, unpredictable breed who were central to police work. They were paid anywhere from a few dollars to thousands, depending on the police agency involved, with the federal government at the high end and local police departments near the bottom. Cops relied on them for successful raids, like the one at the garage. Sometimes they were worth saving from their enemies.

Long silences passed between the undercover cops at the table. They ate quietly, scooping up chicken Vesuvio and smoking cigarettes. I would have thought they were just taking a breather, having story time, in the middle of a pretty good day. But there was anger in their voices, anger that went beyond the groaning of cops about their crummy pay and terrible hours.

The frustration was rooted in what they saw as the department's hypocrisy. Administrators talked about going after the big dealers, but they weren't willing to commit the manpower or money. They talked about reducing the flow of narcotics on the street, but the police brass were restrained by their own stupidity. The war against drugs in Chicago was, if not lost, at best stalemated through stubbornness.

The narcotics unit, for example, had been gutted over the years by old-school superintendents who believed that drug agents would inevitably be the Achilles heel of the department, the most vulnerable to corruption. Even though Martin had once headed the unit and still paid lip service to the war on drugs, he did little to bolster its personnel or equipment.

A recent order prohibited gang crimes officers from serving narcotics warrants. The administration's position was archaic; the gang crimes units—one of which West's group was technically assigned to—were for fighting gangs, not drugs. Of course, the policy ignored the primary reason most gangs existed.

Aggravation led someone at the table to make a suggestion. Think of the money seized in narcotics raids—millions of dollars since a federal law passed in 1984 allowed local police departments to keep a percentage of what they took from drug dealers. Where did it go? You're a reporter, the cops said; you figure it out.

Now there were two questions I asked everywhere I went and of everyone I met: Where's the crack? and, Where's the drug money? Not surprisingly, the first question was easier to answer than the second, and it angered fewer people.

■ ■ ■

Most Chicago cops didn't even know what crack was, insisting it was somehow different from free-base cocaine, or rock, which they had been seizing all over the South and West sides for two decades, though there was no difference other than the method of preparation. But in their minds, because no one in the police department had instructed them otherwise, crack contained a secret ingredient that made people so high, so mad and determined that nothing but destruction could get between the user and his fix.

Base, rock—that was what Richard Pryor was doing when he burned his face off; that was what thousands of dirty junkies on the West Side were hooked on. Old news. Crack was New York, L.A.—not Chicago. Or not yet.

The crime lab technicians knew better. They understood that crack was nothing more than refined cocaine. But in a pathetic irony, they didn't bother to catalogue the total number of crack seizures during the early phase of the drug's spread. Consequently, their statistics never accurately reflected the popularity of the drug and provided a faulty basis for the complacency of the department.

Such were the twisted moves of the cop tango: simple denial of problem, press conference, fancier denial. Police administrators thanked their stars Chicago wasn't Detroit. They came up with grand explanations for their luck. They did everything but deal authoritatively with a situation that was about to blow up in their faces.

■ ■ ■

In the suburbs to the south of Chicago, some of the poorest in the area, everyone already knew everything there was to know about crack.

The severity of the problem became clear during a conversation I had with a suburban police officer assigned to a drug task force that worked south of the city.

"We've seen crack for three years," the cop said. "But nobody worked on it. It was somewhat confined, if you know what I mean." He meant that it hadn't yet spread to the adjoining communities, which were richer, whiter, safer. But that was no longer the case.

"If we don't do something now," Nick Graves, the police chief of Harvey, Illinois, said, "crack is going to tear up this area. It's going to gut everything."

After the denials of the Chicago police, I was stunned by the candid assessment.

I arranged to go see how bad it was.

■ ■ ■

In Robbins, Illinois, a town just sixteen miles south of the Loop, there were no excuses, no cop jive, no professorial calm.

The police station stood in the center of town, a depressed black community where only the trees grew strong and healthy. With no money for sidewalks, the roads were dusty and wide and bordered with summer weeds so they looked positively rural, like somewhere along the back roads and catfish creeks of Kentucky.

I was to meet a Sergeant Harris at 7:00 P.M. in the station. The firehouse next door rocked with jet engine rap music that would loosen the hips and batter the brain. The police station, by contrast, was dead. Inside, its walls painted a washed-out green, it looked like a tenement and smelled like a backed-up sewer. In the radio room, which was the size of a closet, a man in a sky blue uniform, not a police uniform, stared at the silver microphone planted firmly on the table.

The radio hissed back every few minutes. I told him I was looking for Charles Harris, Sergeant Charles Harris.

"I don't know if he's coming in," the man answered. His shirt was soaked with sweat.

In the lobby, a large pool of water spread across the floor. Either the ceiling leaked or the rusted water fountain overran, or it just washed in from the street. No one seemed to mind. People came and went, mostly mothers and their babies, marching toward the swinging door of the washroom as the summer sun set outside.

The police station in Robbins was an outhouse with a two-way radio. Some months there was no money to pay the twenty-six officers, most of them part-timers. The pay, about five dollars an hour, attracted a ragtag bunch of job seekers, many of whom were dangerously unprepared.

About an hour after I had arrived, Sergeant Harris walked into the station wearing a beige lumberman's jacket and a gun, offering a slight apology before he walked out again, expecting me to follow.

Harris had promised to take me on a guided tour of the town, where he had grown up, and which he now called "Rockville." It was a decent town at one time, he said, with decent people. But it had become hellish, overrun with poverty and crack and violence. He chose to live in Chicago, where it was safer.

For Harris, "rock" was crack. It was no more complicated than that. "They started rolling about a year ago," he said in a cold voice. With the spread of the drug he became Robbins's narco-raider, its one-man show, swooping down on the housing projects when they came alive at nightfall.

Outside the police station, we got into a dirty van Harris had borrowed from a friend. There was only one undercover car in the Robbins fleet, and everyone in town knew what it looked like. But it didn't really matter what kind of car Harris drove because everyone recognized him as well.

"Hey, Harris, how you doing?" came the greetings.

"All right. How you doing? Stay out of trouble, you hear?"

"It's a personal thing," he explained as he drove, one arm hanging out the window. "They'll call down to the station just to see if I'm working."

We parked across from the new projects and watched as a stream of cars pulled up to the low rises and waited in the misty fluorescent light.

"They're coming from Tinley Park, Orland Park, Palos Hills, Oak Lawn. What do they want? I guess they came for some rock."

Fifteen cars in five minutes, from all over the suburbs. White kids and black.

"I've been trying to get some more officers from other communities to carry out a big sweep," Harris said as he gazed at the action. He said the words as though they had inherent meaning. Community. Sweep. But there was little hope of either. Long neglected by its wealthier neighbors, Robbins was a dumping ground for more affluent suburbs that watched with contempt as it broke apart. Robbins could destroy itself for eternity as long as the crack stayed within its borders. But it didn't. It attracted users from all over, with no regard for their race or social standing. All that mattered was their form of payment. If you didn't have the ten dollars, a VCR got you a bag of crack, a color television two bags.

The south suburbs had their own drug task force. But selfishness and idiocy dictated that Robbins, which needed the most help, actually received the least, because it had no money to contribute to the task force's operations. Crack houses in Robbins were rarely raided, except by Harris, who fought the war alone, staying motivated by the simple desire to make things right in his hometown.

We left the new projects, taking a left onto a dirt road that led through a trailer park.

"They do a lot of cooking in here," Harris said. He pointed to two houses set back in thick bushes and trees. "It's always dark here, way dark. They deal twenty-four hours a day."

From there we drove past a corner gas station that was lit up like a movie set. A revival meeting. People screaming at the top of their lungs for Jesus. Harris barely noticed.

The town was small, with maybe four main intersections. In a few minutes we had circled back to the projects. A young boy was swinging from a laundry line.

Harris pulled into the parking lot. His movements quick but efficient, as though he was a janitor summoned to fix a boiler about to explode, he trotted, then ran, up to another boy.

"What you got?"

"Two rocks."

"Let me see 'em," he ordered, gesturing toward me. "I didn't bring my man here for nothing."

Harris grabbed the crack, but he didn't arrest the boy. "We're on 'em. But I can't take them all in."

■ ■ ■

The following week I returned to Robbins with a photographer. We took the grand tour again, first to the old projects, then the new. On one dark street, a group of teenagers approached the car, their palms stretching toward us, offering bags of crack.

As long as it's not raining outside, it's peak time," Harris said. "If you want a photograph, we'll go to this old house."

We drove to a two-story bungalow and parked on the front lawn. Inside the walls were cracking. A kitten ran around in circles. A copy of *Contemporary Business* lay on the floor. Windows were covered with shades. A radio played soul music.

"I want the pipes," Harris shouted as he headed up the staircase.

"Ain't got no pipes."

"What were you smoking out of?" he demanded as he entered a smoke-filled room where two men and a woman were stretched across a bare mattress.

"We threw it out the window," a man said.

Harris tore downstairs and ran out the door.

"If I don't do it, what's going to happen?" he asked himself as he searched the grass for the pipe. In a couple of minutes he found two.

■ ■ ■

Since he had guests, Harris was determined to carry out a raid that night. This would be easy, for he knew where everyone sold. The best place for surveillance, he said, was in the old projects, up against one of the buildings.

The three of us ran quietly through the development, Harris in the lead. People looked out their windows as we passed; others outside saw us but didn't seem to think much of it. We pressed against the side of a brick building, stopping at its edge, from where we could see a busy corner about a hundred yards away. Harris lifted his gun from its holster and held it pointing upward next to the side of his head.

"Okay, be quiet," he instructed.

He took off without warning, running toward the corner. The photographer and I exchanged glances, and without saying anything to each other, we followed. Halfway to the crowd, Harris started firing the gun and shouting, "Police. Get on the ground. Police."

The gunshots echoed in the open spaces between the buildings. People hustled outside to see what Harris was up to—everyone, after all, knew it had to be him.

When we caught up with him, Harris stood over six young men who were lying face down on the ground, their chins grinding into the dirt. Their hands were behind their backs, straining upward and arching like fish out of water. Harris collected the crack from each of them. He lectured. He demanded quiet.

One of the boys on the ground even Harris was surprised to see: a sixteen-year-old named Willie, who came from a good family in Robbins and had told everyone he wanted to go to college at Georgetown. Unlike the others, whom Harris freed without charging, Willie was going to the station. There he was met by his mother. The three of them, Harris, Willie, and his mother, stood by the arrest book—actually just a legal pad—which would soon carry Willie's name unless he showed some common sense.

Willie's mother told him that his uncle, a suburban police officer, would soon arrive at the station to beat him silly.

"I kept on telling you, your friends were dropping out of the picture."

"I was just carrying it for the other boys, Mom," Willie said.

"Shut up, fool. I've been listening to you. You had it on your possession. Willie's not on nobody else. You're on your own. Where are your friends now? I told you every day, I keep hearing about the same guys. I keep hearing about them selling drugs, selling drugs.

"I don't understand this. My life has been fucked up before. . . . Your association with those people is going to be your hellhole."

Willie's mother was a strong woman with broad shoulders and veiny, muscular forearms. Her voice boomed, rattling the windows. She had raised her son on her own, with no one else. Hard work, she thought, would set the example. This was her last chance to reach him, and she knew it.

Shaken, Willie, a short boy, round and soft, finally admitted he was thinking of selling because he wanted a Jeep like the other boys.

"I was going to give it to somebody else to sell so they'd give me some money, Mom. I had no money and I thought I could get some money, buy some clothes."

"Brother, you cannot do this to yourself or to me. I know your goals. I talk to you about it every day. You hurt me and you hurt yourself. . . . You saw what it did to me." The woman broke down, her chest heaving, her voice and heart punctured.

Willie wrapped his right hand tightly around three fingers of his left hand, squeezing them out of frayed nerves and a sense of fear he hadn't showed in a long time. He wouldn't let go.

I was invisible. Neither Willie nor his mother looked at me. Their battle would have raged no matter who was in the room.

"They saved you tonight, Willie. Do you hear me?"

"Yeah."

Harris looked at me without emotion. He just kept shaking his head from side to side, not quite believing how sorry his town, his job, and his friends had become.

"I just want people to know," he told me.

■ ■ ■

Aloysius Brooklyn got his story. It ran on page 1, along with a picture of Sergeant Harris dressed in a leather jacket, a couple of rocks of crack balanced on his open palm. Behind him, against a car, was a suspect.

I did a few television and radio talk shows about crack in Chicago. On one of them I sat between Chief Graves of Harvey and Commander Risley of the narcotics unit, arguing whether it was really a problem. Each of them stuck to their positions, Graves predicting doom, Risley artfully praising the cops for keeping the situation manageable.

Within a year there was no more debate. Everyone agreed by then that the city's borders had been cracked wide open.

T E N
...

THE KING OF DIVISION STREET

CABRINI DRUG WAR BREAKS OLD RULES
January 5, 1989

I n the winter of 1989 the cops who worked Cabrini had their hands full with Chuckie D., a nineteen-year-old gangster who had taken over three high-rise buildings and, for a few weeks, changed the drug business there.

I had learned about Chuckie D. indirectly, from the Sheet, which showed one or two new entries every morning recording shootings and snipings at Cabrini. Shots fired. Agg bat—aggravated battery.

A lieutenant in the Eighteenth District explained the source of the gunfire as Chuckie D.'s quick rise, which was no different from the rise of dozens of young dealers, only Chuckie's case showed more chutzpa.

I will always remember Chuckie D. by the enlarged

photo the tactical team in the Eighteenth District kept on file of him in which he sat in an Adirondack chair, gold chains dripping from his neck, rings looping around his fingers, and two of his lieutenants crowding him, one on each side, as they mugged for the camera.

He was a member of the Disciples, one of the largest street gangs in the city. A Disciple leader had appointed Chuckie a "regent," in charge of three buildings in Cabrini. This meant he supervised dealing at the sites, which generated as much as $5,000 a day in profits.

But Chuckie D. decided he wanted to go on his own. So he formed a hit squad of seven young men and supplied them with ski masks and Uzis that he stored in a safe house about three miles north. And, police said, he started buying cocaine from a Cuban instead of through the Disciples' channels, which was the gang's system of guaranteeing every member a profit. Gang leaders routinely dealt with several suppliers, buying up to several kilograms from one or another depending on who offered the best price.

When a Disciple leader sent an emissary to one of Chuckie's buildings to make peace, the hit squad shot him.

"I don't know if he was watching 'Miami Vice' or what," the lieutenant said.

For months Chuckie D. ran his twenty-five-man operation, forcing his underlings to sell their fifty bags of coke each or else face a beating at the end of the week. But when his aggressive tactics led to dozens of shootings, the pattern was plain even to the big shots downtown. The tactical cops intervened, busting Chuckie's runners and reeling Chuckie himself in for a talk whenever they had the chance.

One night I took a ride with a tactical cop named T. Ward, a veteran of Cabrini who was instantly recognizable to residents as he approached in his lumberjack flannel shirt and reddish beard. The night had its peril; earlier that day an informant had told police that Chuckie D. wanted to lure Ward and his partner into an ambush.

Outside the high rises a few kids carried walkie-talkies

in their parkas, removing them to broadcast the arrival of the police. Other than their shouts of warning, the streets were quiet.

Ward liked driving his unmarked car right up to the decaying vestibules of the buildings, throwing it into park and flinging the door open in one motion so that there was no doubt that he, and not just some no-name beat cop, was on duty. Watching the lookouts scatter was the key. Was anyone overly eager to run? Had he dropped something? Was there a bulge in his jacket?

A combination of phony politeness and pure skepticism guided his work.

"Yo, homey, c'mere," he shouted at one of the stragglers, a teenager in a long jacket and a baseball hat.

Ward searched the young man, who had been searched a hundred times before—a hard grab of his crotch, a look under his hat, a finger along its cardboard rim.

"Why you shaking?"

"That's the way I be."

Ward put his arm around the boy's shoulder as though they were at a drive-in together. He checked the boy's license with his free hand.

"You a Libra?" Ward asked. "You ain't supposed to be cranky like this. Why does it say Scorpio on your arm?"

Then, sounding like Columbo: "Did I ever arrest you? Chris, right? I think once I caught you right downstairs here with some reefer. Now I remember. We raided this drug house. You beefed on me. You're a crybaby. What do they call you?"

"C-Mac."

"No, no, no. Don't they call you C-Dog?"

"They don't call me that."

"What's wrong with your throat, C-Dog? You swallow the dope?"

C-Mac looked at me, thinking I was a cop too, and wondering why I was so quiet. That was always an awkward moment, when, after jumping out of the police car and running toward the interrogation, I joined it with my own set of questions—which, compared to the inquisition of the police, were completely abstract. What mattered to cops was the felonious nature of the moment.

"Why you in it?" I asked the kid.

"To belong."

No one knew where Chuckie D. was that night; no ambush took place.

Ward didn't see Chuckie D. until the following week, when the little dictator sat in the Eighteenth District with a group of plainclothes cops who had hauled him in for questioning.

"I wish things could be like the old days. I'm tired," he had said. At nineteen, he had seen too much. Even Ward noted the irony.

Then a strange thing happened. Chuckie D. quit the buildings, handed them back to the Disciples, and started working for the gang again, his visions of grandeur quieted for the time being. And when the shooting slowed down, the cops had less incentive to face the nightly standoffs, so the drug business picked up at a faster pace than before.

It wasn't long before Chuckie D. turned heavily to the drugs he was selling. He spent all his money. His enemies for some reason never killed him, never even shot him. So he wandered around Cabrini, reminiscing about his brief encounter with a limited but potent fame when he had been the boss of bosses.

He went to jail a few times. He lived with his grandmother otherwise. And he survived.

■ ■ ■

Willie Lloyd ran a faction of the Vice Lords on the West Side. He was going to be the next Jeff Fort.

"He's not just a street punk," one prosecutor said. "He's an organized criminalist."

The police knew everything about him—how he had

been convicted for killing a police officer in Iowa; how he claimed to be a legitimate businessman and could afford the most expensive attorneys; and how he divided his time between Chicago and Minneapolis, where his family lived. At thirty-five, Lloyd had lived longer than many West Side felons.

A West Side cop I knew was unimpressed.

"Willie Lloyd is little," he said as we toured some of Lloyd's reputed territory about three miles from the Loop. "He's a nobody. I asked some people why they don't just get rid of him. They said it wasn't even worth it."

Organized criminalist? Or nobody?

One afternoon, a cop called to say that Lloyd had been arrested for possession of a Mac-10 machine pistol loaded with a thirty-round clip. Because Lloyd was a convicted felon, a gun possession conviction carried mandatory imprisonment. Bond was set at $5.3 million. In the hallways and locker rooms of the West Side districts, the consensus among street cops was that Lloyd would somehow raise the cash.

He never did.

The first time I saw him was during a court appearance. He was five feet five inches tall. His teeth were yellow. His sister pawned a gold ring to help raise some money, but her contribution was a fraction of what Lloyd needed. He remained locked up for years, miles from his Vice Lord turf.

■ ■ ■

Power, it seemed, was always fleeting.

Consider the class of '79.

I had gone to visit Eddie Kijowski, then the commander of the violent crimes section in the Grand-Central detective area, when I noticed a photograph pinned to his bulletin board.

"That's the class of '79," Kijowski said, glancing at the picture.

Before he took over the detective area on the Northwest Side, Kijowski had commanded the tactical team in the Fourteenth District, Shakespeare, which included Humboldt Park. He had been older than the average street cop, older than most tac officers, but he could keep up with any of them. And he worked around the clock, taking gang-related murders seriously, as a direct challenge to his police skills.

He knew the class of '79 from back then, when they were a wild group of hotheads, killing each other off so routinely that there was always overtime to be earned. They had lived and hung out in an area known as the Zone, one of the toughest parts of the city.

The photo was taken in 1979 in a Hillside cemetery to commemorate the death of Ramon Vazquez, "Chi Chi," who had been gunned down the year before in a drive-by attack. About twenty members of two or three gangs crowded together, some standing, some lying on the grass, staring icily into the camera and signing with their fingers held up or down in one or another formation to signify their particular gang allegiance.

Kijowski's scribbling along the bottom of the photo identified some of them.

"They're all dead or in the joint. That's how they all wind up," Kijowski said, which turned out to be almost correct.

■ ■ ■

One evening I took a copy of the photograph to a gang cop who knew the Zone. He had worked the area for years, arresting and rearresting the same people. He took one look at the picture and immediately recognized the faces. What looked like an expression of joy sprang to his own face.

"They're all Disciples and Cobras," the cop explained. He was willing to help me track them down as long as I didn't use his name.

"That's Hippo. He's dead. Killed on North Avenue. Baby D. He's doing time for murder. Fernie, sentenced to natural life for a triple murder. Rivera, he's selling dope in the Zone. Angel, he used to work for the intervention network. Chino is doing time for narcotics and awaiting trial for murder conspiracy. Monet is in Puerto Rico. Garcia is in the pen for dope. Matthew, he's a stone-cold killer. Here's the guy who died in the barber's chair, I don't remember his name. And Ramos, he's around."

I went to visit a source—call him Luis—who lived in Humboldt Park, a former gang member who knew just about everyone in the neighborhood. I had met Luis years before, when I first arrived in Chicago and was working on a story about graffiti crews. He was a charismatic young man with a criminal past who insisted he had found God and was going straight. I kept in touch with him, visiting now and then in Humboldt Park, especially after I moved to the police beat. He always had a pretty good idea of what was going on.

Luis too looked at the picture in disbelief. We stood on North Avenue as a group of high school kids walked by, Luis recognizing, it seemed, how his youth had slipped away. He also recognized that he had been luckier than nearly everyone in the photo. He was trying to build his own business, and was learning about politics. He could have a future if he wanted one. These toughs in the picture, except maybe two or three, were lost.

With Luis's help I found three of the former gang members in the photograph and arranged to meet with them in a Humboldt Park coffee shop. They were a decade older than at the time the picture had been taken, and it showed in added girth and receding hairlines. I treated them to long slabs of ribs and cold Heinekens. Then I passed the copy of the photo around the table.

"Looking at the faces you can see pain and hurt," Shank said as he sipped a beer.

He was large man who kept a hairbrush in his back pocket at all times. He told me he had a job as a laborer, but later he said his job was helping his invalid cousin part-time; I could confirm neither story.

They joined for the same reasons most kids join gangs, for fraternity and excitement. They raised money to buy their $40 gang sweaters decorated with crowns from selling nickel bags of marijuana. At night they'd sit around in a friend's basement in their gang colors, smoking reefer and listening to music or watching gangster films.

"We had our own castle, our own laws," said Angel, a wiry twenty-eight-year-old who had kicked a drug habit and was involved with an antigang program on the Far North Side. "We didn't have a Boys' Club. We didn't have anything."

Eventually the reefer and the music and the sweaters weren't enough. So they chipped in $10 or $15 apiece to buy a gun—a nickel-plated .38-caliber revolver sold to them by a heroin addict, who gave them four bullets as a bonus. They tested the gun and ammo that night in an alley, an exercise that made them want more guns—which they soon obtained. They strapped the guns to their waists as the finishing touch to their uniform: "Godfather suits, old man suits, pleated pants, Stacy Adams shoes, vests, pocket watch—the Look."

By 1978 the gang had run the older heroin dealers away from the neighborhood. The firepower got heavier. By then you could get machine guns. Cocaine was suddenly everywhere.

And then, Chi Chi was killed on the street as he stood talking with his girlfriend.

"We said, Fuck it, we're going to kill the guys who killed Chi Chi," Shank said.

"A typical night was like a war zone," he went on. "A car would roll down Rockwell Street with its headlights off. Half of the guys would ride hanging out the windows with shotguns. We knew which cars they had. If you didn't have a gun, duck. If you did, shoot back. After a while, it became second nature to us."

I met with them three or four times, always in their neighborhood. Each of them, it seemed, had the intelligence to break loose. But like Chuckie D., they stayed close to home, mixing with the same people, always just a dime bag from trouble.

■ ■ ■

On a Saturday night I was driving with my girlfriend east along Division Street. I had just pulled away from an intersection alongside Cabrini, one of the most ignored stop signs in the city, when up ahead I noticed police cars with their blue Mars lights flashing.

As we approached I saw two officers, their guns drawn, chasing a group of men past one of the high rises. One of the men fired his gun and the police fired back as they ran, the end of each pistol lighting up with a blue flare. Part of me wanted to get out a pad and take notes, to try to figure out who the cops were chasing and why, and where they fitted on the giant flowchart that someone, I was sure, was keeping somewhere in police headquarters under lock and key.

A few months earlier the chart would have shown Chuckie D. near the top of the pyramid. By that night, he would not even have appeared; he was already ancient history.

In other projects, in other neighborhoods, other temporary kings ruled.

E L E V E N

. . .

LEGS

We are responsive to public pressure like everyone else.

Police official, June 25, 1989

I t would take more than a crack epidemic among the poor or shootouts in the projects to hold readers' attention.

It would take more than a short-order cook stabbed to death behind the counter of a greasy spoon for $100 wedged into the cash register; more than a cabbie shot to death as he drove a fare to the projects; more than six schoolgirls raped in an abandoned building, or an eighty-year-old deacon murdered in his church, or a twelve-year-old girl fatally beaten with a bat, most likely by her father.

Every one of these stories was buried beneath other news, of crabgrass alerts and city council hearings. Readers had developed an aversion to bad news that did not play out on an epic scale. Big tragedies, floods and earthquakes, lingered for a couple of days, but even they soon lost their emotional grip. The speed of events dislodged them, one trauma overtaking the next. Exactly what appealed to the newspaper audience was still a riddle. But anemic circulation figures in the industry made it clear that readers everywhere were tired of the same old thing.

It took an unpredictable combination of ingredients to reach people with tales of the city gone awry, especially at a time when about two-thirds of the *Tribune*'s readers lived in suburbia. Filtering out stories of urban turmoil became possible when the paper instituted an aggressive program of zoning, which, with the aid of advanced printing facilities, enabled editors to fill entire sections with news relevant to the various geographical communities they served.

Residents of Du Page County, for example, a wealthy, white-collar suburb twenty miles west of Chicago, received a local section featuring daily political and economic coverage of the county. Such target-marketing was necessary to avoid what many in management referred to as the *Newsday* scenario. The *New York Times* and New York City's other dailies' neglect of suburban Long Island readers had allowed *Newsday* to monopolize the lucrative market outside the city, and its success in turn funded a new, competitive city edition of *Newsday*. At the *Tribune* the decision had been made high up, up where the Tower intersected the clouds, never to let a *Newsday* find root in Chicago.

Zoning became increasingly precise. Readers on the South Side of Chicago received a different paper from the one those on the North Side got. At the city desk each night, putting out the paper was like fitting together the pieces of a jigsaw puzzle, with snap judgments being made as to which stories should appear in which zones. Did readers in Du Page County need to know about a murder on the South Side? Some editors argued yes, suburban readers wanted to revel in having escaped the old neighborhood, while others insisted they no longer wanted anything to do with the craziness left behind. The latter argument usually won out.

To fill the zoned editions, each section carried a healthy dose of agate about people arrested for drunken driving or stealing cars, gallons of milk, or pink flamingos. Most city news, unless it had regional appeal, or "legs," was boiled down to a few paragraphs on a summary page.

Fledgling reporters soon began to hope for tragedies with legs as intensely as Bronx County prosecutors dreamed of the great white villain in *The Bonfire of the Vanities,* Tom Wolfe's novel about a bond trader whose actions so defied his social station that everyone, in every zone, followed the story.

We came close to such outrages when I first started on the beat. A young couple from Wheaton, Illinois, disappeared one summer night in 1988. Their red BMW was found in an alley behind Orchestra Hall, its engine warm, its ignition key in the off position. The missing were white, middle-class, and seemingly innocent. A nationwide search for the Wheaton whities, as they were known among reporters, began, involving dozens of Chicago cops. The worst was feared. The story dominated conversation in a way local stories rarely do, until the couple turned up alive, tanned and healthy, in San Diego, where they had run in search of "perfect love."

■ ■ ■

The one other story with legs in my first year at the Cop Shop was the saga of Rodolfo Linares.

It unfolded in late April, a few weeks after Richard M. Daley was elected mayor, replacing interim mayor Eugene Sawyer. For weeks most news had dealt with the election, the failure of any black candidate to assert leadership, and the questions about Daley's ability to unite the city. Daley had stepped lightly since the election, taking care not to insult or inflame any minority constituency. In a clear signal to the black community, he pledged to keep LeRoy Martin as police chief. The biggest issue as it affected my beat was thus settled.

It was pretty much business as usual when the radio fired up on the morning of April 26.

"A gun-wielding Cicero man held hospital workers at bay as he removed his fifteen-month-old son from a life support system. . . ."

Thank God it wasn't another fire.

By the time I got out of bed, I had learned that the boy, Samuel, was dead. His father was charged with his murder.

I got dressed. Got showered. Got out to the Linareses' neighborhood in Cicero, once the headquarters of Al Capone, now a corrupted suburb featuring sex shows and drive-ins.

I looked forward to going. I knew some detectives in the Harrison area near the hospital who could help me with the details. I had a plan.

■ ■ ■

On the street where Linares lived the talk was of courage, bravery, heroism. He had acted alone and against the system to end his son's and his family's misery.

It was one of the biggest journalistic swarms I had ever seen. We hunted in packs for Linares's wife, Tamara, his mother, his car-waxing buddies. Everyone willing to be interviewed expressed an eloquent and powerful defense of his actions.

On the surface, Rodolfo Linares hardly seemed capable of an act of tenderness. He was a big man who looked a little like the Indian in *One Flew over the Cuckoo's Nest*. He liked to drink, and he wasn't afraid to fight with cops. But on the August afternoon his son swallowed a balloon, Linares, by all accounts, was transformed.

He grabbed his son and rushed him to the fire station a few blocks away, into the arms of the paramedics.

"My child isn't breathing," he shouted.

The paramedics pulled the balloon out with forceps, but the damage had been done. For months, Samuel remained in a tiny hospital bed, staring straight ahead, in a vegetative state.

In April, the hospital left a message on the Linareses' answering machine: Samuel was to be transferred to an extended care facility. Hopelessness was now made official. The emotional and financial drain would continue indefinitely.

Linares took his .357 Magnum and drove with his wife to see Samuel one last time. Shortly after 1:00 A.M. they entered the pediatric intensive care unit, walked to their son's bed, and looked at the tubes that looped out of him.

Tamara left the room at about 1:20. Linares approached a nurse and asked her how long it would take for the child to die once he was removed from the machine.

The nurse said she didn't know. Linares then brandished his gun and ordered her out of the room. She gathered up the other children in the twelve-bed unit and hurried out.

Linares quickly unplugged the respirator, lifted Samuel from his bed, and cradled him in his big arms. He held the gun tightly beneath the boy. A few hospital staff members and security guards gathered at the doorway. They could do nothing but watch.

Linares stood in the center of the room until Samuel's heart monitor sounded a flat tone. The nurse ran in, pleading with Linares to reattach the respirator, but he ordered her out.

A few minutes later, Linares asked for a stethoscope, which a doctor slid toward him on the floor. Linares placed the suction cup against his son's chest. He listened closely. When he heard nothing but the sound of his own breathing, Linares handed the boy back to a nurse, along with the gun. Then he collapsed in tears. As he was led into a West Side police station to be charged, dozens of reporters crowding around him, Linares said, "I did it because I love my son and my wife."

I sat with an editor that night, plugging in a few details and rewriting until he was satisfied.

"Every paper in the country should carry this story tomorrow," he announced, and many of them would.

■ ■ ■

The Cook County state's attorney, Cecil Partee, decided in May not to prosecute Linares, for whom there was massive public sympathy. Letters, calls, and donations for Linares poured in from all over the country.

Nevertheless, Linares's life got harder. By the summer, his name would be mentioned in the media only when he was hauled into a Cicero police station for drunken driving or a minor dope charge. The story of his decline, unlike that of the day he ended his son's life, had found a place in the back pages of the metro section, where it belonged.

■ ■ ■

Meanwhile, black and Hispanic teenagers were dying by the score, and there didn't seem to be any way to keep their memories alive. Too many had fallen from grace to make big news.

Then, early on a Sunday, a story was breaking that wouldn't move people the way Linares's had, or anger them as the Wheaton couple ultimately had; rather, it would frighten them in a way that I had almost stopped thinking was possible.

Early that morning Dana Feitler, a twenty-four-year-old woman who was about to start a graduate business program at the University of Chicago, climbed out of a friend's car and walked into the entrance of her apartment building on

Dearborn Street, in the heart of the Gold Coast. Feitler and her friend had spent much of Saturday looking for an apartment in Hyde Park, then dined at a nearby Mexican restaurant. She turned to her friend in the car and waved good night as he pulled away. It was 1:30 A.M., June 18, 1989.

Feitler opened the aluminum mailbox, pulled out a few envelopes and a cassette tape, and placed them on a wooden ledge. She was about to unlock the lobby door when, according to the early police accounts, three men walked into the entrance, grabbed her, and forced her back onto the street. Her mail scattered on the floor.

The four walked north to North Avenue and then west to Clark Street, passing the stately mansions and town houses that lined the streets of the exclusive neighborhood. They were especially impressive at night, when chandeliers and mantislike halogens illuminated the comforts inside, the grand pianos and perfect Mondrian-imagined kitchen cabinetry, the long shadows cast by the gentry as it prepared for rest.

The three men wanted some of that good life, if only a smaller, short-term yield. Their destination: a cash machine in a glass-enclosed vestibule of a bank at the corner of Clark and Germania.

Outside, the streets around Rush Street pulsed with the tequila-soaked dreams of sailors on leave and rowdy conventioneers. On weekends Rush and Division was their Mecca, a sundown-to-sunrise party spilling out from two dozen bars as uniformed and mounted police tried to prevent sloppiness from becoming something uglier. Usually the presence of a line of squad cars and hulking police horses was enough to deter trouble.

Feitler held the hand of one of the men, her arm, her legs, her whole body stiff with fear. Her eyes blazed with the message that she was not there by choice, so much so that a woman walking her dog stared into them for twenty seconds before deciding not to dial 911.

The four walked into the brightly lit cash station. Its

marble floor and oak trim suited the style of the local customers, primarily young professionals and their bosses who needed the machine at all hours.

At 1:50 A.M., Feitler withdrew $200 from her savings account. At 1:54 she withdrew another $200. That was all she could get from the machine. A security camera recorded her movements. She wore a navy blue sweater, white jogging shoes, and flower print shorts.

From the cash station, according to police, they cut through an alley, stopping a block from Feitler's apartment. One of the men, identified in court statements as Charles Guyton, turned to the others and declared, "I'm going to knock this broad." And there, in the dark, narrow drive, he removed a .22-caliber pistol from his waistband and, as quickly as he had spoken, placed the gun at the base of Feitler's neck and fired one shot into her skull.

A doorman nearby saw three men running from the mouth of the alley, two in one direction and one in another. All he could see was that they were black.

Feitler lay in a pool of her blood for twenty-five minutes until a passerby found her and called the police. In her purse a few feet away were credit cards, the bank card, and seven dollars in cash. She was speeded by ambulance to Northwestern Memorial Hospital half a mile away, where she lay in a coma, near death.

■ ■ ■

The Sunday *Tribune* staff, which got the first crack at the story, didn't overreact, placing it on the front of the metropolitan section. I imagine the response was somewhat muted because Feitler was still alive. The *Sun-Times,* for its part, displayed the attack prominently on page 1. Every television newscast Sunday night led with the story, which was only a hint of what was to come.

Twelve hours after she was shot, Feitler was a celebrity victim, the first in a long time—that is, she was young, attractive, intelligent, white. The youngest of four children, she had grown up in an affluent suburb of Milwaukee, graduated cum laude from Colby College in Maine, and worked for Continental Bank before leaving in June to pursue graduate studies in business. Her father was president of the Weyenberg Shoe Company in Milwaukee. Shortly after the shooting, a $25,000 reward was offered by her family for information leading to the arrest of her assailants.

I had been out of town Sunday and didn't hear much about the crime until late that night. When I did, I knew that the course of the coming week was set.

Arriving at Eleventh and State the next morning, I started making calls. The detectives at the Belmont area had little to go on. The bank's camera had photographed only Feitler during the transaction; everyone else was a blur. More than a day after the attack, police had no eyewitnesses.

Was there a pattern of robberies in the area? That was the logical place to start investigating. A computer at the Belmont detective area spit out a list of twenty suspects involved in strong-arm robberies of women, and a separate list of men who committed robberies with two or three accomplices. Already there was a feeling that the suspects would not be found through a high-tech search.

"We don't have a crime wave here," the Belmont commander, William Callaghan, insisted. "We have an incident that's tragic."

What police also had in the Belmont area was the first high profile "heater" case in a long time. You could tell from the friendly but mildly desperate tone in their voices.

"With your cooperation, we may be able to find somebody who may have seen this young lady," Callaghan said, echoing an appeal he was no doubt making to everyone he knew in the media. He was all too aware that the first forty-eight hours after a crime were crucial to the success of an investigation. "It's in the minds of people watching the news," he explained. "In two or three days, that will wear off."

Two or three days was a long, long time to hold the

public's attention. But the Feitler case was in that category of news, somewhere between killer hurricanes and Bears playoffs.

With so little new information on the police investigation, at first the story lingered as a death watch. Video crews, reporters, and producers camped outside the Northwestern Hospital pavilion where Feitler was being kept alive by asthmatic-sounding machines and pumps. A doctor updated the press several times a day at our post on the steps of the building.

"She's somewhat better than she was yesterday," Dr. Robert Levy, a neurologist, announced on Tuesday afternoon. "She's breathing on her own and responding to powerful stimuli, withdrawing her arms and legs. We still need to wait to see if she'll wake from the coma. Should she wake from the coma, there is the potential for significant neurological recovery and significant life. . . . I'm encouraged."

Suddenly the story took on an entirely different tone. You could sense people rooting for her to snap out of the coma, return to school, graduate with honors, do "Oprah."

I went to the apartment on Dearborn, thinking I might come across someone who knew Feitler, a relative or friend, perhaps the friend she was with that night. Sometimes I got lucky in these situations, finding just the person I needed.

Poor people always seemed to have time to talk to journalists. They welcomed you into their living rooms, they vented their grief, they spoke without inhibition. People who were better off considered your presence an affront and an invasion. The only time I came close to getting into a fistfight in my career as a reporter had been a few years earlier at the suburban home of a slain oil company executive. A young man, a fraternity type, came out on the porch and with a stiff arm shoved me down the stairs. I could understand how he felt. But nothing like that ever happened in all my trips to Englewood or Wentworth, where death was marked by a louder, looser decorum. In bleak parts of town, where nothing was expected, people rejoiced when any attention arrived, whatever its form.

Feitler lived in a five-story building of chocolate brown bricks, nothing really fancy apart from its location. A sign in the lobby advertised a one-bedroom apartment facing the street that rented for $695 a month, high for Chicago. I walked from there to the cash station, cutting through the alley to eyeball the spot where she had been shot. The alley, cleared of yellow police tape, looked normal again, its peaked-roofed garages lining each side of the cobblestone road.

I collected a few quotes from a neighbor, who was of course shocked by the violence—shocked that it could happen there, shocked to the point of fear.

Dana Feitler became an obsession, especially for residents of the Gold Coast, Lincoln Park, and other upscale enclaves in the Eighteenth District, people who were unaccustomed to facing savage crimes against one of their own.

The Near North Side, and the Gold Coast in particular, provided a picturesque view of city life. The only visible affliction was rampant consumerism. The main thoroughfares were lined with boutiques and good restaurants, and on weekends the neighborhoods bustled with such glee that it was hard to imagine the economic suffering people living no more than a few miles in any direction were experiencing.

The area was insulated from violent crime more than other parts of the city in large part because the police there paid more attention. Cops in the Eighteenth District knew you didn't just hang up on callers; you never knew who they knew. There was a mandatory responsiveness that didn't exist elsewhere.

And the police paid attention to Dana Feitler.

The first place they looked for Feitler's attackers was in Cabrini-Green. The project was only a few blocks west of the crime scene, and every cop had imagined that sooner or later the clash of cultures would lead to just such a crime as this. The shooting had taken place just beyond Carl Sandburg Village, a wall of high rises literally cutting Cabrini off from the lakefront and its posh environs. There were apocryphal stories about snipers shooting out the windows of Sandburg Village, but for the most part the violence in and around the Green took its toll on the project's residents.

Everyone who had ever helped the cops out with information was summoned. Had anyone heard anything, anything at all?

A thirty-six-year-old man, Lee Harris, who lived in Cabrini and who had helped the police out in the past, offered what sounded like an interesting lead. That night, Harris said, he had seen three men running from the alley where Feitler was found. He was sitting in a Dunkin' Donuts shop, looking out the window, minding his own business, when he observed the men, two of whom he recognized as "Ford" and "Cheese."

"You involved with this one?" a detective asked Harris.

"No way in the world could anybody put me in that alley," he answered emphatically.

■ ■ ■

Dana Feitler was taken off life support on June 29. Dr. Levy issued a statement: "No extraordinary measures will be administered to sustain life."

She died on July 9.

Taking on the same amplified quality of the entire case, her death suggested a larger truth about the media—and which victims counted the most.

■ ■ ■

Two months later, Feitler's killer was still free. The story on Ford and Cheese didn't check out. When the cops went back to Harris, he changed his version of events.

Yes, he had seen Feitler walking with two other men near the cash machine; he had tried to sell the three of them drugs. He had been there when one of the men shot her, but he swore he had nothing to do with it.

The detectives had always considered Harris more a con man than a violent criminal, but they were revising their opinion. His rap sheet showed that he had pleaded guilty to burglary and not much more. Around Cabrini, especially at a corner drugstore where he liked to hang out, weaving tall tales, he was known as a thief and a storyteller, but not a bad guy.

Meanwhile, the detectives continued paying Harris $10 or $20 for each session with him. They also put him up at several cheap motels so that he would not be imperiled staying in Cabrini. Two weeks later, as he was being driven to the Belmont area station by a detective, Harris changed his story yet again. This time he cried as he spoke.

On that Saturday night he had met two men at a sleazy bar across the alley from the Eighteenth District police station. The three of them shared a bottle of cheap wine and talked about finding someone to rob for drug money. They left separately to scout for potential victims. Within an hour, Harris said, he ran into the others walking with Feitler. The two men were arguing over whether to kill her. In the alley, he said, Guyton shot her.

That fall, twelve weeks after the slaying, Harris was charged with the murder. Although he named two accomplices, Guyton and Vincent Hills, neither of them was charged because police had been unable to gather any independent evidence. The gun, Harris said, had been thrown into the Chicago River, but although police divers dredged for it, they came up empty.

The evidence against Harris was weak, and the police knew it. But they needed an arrest, and they moved ahead with what they had: Harris's conflicting and self-incriminating statements: an "almost positive" identification of him by a woman who had seen Feitler when she was walking her dog that night; and a remark Harris made to an inmate in the Cook County Jail, saying that he had been the triggerman.

It took a jury only four hours to convict him. Harris's public defender had urged the judge not to be swayed by "the character and status and class of the person who died." The public defender cited a study that most death sentences are handed down to black men convicted of crimes against white women. The judge sentenced Harris to ninety years in jail.

■ ■ ■

There was something unsettling about the minute-by-minute attention paid to the Feitler shooting. At one time I felt personally offended whenever someone suggested that the *Tribune* neglected crime-ridden minority communities in its coverage. After all, I'd argue, I spent the bulk of my time reporting on crimes that had been committed in bad neighborhoods. When a writer for a weekly newspaper in Chicago compared the police coverage of the *Tribune* and the *Sun-Times,* I was pleased he credited the way the *Tribune* handled "cheap" crimes that might otherwise have been ignored. But the longer I worked the beat, the better I understood that the reason I wrote about such crime was that there was little of anything else. Dana Feitler was an aberration. The truth was that I hadn't dug into the lives of most victims with as much enthusiasm as I had into Feitler's, because the public's interest lasted no longer than a day, if that long, which was hardly enough time to piece together an accurate portrait of who they had been.

Out of curiosity, I checked the Sheet to see if any other shootings had occurred the weekend Feitler was shot. It was not a wholly original idea. The *New York Times,* for example, had run an insightful piece shortly after the Central Park jogger was assaulted in April 1989. It chronicled the twenty-eight other rapes or attempted rapes committed in New York during the week of the attack. Nearly all of the victims were black or Hispanic women; their cases received scant public attention. The aim was to open a discussion of the shifting standards guiding news judgment, standards that were invariably based on the race and socioeconomic status of victims and where they had lived and worked.

There had been a murder on Friday morning, forty-three hours before Feitler was shot. The victim was Denise Farmer, forty, who had died of multiple stab wounds.

Cop questions nagged me: Okay, but was she a hooker? a junkie? Skepticism was a reflex at Eleventh and State, and not just among the police. Every morning the City News reporters went through the medical examiner's autopsy lists, spot-checking each death for unusual circumstances. In most cases the home office directed them to "cheap it out," which meant not to bother investigating; the death was too routine. Hundreds of murders, overdoses, and suicides thus fell from public view, since if City News didn't report a crime, the chances were slim that any other news organization would pursue it. But as the murder rate rose, the standards that dictated whether a killing was considered newsworthy became exceedingly difficult to meet. There had already been 328 murders in Chicago that year, and Farmer's was simply one of them. Barely a sentence had been written about her.

For the story I had in mind, that was ideal.

I scribbled down the address, 6217 North Winthrop. It was in the Twenty-fourth District, under the supervision of the Belmont area detectives, the same ones investigating the Feitler case.

"Yeah, we're handling that one," the desk sergeant said. "She was a security guard over at Columbus Hospital. Looks like a robbery. Her pockets were turned out."

Other than Farmer's family and friends, no one had heard of her slaying. There were no police press conferences, no public appeals for witnesses, no reward money offered for the capture of her assailants. There had been no extraordinary measures to sustain her life, not that they would have made a difference: Her attackers had practically cut out her heart. There was no all-out search by police for suspects because she happened to have been killed at about the same time as Feitler, whose murder soaked up the available manpower.

Farmer's friends and relatives were angry, believing that police had paid less attention to her death because she was a black working woman living in a rough neighborhood. And they were right.

Even Wodnicki knew it: "We are responsive to public pressure like everyone else," he said.

As he explained it, the priorities in an investigation were set by the media. "The media decide what's important and what's not—not us." More news coverage meant more leads. That was the simple fact. If a crime didn't make the papers or TV, especially TV, the leads often dried up.

The leads in the Farmer case were at best slim. On Friday morning, Farmer had gotten dressed in her work uniform: blue jacket, pressed white blouse, gray slacks, and shiny black shoes. At 7:00 A.M. she walked down the back stairway of her apartment building on her way to her parking spot at the rear of the building. At the bottom of the stairwell she was grabbed, slashed with a knife, and robbed. Her body lay near the stairwell for half an hour before it was found by one of her neighbors in the building.

The autopsy revealed that she had been stabbed more than twenty times; four wounds penetrated her heart, and another four punctured her left kidney. Her forehead had been opened up with a gash two inches wide. The police began investigating the killing, but when Feitler was shot, the leg work was put on hold.

Denise Farmer did not live in the Gold Coast. She lived on a block populated by transients, college students, and dope dealers. It was a bad street—you could see that just driving by. On the southern corner was a liquor store, which seemed to attract noise and trouble. Here the dealers would set off car alarms to let everyone know when the cops arrived; alarms wailed throughout the day.

Farmer didn't come from a well-to-do family. The oldest of three girls, she was born in Cairo, Illinois, on August 4, 1948. She moved to Chicago with her mother at the age of five. By 1969, the entire family was living on Division Street in Cabrini-Green. She married, had two children, and moved out of the project. When her marriage failed, she sought work as a security guard because, as her brother said, "She wasn't scared of anybody."

"She was a nice person who would do anything for anybody until you got on her wrong side," her sister said.

She wasn't scared of the dealers in her uptown apartment building. Two weeks before her death she had complained to the management of the building about the dime-bag hustlers working the hallways. Police raided the building twice, but it didn't seem to have any effect. After that she told relatives she was going to move, because the neighborhood had become too dangerous.

Most of her family lived on the South Side, which is where I went to visit them. We sat in Odessa Guest's well-tended yard, drinking lemonade and talking about the daughter who had done right.

"It's total discrimination," said Farmer's son, Ernest, a college student, who, like his mother, had defied the odds and was on his way to a degree. He was a handsome young man with anguished eyes.

If only they had money, Guest said, they would offer a big reward. But they didn't, and so they would have to wait.

■ ■ ■

The police arrested Denise Farmer's killers on December 21.

"It was all over dope, all over cocaine," Commander Callaghan said.

The suspects had been angry at Farmer's attempts to

stop them from dealing in her building. So they decided to kill her for revenge, the police alleged. Five people had participated in the attack. All of them lived within a few blocks.

■ ■ ■

Race relations in Chicago that year were remarkably calm. If the black community expected the worst from Daley, it was surprised by what it got. It wasn't that the white Irish club didn't assert itself, but there was something outwardly mild about Daley's politics that helped keep the peace.

In return for the mayor's support, Superintendent Martin became Daley's valuable ally and, at a crucial moment, repeated the magical feat he had performed in front of Oak Woods Cemetery. In the fall of 1989, when a group of aldermen held hearings in City Hall on the issue of police brutality, Martin single-handedly defused the matter by taking black leaders to task for what he called a smear campaign against his department. The only brutality being perpetrated, he argued, was political.

"This city has gone upside down, almost insane with this bull about brutality," Martin lashed out in an interview with one of the *Tribune*'s political reporters. "There are so-called leaders organizing the black community through fear and hate, and that has got to end.

"Is there a litmus test that we blacks in leadership positions have to take? Is it that we become antiwhite? Is that what some so-called leaders want? Is that what this city's come to? All blacks in lockstep against whites? It's sickening, it's frightening, and we have to stop it now. Responsible people can't play those games."

The brutality hearings led nowhere because they dwelled on old, ambiguous cases. But they also died because Martin quashed them. He denied he was helping the mayor who had kept him on. He insisted he was only speaking his mind.

Even without Harold Washington, Martin remained untouchable for a long time. He seemed determined to retire in two years at the age of sixty-three, max out with a hefty pension, and do so with the least amount of personal and professional pain. He was thrilled not to have to deal with overt racial tension, even as a subtler form of discrimination was ignoring the inner city to death.

■ ■ ■

I had found a pretty good groove on the beat. Crimes came up and I jumped on them, writing what I could in a day or two and getting it into the paper. Even the piece I wrote comparing the Feitler and Farmer murder cases got a good ride, which made me think that covering crime might not be a losing battle—that in fact people *were* concerned about the unwarranted deaths of their neighbors, and maybe I just had to write more about them.

It was still a struggle to get people to take notice unless the violence had a cinematic twist, a true-crime swagger and a big finish. A sixteen-year-old girl gunned down by mistake in a drive-by made it onto page 6. A story about a fourteen-year-old pregnant girl who was beaten with a bat, page 4. An alleged bigamist and con man who was bilking women of their savings, page 1 metro. A plane crash in Iowa in which half the passengers died and the other half were saved by a heroic pilot who landed the plane with one engine, page 1. A twelve-year-old boy paralyzed from the waist down by stray gunshots, page 5. A nine-year-old girl stabbed to death in an abandoned building, a message scrawled on the wall above her: THE SYSTEM OR THE POWERS OF SATAN. NOTHING CAN HURT HER ANYMORE. SHE PASSED JANUARY 9, BETWEEN TWO-FOUR O'CLOCK. HER MOTHER. Page 3.

I had the best chance of getting out front on Fridays, writing for the Saturday paper. If I could put together a crime feature, I could get it onto page 1. I wrote about a white security guard and a black public housing resident who were both killed in a gang shootout, and a triple killing over half a kilo of cocaine. I would try to imagine how such stories went down with a leisurely Saturday breakfast.

■ ■ ■

The Sheet marched on.

DEATH INVESTIGATION / Kurt Lange / male / black / 26 / 244 E. Pearson / Body found 200 block N. Cicero Avenue / Last seen by doorman July 26

There were enough inconsistencies in the paragraph to be of interest. A Gold Coast address, a doorman building. The body was found on the West Side after the man had been missing a day.

"It looks like dope," the officer who was first at the scene told me. "No signs of violence. When we found him he was talking nonsense, that someone was trying to kill him before he crawled under a squad car and passed out. The next second he stopped breathing. Pronounced dead at Loretto Hospital."

"Who was this guy?"

"He was a doctor at Northwestern. A black kid."

This information alone was enough to build a piece around. And the story got more disturbing.

Lange had been a resident at the hospital. He had grown up on the South Side, gone to Phillips Exeter Academy in New Hampshire, then to Emory University in Atlanta, where he graduated Phi Beta Kappa, and finally Cornell Medical College in New York. His was a stellar rise from the inner city of Chicago. And it ended on a filthy, drug-infested West Side street. "A hangout for pimps, robbers, and junkies," according to a detective on the Northwest Side who spent a few days investigating the case.

Everyone I spoke to that afternoon was shocked. What had Lange been doing in that area? He was so smart; he had come so far.

He had been raised by a single mother in a government-subsidized apartment on the Near South Side. He attended Exeter as part of a special program for disadvantaged minority students, returning to Chicago in the summers to work part-time to help his mother.

At Emory, according to a relative, he decided to become a doctor because he "enjoyed helping people and he had a fascination with medical programs on TV where they're cutting up people and replacing hearts."

By all accounts he was excited to be returning to Chicago, to Northwestern, his first choice for a training hospital.

Lange had spent the Saturday before his death with his mother. They bought a stereo and took it to his apartment near Northwestern Memorial Hospital. They met later in the day for mass at St. James's Catholic Church in his old neighborhood, where he carried the cross down the aisle and stayed afterward for a potluck dinner to celebrate the feast of St. James. The whole time he kept spotting and greeting people he hadn't seen in years.

His family, his teachers, and his peers agreed on something else: It couldn't have been drugs that killed him. No way. He never got close to them.

But the feeling on the desk that afternoon was just the opposite—so much so that no one shrugged when I pitched the story. It was as though, one way or another, death through drugs was the expected fate of a twenty-six-year-old black man. He had climbed out of the ghetto, become a doctor, and ended up dead on the West Side. So what? It sounded like a drug overdose; why should anyone care?

It wasn't only, as I first believed, the old reporters who had lost their sense of outrage. It was the editors, the cops, the corporate executives, the football fans, and waiters. Just about everyone, it seemed, could ignore the body count unless it involved an athlete, a nun, or some hero like Rudy Linares, whose story could easily be reduced to a movie of the week.

Denise Farmer was invisible. Kurt Lange was invisible.

Seventeen-year-old Emma Jean Wales, who had been working her way through college, and whose naked body was
found in Washington Park in late 1989, was a nobody. When
I told an editor about her murder, he asked: "Is she black?"

In the north zones the next day, her death was reported
in a paragraph.

■ ■ ■

For three days after Kurt Lange's death I stayed on top of
the police and the medical examiner. An early police report
mentioned a woman, possibly a prostitute, who had been
with Lange at the time of his death. But there was no name.
The cops were certain it was not murder. I begged his
mother to sit down with me to talk some more, but she
wouldn't, saying only that she was moving to St. Louis; she
had had enough of Chicago.

Two weeks later, a toxicology report showed that Kurt
Lange had died of cocaine intoxication. His motive remained a mystery. Reporters at the city desk had speculated
that his death resulted from an inability to cross the cultural
divide from impoverished neglect to acceptance; his story
was much like that of Edmund Perry, the black teenager who
had graduated from Exeter and was on his way to Stanford
when he was fatally shot while trying to hold up a cop in
Harlem. I couldn't accept that theory. Lange had already
become a responsible and successful adult; why would he
want to throw away everything he had achieved? I had heard
that his father had been murdered in Chicago, but without
the cooperation of his family I couldn't track the story down.

And when the medical examiner issued his final report,
some people said, "I told you so."

T W E L V E

...

TWO POLAROIDS

POLICE SAY BURNED BABY HELD IN TUB
August 16, 1989

Sixteen months as a police reporter, and I thought I was rock solid. I had covered rapes, drug busts, epic car wrecks, arson, gang wars, and a variety of murders including several double and triple slayings. Victims could be cabbies, actors, immigrants, schoolteachers, kids with ambition, graduate students in debt, small children—an eight-year-old, a six-year-old, an infant. I still thought I could endure the daily grind of the Cop Shop without becoming a brute or a racist.

The beat required chasing. On good days you hit the streets, knocked on strangers' doors, and walked in past rumpled carpeting and holes in the floor—past pictures of Jesus in cheap wooden frames, past singed vats of beans and bacon grease—into the room of the son who had been stabbed to death, of the daughter who had been shot to death, where golden trophies tumbled over each other and posters of Ferraris or Michael Jordan drooped from the walls. You took a seat at a Formica table in the kitchen and listened as a parent told the child's whole life story to you and no one else.

You couldn't care every day. I'd see reporters come back from these interviews and stay hurt for weeks. Most cops I knew had become hardened, their hearts empty; they were no longer capable of worry or outrage at the atrocities they were called on to investigate. Either extreme was dangerous.

I had reached the point that I felt emotionally prepared for ever-larger disasters, for *Hindenburg*s exploding, planes crashing, mass murders, knowing that such stories would involve untold gore. There was something almost pornographic about this sense of anticipation.

At the same time, I wondered when the horrors I reported on would finally back up, overtaking me one night in my sleep. The nightmares hadn't arrived, and I began to think they never would. But I knew that reporters, like most cops, had to face that terrifying moment that gauged how much of their compassion was left and how much had melted away.

■ ■ ■

On the AM station I awoke to every morning, the newscaster spun out the details.

"An eleven-month-old boy is near death today after allegedly being forced into a tub of scalding water. Chicago police have charged the mother's live-in boyfriend with aggravated battery. More after this."

The news set off a mixture of disgust and exhilaration in my stomach. I twisted for a moment, wondering if I wasn't still asleep.

I got out of bed, showered, and called the city desk for

the boy's address. I was still able to sound enthusiastic on the telephone, eager, and the editors on the desk appreciated it. They punched up the wire story on the computer and passed on the information that was available.

The mother's name was Karen Miller; her son's was Benjamin. They lived in Hyde Park, a few blocks from the University of Chicago.

It took five or six maneuvers to extract my car from the driveway behind the house, an inconvenience I accepted; the car had already been broken into once. I switched on the AM radio and the two-way, which hissed every few minutes with the morning's photo opportunities.

"Forty-three to Tower. I'm cleaned up on the two-eleven. What else you got?"

"How 'bout some features, Forty-three?" A "feature" generally meant an upbeat subject—a kid drinking from a water fountain, say, or better yet, a dog drinking.

I found a certain comfort in the banter when I recognized a voice out there, especially when it belonged to one of the veteran photographers who liked covering cops, and whose job, more than that of the average reporter, resembled my own. We spent a lot of time driving to the same crime scenes, pleading and cajoling with families and witnesses, demanding information and photographs—"handouts," as they were called—and winning small victories when we bagged them.

I navigated the side streets of Ukrainian Village, taking in its early-morning serenity, its old trees separated by long stretches of unfortunate sidewalk and gray-shingled bungalows. Getting on the Dan Ryan, the bullet route to the South Side, I sped past the outer perimeter of the Loop with its high rises and lofts, past the old factories and warehouses along the Chicago River, past Comiskey Park and the outside wall of the Robert Taylor Homes, past the ten-story antennas of Wentworth area detective headquarters, to exit at Fifty-fifth Street, a wide boulevard that led to Hyde Park.

I stopped for a cup of coffee in a busy strip mall to clear my head. In the next hour, if I was lucky, I would interview a witness, a neighbor, a friend, a relative, the mother, the grandmother, the police. With any two, it was done; three voices or more, a simple plot, and it was better, a story, something your friends might read.

It was early, so there would be plenty of time to collect and arrange the facts before deadline. How could someone dunk a kid in hot water? There were official explanations, even for a horror such as this: The baby wouldn't stop crying, or the baby peed in his diaper, or as the cops would say, "Who knows? Mamma's boyfriend was high on cocaine. Mamma's boyfriend was drunk. Let me tell you something, in these cases it's always Mamma's boyfriend." That analysis reduced the crime to a manageable existential size, but clearly the causes were graver, like a shifting of the plates of the earth or some other cataclysm.

Every week seemed to begin and end with the same kind of trauma.

The big questions about motive (How could anyone *do* such things?) would persist until I arrived at the scene; once I was there, I would feel a letdown as the inexplicability of what I saw sank in. The big answers were buried much deeper than newspapers or television could reach. In Hyde Park, as elsewhere, I was willing to settle for facts. I was beginning to understand the refrain from "Dragnet": "Just the facts."

I parked on University Avenue, a pretty street on this summer day, its cream-colored prewar buildings basking in the gentle light.

It wasn't the ghetto—that was a plus. In the ghetto, three dead was usually the minimum requirement to transform tragedy into a news story of any significant length. A crime on a tree-lined street where the houses and apartment buildings hadn't been abandoned or burned down or claimed by drug dealers was much more likely to make it into print.

Standing in a tiny lobby, I pushed the bell for Apartment 308 four or five times before a shrill buzz let me in. I didn't expect to find anyone willing to describe what had taken place there. Everyone involved, I feared, must be in jail, in the hospital, or in hiding.

As I reached the third-floor landing, a woman in a blue-and-white striped bathrobe stood in a doorway, her wet hair pulled back, her bare ankles dripping water onto the floor.

"Can I help you?" she asked.

"Miss Miller?"

"Yes."

"I heard what happened. I'm so sorry."

This had become my standard introduction, polite but restrained, though always at these times my heart would race at the prospect of an important interview. I handed over my card with its red-white-and-blue embossed logo. She hesitated for a moment.

"Come in."

Cheap bamboo shades locked out the sun as they knocked gently against the window with the breeze. The studio apartment, about four hundred square feet, was crammed with neatly arranged furniture and jumbo baby supplies.

She took a seat on the couch, propping her legs up on a glass coffee table. Smoking a cigarette, she tried to stay calm, but everywhere she looked she saw her son: a fire truck sticking out from under the chair. Cans of baby formula stacked on the refrigerator. Half a dozen pairs of little sneakers. A pile of fresh white diapers. She smoked harder, holding each drag way down in her lungs, then exhaling slowly as though it was an exercise.

"How old is he?" I asked, even though I had heard his age on the radio. It was always a good idea to start with the basics. It was one of the few rules propounded in journalism textbooks that worked. After that you were on your own.

Already Miller seemed different from most of the people I had met under these circumstances, who either were incapable of speaking or did so in bursts of emotion after having been drawn out through the most manipulative ways of reporters.

"Eleven months the day it happened," she said quietly, staring straight ahead.

She was a nurse at Chicago Osteopathic Hospital and understood the bleak prognosis. "He was burned so bad, they say it's a one in one hundred chance he'll make it."

She was preparing for her son's death, packing up memories of him.

He was a climber, she said. On the floor was a king-size mattress, and on top of it a crib with no legs.

"That was just something I thought of," she explained as she studied her makeshift architecture. "When he fell off the bed I said, 'I'm going to fix you, Benjamin. You ain't gonna fall out of the bed no more.' "

So she placed the crib beside her when she slept. When she moved or stretched, it tossed like a canoe.

Her boyfriend, Clarence Gaunt, had slept in the bed next to them. He was a friend of her family's, and they had known each other for years before going out seriously. When Gaunt moved in a few months earlier, he had offered to babysit, which she thought was a fine gesture.

"I was real funny how I liked Benjamin cared for. I liked to keep his skin smooth. Clarence gave him his bath sometimes, fed him, washed the tub."

Gaunt and Benjamin seemed to get along fine during the two or three shifts a week Miller spent at the hospital. There were never any signs of violence, no unexplained marks on the boy's body, no tension between them.

"I was real close to Benjamin," she said. "I feel he would have let me know in some kind of way if Clarence had hurt him."

Miller was a beautiful woman, even in her sorrow. In her bathrobe you could see she was muscular and broad. She had lifted weights until she was five months pregnant. A bench press sat in a corner of the room. Her strong black features betrayed her pain only briefly, when her mouth drooped and her eyes gave way. She lifted a photo album from the coffee table, gripping its plastic cover as she slowly turned its pages.

"I tried to take pictures of him every day."

The album contained the milestones of her son's short history. He had crawled at six months. At eight he spoke. Then at eleven months, he was submerged in a tub of scalding water. His life had been so normal and happy until then. Now glossy photos, some bent at the edges, some out of focus, were all she had left. She clutched them tightly to her chest.

Miller held her breath momentarily, as though teased by the possibility that she was in the middle of a bad dream. She exhaled mightily, realizing again that she was about to lose her son, looked toward the ceiling, and cried.

■ ■ ■

From the description on the radio, I hadn't thought Benjamin Miller's case would be the worst I ever covered. But from the minute I sat down in that apartment, it became just that.

I had expected to find a broken home with signs of neglect all around, choking heat, the smell of gas leaking from the stove. And on leaving, I expected to congratulate myself for stomaching it, as though I and not the people living there had endured some inconvenience, some pain.

Now as I looked at Miller I heard my own voice when I spoke, an interior echo I remembered from the one time I passed out, in a doctor's office.

I battled for composure. I started paging through the photos of Benjamin myself, looking for close-ups; they reproduced best in the paper. I chose two in which he smiled broadly, his face round, his ears prominent, a plastic bib decorated with miniature hot-air balloons draped over his chest.

Miller ran her fingers over the outline of his face.

"Now either he's going to die or he's going to have many years of pain," she said.

I had to remind myself that by any standard this was a good story. Here were people readers could relate to: a working woman struggling to get by; an angelic baby surrounded by toys, who had been dunked in hot water. I checked my watch. Almost noon.

I slipped the photos into my shirt pocket.

"Please, tell me what happened."

Miller didn't seem to mind. She sat stoically and continued to look straight ahead as though she was watching the events of that day unfold on a television screen. Outside car horns honked, mothers yelled at their kids, jammed windows were forced open, scraping away old paint, rusted chains squeaking loudly.

On August 13, 1989, Miller had begun a double shift at the hospital. At three-thirty that afternoon she stopped home for lunch, loaded batteries into the fire truck she had bought Benjamin, then returned to work.

At about six-thirty, Gaunt called her at the hospital.

"Karen," he said, "come home right away."

When she rushed through the door she could see Benjamin curled up on the floor, burned from top to bottom. Gaunt could barely speak.

"I knew then what had happened. . . . I wrapped Benjamin in a cool blanket and I called the hospital," she recalled, still smoking a cigarette. "His skin started peeling. My baby was in shock too. I didn't touch his body. I just touched his face. I said, 'Oh, Benjamin, you'll be okay.' He was moving around a little bit. He was trying to cry."

In the hours that followed, Gaunt insisted he had done nothing wrong. He had been rinsing a mop in the tub, and he left it there, clogging the drain, and the water kept running and the boy climbed in. He swore to it. Then he heard Benjamin scream, saw him in the water, and yanked him out.

Miller stood up and led me to the bathroom. She pulled aside a pink ruffled shower curtain and turned on the hot water faucet, demonstrating how it steamed within ten seconds. The tub had a cheap whirlpool attachment. A gray steel bucket and a mop leaned against the wall.

"There's no way I could believe he put my baby in the water like that."

The detectives reached a different conclusion. Benjamin's burn marks showed that he had been suspended from his left hand into the tub. He used his right hand to cover his genitals, so it was burned like the rest of him. The boy was dangled over the water and forced in feet first until only the top of his head stuck out. And only one person, in the detectives' view, could have done it: Clarence Gaunt.

Police charged him with aggravated battery, but like the doctors, they foresaw the boy's death. So they prepared murder charges too.

The detectives said he did it because the baby wouldn't stop crying.

■ ■ ■

We returned to the couch and sat quietly for a few minutes. She glanced at a photo she kept of Gaunt on the night table.

For her sake, I wanted to believe her version of events, but I couldn't muster much enthusiasm for it.

I asked Miller if I could use her phone.

I dialed the city desk. I wanted to tell someone, but what could I say? That I could no longer tell who was lying and who was telling the truth, who was right or wrong. That in the midst of the worst sorrow of her life this mother did not run, but stared the pain down and kept her dignity, and maybe her illusions. Others would be screaming for blood, for revenge, like the mother of a slain cop who told me in court that she truly wanted to pull the switch that would unleash the electricity into her son's killer. Or the women I had spoken with in a beauty shop on the South Side who talked excitedly about castrating a rapist who had been terrorizing the neighborhood.

When the editor answered, I told her what I had. An interview with the mother. Pictures of the boy. I went over some of the details with Miller at my side.

"Sounds like you got great stuff," the editor said. "Is he dead yet?"

I carefully put down the phone. You can't cry, I told myself. The mother's not even crying.

From the first day I started on the crime beat, children were dying by the dozen, vanishing, like teenage Brazilian pickpockets, like gypsies. And every one of them might have been safe with a mother like this, with that wobbly crib and the baby toys and the clean diapers. And still it had happened here, in this cool, shady apartment.

And for the first time, I pictured the moment it happened. I imagined Benjamin's fingers splashing in the liquid heat, stretching toward the smooth edge of the porcelain tub, imagined a leap, a splash, imagined his body submerged. And rising from the water was a tiny hand reaching out for help. There was not a single story I had covered in which there wasn't someone reaching out for help. I could give nothing but my notebook, which I filled with brittle grief. That was the business I was in.

I held Miller's hand in both of mine.

If he died, or if I could write it as it really was, make the reader laugh and cry, the story would probably get on the front of the metro section. It wasn't the front page of the paper, but it wouldn't be lost either.

Miller saw me out. She would piece her life back together. She would put her son's fate in God's hands.

Outside I breathed in the warm air.

As I drove away, the photos of Benjamin sat on the passenger's seat next to me. Maybe if I write this one just right, and a few more, I thought, maybe I can get the hell off this sorry beat.

■ ■ ■

The following morning, in longhand, a detective on the fifth floor of police headquarters wrote into the Book of Death the name of Benjamin Miller, the 437th murder victim of 1989.

He would join 740 others by year's end, a 12 percent increase from the year before. No one in the police department could explain the rise other than to say that the murder rate was unpredictable. It worked in cycles. Next year would be better.

There Benjamin's name remained, even when, a year later, a Cook County judge ruled that Clarence Gaunt was not guilty of killing the boy.

I told the story in twenty inches, Benjamin's photo anchoring the article on the jump page. All day long friends called to say how terrible it was.

Though I had promised to return the photos to Karen Miller that day, I kept them for two weeks. They were tucked into a leather flap on my address book. Every time I opened it to find the names and numbers of police detectives, I saw her baby's smiling face.

THIRTEEN
. . .

SUPER RAT

DELUXE

MOB TURNCOAT TELLS HOW HE LED TWO LIVES
February 9, 1990

F or a mobster, B. J. Jahoda was taller than I had
expected.

We met late one afternoon in early 1987 in the back
room of a seafood restaurant called Bristol's as the waiters
changed the red checkered tablecloths. He stood to greet
CrimeFighter O'Brien and me.

Jahoda had broad Eastern European features, thinning
gray hair that whirled around his head, and a drooping mustache. He wore a buttoned beige shirt outside his pants.

Like a good sports columnist, O'Brien inspired readers
to rearrange the universe so that the characters he wrote
about seemed, at least momentarily, to be the only people
in the world who mattered. He was one of a handful of jour-

nalists in Chicago who knew the mob game and appreciated its twisted world because the story of gangsters and their children said something meaningful about the way people, cities, and the law worked.

O'Brien placed his bulky first-generation cassette player in the middle of a mahogany table that was shellacked to a magazine cover shine. Jahoda studied the machine, watching its black pins turn in little circles until he seemed almost mesmerized, then jerked his head away. He loved cassette recorders because they were of his time. What else did a man need but a decent sound system and a private cabana poolside in Melrose Park?

But he was also leery of the machines. A few voices caught on tape speaking the wrong words—bragging about a card game or alluding to some gravesite—and there'd be a racketeering enema. That's why one of Jahoda's responsibilities was having the homes of mobsters swept for electronic bugs. Tapes and listening devices were the tools of rats, squealers, and FBI agents, none of which, he swore, he would ever be.

Jahoda was a gambler. A numbers whiz. That was his reputation among mobsters, and among people whose job it was to watch mobsters. He had always been good at math, even in grade school, parlaying it into Monopoly for real money, then a career in gin rummy and blackjack. He was smarter than most of the people he hung around with. Not only could he count, he could spell. A Bohemian among Italians needed a shtick.

He was also a careful reader of newspapers. I had learned that the previous week, after Jahoda's name appeared in a lengthy article O'Brien and I had written about organized crime in its new frontier, the suburbs.

Jahoda was an all-star, by our count one of the top ten hoods living in Du Page County, and was believed to be in charge of an extensive suburban gambling network.

The fat men and thugs who made our list didn't have much say in the article about their relocation to suburbia.

We didn't expect them to comment, and who wanted to knock on their doors anyway? That was our first mistake.

The second was the address we published for Jahoda.

He told me that himself when I picked up the phone.

"This is B.J.," he said in a gravelly, whiskey-soaked voice.

I grabbed the article we had written from a pile of newspapers on my desk. There he was, at the top of our roster: the gambling boss. The operation he oversaw raked in hundreds of thousands of dollars each month from high-stakes card games and wirerooms all over the suburbs, which made him fairly important in the hierarchy.

More than drug dealing, extortion, or loan-sharking, gambling bankrolled the mob. Yet it was almost tolerated by the law, and when it wasn't, a little negligence could be bought at a reasonable price.

Jahoda allegedly ran the day-to-day numbers operations for mob boss Joseph Ferriola, a paunchy man with a steroid-impregnated nose who lived in an Oak Brook mansion, and then for Ferriola's lieutenant, Rocco Infelise.

"What kind of journalists are you?" Jahoda complained. "You didn't call me, you didn't come to my house. And even if you had, you wouldn't have found me, because I don't live there."

It was one of those crimes of journalistic laziness that must be avoided at all costs. I had called someone a mobster in print, then published the wrong address. So I said, "Why don't we get together and talk about it?" The invitation was a formality; I didn't expect it to lead anywhere.

Except that Jahoda said, "Sure—name the place."

Bristol's, in the back, at 3:00 P.M., when the lunch crowd would be gone.

■ ■ ■

Before I started at the Cop Shop, crime to me was either white-collar clean—Michael Milken, say—or out of the way and dirty, in the ghetto. Writing about the mob, which seemed to be right in the middle, I was compelled by *Godfather* nostalgia—drawn to the enigma of men with names like Ferriola, Infelise, Senese, Solano, and Jahoda, who tooled around in Lincolns, smoked with feeling, and in parking lots calculated the old math of skimming and percentages.

I had known gangsters only from books and movies. As a teenager, the closest I came to the syndicate was starting against a yeshiva student named something like Danny Lipschitz, the greatest five-foot-seven-inch basketball player on the Lower East Side, whose father was rumored to be a gangster.

I was naive enough to think that if I could get to know a few mobsters, or at least understand them a little better, it would give me a limitless store of material for novels and screenplays. That thought guided me through some of my worst moments.

The first lesson I got about mobsters from O'Brien concerned their unique methods of finance. For intervening—ordering a sheriff to back off a betting room, for example—they were paid. For extending credit, they were paid. For getting rid of someone, they were paid. The beauty of their system was that for not intervening, for doing nothing, for agreeing not to kill, they were also paid.

The way I understood the system from O'Brien and other experts, mob bosses were at the peak of a pyramid, vacuuming up profits from the streets. Somehow the dealers working out of an abandoned building on the West Side answered with a percentage to those on top, and finally to the man at the very top, an alleged gangster named Tony Accardo, who lived in semiretirement in California. But no one—not the FBI, not the IRS, and certainly not the newspapers—could prove it. There were only allusions to it. Everyone waited for a criminal case that would show the connection between traditional organized crime and street gangs. Late in 1989, the feds believed they finally had it.

In a predawn raid, agents arrested Rick Miller, a thirty-year veteran of the Chicago Police Department, who had been running a drug operation from a decrepit West Side hotel. The drugs, government agents maintained, came through a local Sicilian connection.

Instead of patrolling a hospital, which was his official job, Miller spent nights cutting drug deals with West Side gang leaders whom he managed to bully. For the privilege of selling his dope, they paid him.

Miller was convicted and sentenced to thirty years in prison. But the case, contrary to what the feds had hoped, shed little light on the syndicate. Miller's supplier, an Italian butcher, was also convicted. La Cosa Nostra, the Mafia, wasn't even mentioned. In that respect, the case was a bust.

Chicago had more mob-ologists per capita than any other American city, and they turned up tending bar, riding mountain bikes, and delivering pizza. Organized crime was a popular spectator sport. In a city not infatuated with celebrities, gangsters were on a par with high-priced athletes, veteran politicians, and Coach Ditka. Tour buses stopped at mob haunts such as the Biograph Theater, where Dillinger was killed, the lot on Clark Street that was the site of the St. Valentine's Day Massacre, and the empty Capone vault once lamely sifted through by Geraldo.

The professional mob watchers worked out of the Chicago Crime Commission. Their chief investigator, Jerry Gladden, perhaps the most learned in the field, always kept informed about who was in power and why. A former Chicago cop who once wired his mother to catch a marijuana dealer, Gladden had friends on both sides of the law. He was the source most reporters flocked to for background whenever a gangster turned up buried or blown away.

But I heard one of the best interpretations of mob life in a taxi on the way to the Cop Shop. The cabbie, a Jewish guy who scraped by on $20,000 a year, claimed to have a degree in criminal justice. When he asked me what I did and I told him, he launched into what I'll call the Melrose Park theory.

"Pull over and keep the meter running," I ordered.

"This is how it works," his lecture began. "Mafia. M–A–F–I–A. They're the aristocracy. They're made. Accardo is made. Paul the Waiter Ricca, made. There are maybe—maybe fifteen hundred made members in the country. That's all. Then you got your Italians who are not made. And finally, you got your hangers-on, like the Jewish guys in the card games."

A beefy man with a double chin, the cabbie spit onto the corners of his mustache as he spoke. The meter clicked at twenty-cent intervals.

"All crime is licensed by Tony Accardo. Everyone pays. Some people call it street tax, but it isn't street tax, it's 'license to operate.' Everyone is licensed to operate, even the Rukns, the Vice Lords, the Disciples."

"Why do the gangs need the mob?" I asked. "Why not be independent?"

"Why, you ask?" the cabbie shouted. "Because where are they going to get a hundred thousand bucks for their business? The schvartzes, on their best day, their *best day*, never compiled a hundred thousand bucks! So what they do is go to Melrose Park to get a hundred thousand for dope. Then they sell the dope on the street and turn around and give a hundred fifty G's back to Melrose Park. That's how they're licensed. To take five thousand bucks out of the mattress is not going to help a five-thousand-member gang."

"And where does this transaction take place?" I asked in a mocking tone. He eyed me in the rearview mirror.

"Look, they're not schmucks. Tony Accardo doesn't go to Sixty-third and Stony Island to meet Jeff Fort's guys. He talks to somebody who talks to somebody who's got one foot in the schvartzes' craw. A suitcase makes it to Sixty-third and Stony, and they're off to the races."

■ ■ ■

The average citizen did not deride the mob but cherished it, like a proud relative. When I wrote a story about Lenny

Patrick, Chicago's best-known Jewish gangster, a group of old card players without connections to the syndicate heaped praise on him—he was a fine man, a good man, a brave man who, like themselves, had once been a poor schmuck from the West Side.

"What is he now?" one of the card players asked. "A seventy-eight-year-old man who was nice to people his whole life." It mattered little that Patrick, a hunched-over fiend, was still extorting money from car dealers and restaurants and threatening to blow people's heads off.

The same admiration and respect existed, albeit in different circles, for Infelise, Ferriola, Accardo. Even the people who lived down the street from them loved them. "They keep their lawns so nice," said a neighbor of Dominic Senese, the head of a powerful Teamsters local, after a gunman blew half of Senese's face off as he drove through the gate of his Oak Brook subdivision.

The neighbor I interviewed the day after the attack also said: "He'd always give the best candies on Halloween."

The Chicago mob was still at the heart of the city's identity. Citizens assumed that politicians were dirty, that backroom deals greased every license, law, and permit. It was simply the eternal rhythm of the town. There were no longer the fireworks that defined the mob in New York, no Gotti, no caterer of annual block parties. During Capone's reign there had been, peaking with the St. Valentine's Day Massacre. Since then the violence was carried out much more quietly.

In a quiet way, an estimated 100 syndicate murders were committed between 1970 and 1990. Only a handful were solved.

In a quiet way, politicians from the First Ward, which included the Loop, Chinatown, and Little Italy, met each afternoon in Counselors Row, a restaurant across the street from City Hall. There in Booth One, they talked about who was to be bribed and when, their greedy words, operatic hand movements, and calorie count ("I'll have the belt-buster, honey") recorded by a video camera hidden beneath one of the seats.

In a quiet way, the First Ward alderman, Fred Roti, would stand in City Hall, his pants pulled up over his navel, his arms outstretched, as he dispensed advice to politicians and reporters. ("You—you asshole," he had said to me when I asked him about a land deal in his ward. "Why are you grinning like a Cheshire cat?" He stood with his palms open, as if to say, Look at me, I'm clean. I've got nothing to hide, and if I did, you wouldn't find it.) Roti too would be convicted of corruption.

In a quiet way, they did what they wanted. New gangs, led by kids with machine guns, were making all the noise.

■ ■ ■

I once went to visit Ferriola.

The *Sun-Times* had published a story alleging he had met with Ed Vrdolyak, a powerful Chicago alderman who was running for mayor. The charge was adamantly denied by Vrdolyak, who wound up suing the paper over it. My job was to get some reaction from the mob boss.

Ferriola's lawn was immaculate. There were no guardhouses, no electric fences, no dogs—just a bell and two conventional doors, the outer one glass.

No one answered.

Three hours later I returned, and again, no answer.

At about four on that frigid afternoon I went back one last time. I could hear the doorbell chiming inside. I imagined it playing the theme to *The Godfather.* Then I heard footsteps.

The door swung open.

"Yes, can I help you?"

The woman standing in the door was attractive, with salon hair and hip-hugging pants. She looked as though she might have been taking a break from ice-skating, just done drinking hot cider spiked with rum.

"Is your husband home? I'm a reporter from . . ."

"O God, I thought you were the pizza delivery guy. I never would have opened the door."

"I'd like to speak to your husband."

"He's asleep."

"Well, would you mind waking him up?"

"I wouldn't even think of doing that."

"Why not?"

She started to retreat.

There I was, at the doorstep of the supposed head of the Chicago mob, a few yards from the couch where he rested his alleged extortionist feet, feeling defeated, when a baby blue Mercedes screeched into the S-curved driveway.

I had him. What was he going to do? Shoot me? It would almost be worth it for the next morning's tabloid headline: TRIBUNE BIGGIE SLAIN BY MOB BOSS; MOLL WATCHES.

A man struggled to climb out of the car. When he emerged, he was holding two boxes of pizza.

"Thanks so much, Vinnie," Mrs. Ferriola said.

"You from the paper?" he asked.

"Yeah."

"Tell your bosses I see their truck parked out here all the time with their binoculars. They're fooling nobody. You guys can't respect nobody's privacy. You tell them that."

I had no idea what he was talking about. I knew there were no other reporters staking out Ferriola's house. So who were the "reporters" in the truck? Impostors, obviously. FBI perhaps. This was getting to be too much.

Ferriola never emerged that afternoon. But two weeks later another reporter, a crazy Greek woman, ambushed him as he was leaving his house.

"I don't know nothing about nobody," he said.

That was the usual response.

■ ■ ■

About a year later, Jahoda called.

Contrary to what the federal government claimed, he denied that he had worked for Ferriola (who soon after died

199

while waiting for a donor heart) or Infelise. He denied he knew anything about the mob, let alone running a $20 million-a-year sports betting operation for it. He denied he knew anything about the murder of an independent bookie named Hal Smith, who had been savagely beaten. He denied everything.

"I know people socially. I'm not going to mention any names. But as far as any working relationships, no, I have none. I don't believe what I read in the newspapers. Please don't take that personally."

Oh, he was an expert on the subject of what he wasn't.

"They are looking for me to commit felonies. I don't. They are looking for me to do interstate gambling. I don't. They are looking for a gambling conspiracy. I'm not into that. They are looking for extortion. I'm not an extortionist. They are looking for a gangster, but I am not a gangster. I don't threaten people. 'Cause those things carry time. 'You owe me the money, pay me or I'll break your legs.' I'm not that way. I'm very careful with my clientele. I don't go overboard."

Smoking cigarettes and drinking scotch, Jahoda gave us a brief history of his life. His story, he admitted, had everything to do with gambling, but very little to do with organized crime. He had been born in Cicero, Illinois, to Irish and Bohemian parents. His father was a fireman. In the early 1970s he was a suburban newspaper editor who played gin rummy in Joliet and Lyons and Chicago. He had no trouble making $100,000 a year and boasted to friends that wagering was "the biggest growth area in America."

As a gambler, he was a clearly among the best. He didn't have a system, only a web of instincts that had proved reliable.

"I'm not that skilled, but I'm also not stubborn. The only thing I've got going for me is I know when I'm outclassed, so I just back off. I don't believe in luck on a consistent basis. I know when I'm overmatched."

The IRS played its hand in 1979 when it busted Jahoda for not paying enough taxes.

By the time he got out of prison in 1981, the IRS claimed that Jahoda owed $119,000 in back taxes and penalties; by the end of the decade the figure was more than $600,000. Agents raided his home in search of gambling records. On three occasions they seized his cars as payment for his tax bill.

One raid he thought would be the last.

"When they come, you never forget it, never. I thought it was a hit. I thought I was dead in my own house. I was down in my basement. I was talking to my kid on the phone, he was going to Marquette at the time, and I heard a bang. It was just—a bang. As I'm going up the stairs, there's a shadow at my front door. I heard somebody scream, 'B.J., open up this fucking door.' I saw a shadow. Someone was coming down with a sledgehammer. As I saw this I heard a crash on the other side of the room. Someone was coming in through the patio door. I've got no way out of this house, I've got no way out of this basement, and I heard nothing but footsteps. I'm in the bathroom now and I think I'm absolutely dead in this house because now I hear at least four sets of footsteps. I'm screaming, 'I've got a shotgun, don't take another step or I'm going to shoot you.' And then somebody said, 'Federal agents with a warrant.' I was shaking for twenty minutes. They actually had to sit me down. I says, 'I've never been happier to see you guys.' "

He wasn't happy for long, for as the agents quickly told him, there *was* a mob contract out on his life.

"They invited me into their witness protection program, and I told them point blank, I said, 'Number one, there's nothing I could really help you with. Number two . . . I would rather be shot on the street than be the only square in the witness protection program. Because everyone in the program is a fink and a rat and I just don't qualify.' "

It was near the end of the interview, and Jahoda asked me to turn off the tape recorder. He had a few things to say about Hal Smith the bookmaker. Sure, he had known him. He had even seen him on the day he was killed. But that was all he knew.

In my notebook I wrote: "Denies knowledge of Smith murder."

■ ■ ■

O'Brien and I walked Jahoda to his car, a rented Oldsmobile with a velvet interior. He looked over his shoulder to check for the government. As he drove away, I found it hard to believe I had met one of the mob. I was inclined to think Jahoda—this gambler, this hustler, this well-trained card shark—had been telling the truth. CrimeFighter was less convinced, but we were both excited that we had made a good contact and collected enough material for an entertaining story.

■ ■ ■

The interview with Jahoda finally appeared in the Du Page section of the newspaper about a year later, after I had started at the Cop Shop. The paper, as it turned out, wasn't interested in a short biography of a suspected mobster. But one person who was interested was Jahoda's boss, Rocco Infelise.

Infelise shoved the newspaper into Jahoda's hand as they stood in a parking lot in—where else, Melrose Park. The interview, though it had seemed harmless enough when he sat for it, suddenly posed a monumental problem, not because of what Jahoda had said, but because of the timing of its publication. Beneath Jahoda's polyester shirt, two plastic pins were spinning around, recording for posterity Infelise's instructions about gambling, extortion, and bribery. On that day, B. J. Jahoda had turned into Super Rat Deluxe. And the first tape he would turn over to the government in his role as informant, to be played at his trial months later, was of the mad dog lecture delivered by Infelise about the story we had written.

"What the fuck is this?" Infelise asked.

"That's about the Internal Revenue four years ago," Jahoda answered nervously.

"Four years ago. There's a lot of shit that just happened in here. . . . I'm going to tell you something. I told you don't ever talk to these motherfuckers."

"I remember, Rock."

"I'm going to tell you right now. This ever happens again, you might as well pack up and leave because you're through with us. I got more fucking ass-chewings over this motherfucking thing. I didn't even see it. This was in the Du Page paper."

"Rock, I didn't think three people in the whole world were going to read the fucking thing."

"Well, it's in Du Page," Infelise shouted. "A lot of guys live in Du Page, B.J. Now you had to tell these motherfuckers to know this shit. Don't lie to me."

"I'm not, Rock. I'm negotiating with the IRS back in eighty-four, eighty-five—"

"There's shit that just happened. Don't let this happen again. I'm fucking telling you, you know."

"On the square, Rock, I'm not that way."

"But if this is what you want to fucking do, tell me, and then—and then just break all fucking relationships, forget about anything. I just don't give a fuck, you know. I don't mind going to bat for you, but—"

"I wouldn't do anything that stupid, Rock."

"Well, this is a fucking book."

"This is the last time. . . . I—"

"B.J. It's over with. I took the fucking cigar for it. And I don't want it to fucking happen again. Now I'm fucking dead serious. Another thing. Change your fucking phone number."

■ ■ ■

The tape recorder spun for seven more months, five thousand hours or more, making B. J. Jahoda the biggest rat the

Chicago mob had ever known. He had agreed to turn state's witness, his lawyer explained, because he "just wanted to get out of this life." But he was also prodded by the IRS, which reminded him that it would soon be time to pay off the gargantuan debt. Some say the agents finally convinced Jahoda that he was in danger of being rubbed out.

As informant, Jahoda lived in a government-rigged luxury apartment overlooking Lake Michigan. Whenever Rocco or Sal visited him there, the machine ran. At the same time, Jahoda managed Infelise's gambling business in Lake County, a twenty-mile drive north. For his cooperation, Jahoda expected a reduced prison sentence and a much smaller tax debt.

In all, twenty people, including Jahoda, were indicted as a result of his undercover work. They were charged with conspiracy, racketeering, and three murders, including that of Hal Smith. By the time he got to court, Jahoda admitted having watched his colleagues beat Smith in a kitchen in suburban Long Grove.

"If the Chicago outfit had its way," Jahoda told another reporter after his role became known, "I'd be nailed with railroad spikes through my tongue to a frozen telephone pole in Cicero."

The tapes were masterpieces. Infelise could be heard telling Jahoda that for $10,000 a month, the Cook County sheriff "never bothers us." He bragged about having helped get Richard Daley elected mayor, and how he had sought the help of a high-ranking Chicago police officer, "the chief downtown," to transfer vice officers who were investigating some of the mob's gambling operations.

It was assumed in the newsroom that by "the chief downtown" Infelise meant Leroy Martin. Even if Infelise was simply blustering, we were going to report it, which meant I had to call Martin for his reaction.

When I reached him at home on the night the transcript of the tape was leaked he was busy packing for a vacation in Mexico. But he had time to say, "I could sleep good because there's no tape with my voice on it, no money with my prints on it."

It was the first time since he had become superintendent that Martin's integrity had been publicly questioned. The allegations against public officials were chilling, even if they were made by a gangster. In responding, Martin had chosen words that, as always, were so brazen and, if you listened closely, so crafty, that I understood again what the public liked about him.

■ ■ ■

By the time Jahoda entered the witness protection program, thousands of informants and criminals had preceded him. Since it was established in 1971, the government had sheltered fifty-eight hundred witnesses, and its effect had snowballed. As more people survived turning state's witness, more were willing to take the chance to save themselves or their families.

But one of the first persons to enter the government program turned up dead on the Eisenhower Expressway early in 1990. His name was William O'Neal.

Henry would have tormented me about pursuing the story if he had been around. He had died of cancer in early January. I wondered if I could truly dislike him at his end. I couldn't. A picture of him was pinned to the bulletin board, and a vial of red ink that looked like blood sat next to the fire ticker. On the vial was a piece of masking tape with his name on it.

If Henry had heard about O'Neal, he would have said he was nothing but a punk—which was true. But the teenage car thief had been turned into a spy and provocateur by a white southern FBI agent named Roy Mitchell.

After arresting O'Neal in 1966 for stealing a car from O'Hare Airport, Mitchell taught him the art of infiltration. It was the beginning of a long, complex, and incongruous relationship. From supplying his handler initially with information about any crime committed on the West Side, O'Neal ultimately became a primary informant on the FBI's main target, the Black Panthers.

In 1968, O'Neal went to the Panthers' newly opened office, volunteered for handiwork and odd jobs, and rose quickly in the organization. As "captain of security," O'Neal was responsible for rooting out informants and stockpiling weapons, which became a priority after the onset of a power struggle with the Rukns.

O'Neal kept Mitchell informed of every move within the Panthers' Chicago organization. Then, late in 1969, O'Neal provided the FBI with the floor plans of an apartment shared by several Panther leaders. On December 4 the apartment was raided by police assigned to the Cook County state's attorney's office. Although the official purpose of the raid was to search for weapons, local Panther leaders Fred Hampton and Mark Clark were killed in a fusillade of bullets. A later investigation would show that the Panthers had fired only one shot at the police, leading to charges the police had carried out an assassination.

In 1973, after his role as an informant became public during a murder trial unrelated to the Panther case, O'Neal joined the witness protection program. For the next fifteen years he regularly changed identities and residences. According to friends, O'Neal had been arrested more than a hundred times, but the charges never stuck. He moved back to the Chicago area in 1988, remarried, and began working as an investigator for a lawyer he knew.

Six months later he ran headlong into traffic on the expressway. The medical examiner pronounced his death a suicide.

As a kid growing up on the West Side, O'Neal would run from his apartment to the road where he would die. He would sprint a few hundred yards, then charge down the ditch to the asphalt edge of the expressway, shrieking with glee. He said he loved the road because it was so wide and stretched so far into the distance to exotic places he wanted to see someday.

Before his death, O'Neal was interviewed for the television documentary "Eyes on the Prize," a series about the civil rights movement. He expressed remorse about the deaths of members of the Panthers, a group he had come to respect almost as much as the FBI. His friends speculated that it was that conflict that led to his death.

"They made him into Dick Tracy, into Spiderman," an old friend of O'Neal's told me, "but when it was over, there was nothing left for him."

It was a small funeral.

There was no van parked in front of the entrance to impede rival gang members looking to disrupt the occasion. There was no commotion as there had been a few weeks earlier at a funeral parlor on the West Side, when a young man walked in, pulled a knife from beneath his coat, and cut off the ear of the deceased.

The funeral home had a banquet hall feel to it, with several services going on simultaneously. The wallpaper had an olive velvet paisley design on a cream-colored background.

A picture of O'Neal on the program showed him with a mustache and sad eyes. A short prayer printed inside ended with the tantalizing lines "So do not stand at my grave and cry. / I am not there—I did not die."

■ ■ ■

I always wondered what Jahoda's fate would be.

One afternoon, when he was already in government custody, Jahoda called me at my desk. He wanted to know why the profile about him didn't have my byline on it. I told him that it did, right below O'Brien's.

"You want to bet?" he asked.

"Bottle of Dewars."

"Fine."

Just to be sure, I pulled out the article. I had won a bottle of scotch from the king of gin rummy.

Later that night he left an incomprehensible message on my answering machine at home.

"This is Ali Baba," he said. He sounded drunk and angry, part of the cost of flipping from one side to the other. I wondered whether he would make it.

In court, he was an ideal witness.

The Infelise crew hired some of the best lawyers in town, but they couldn't get to Jahoda. No matter what they threw at him, he retained his composure and his mastery of details. Infelise was convicted of racketeering and murder conspiracy.

The case marked the beginning of an aggressive federal program of taking on one mob crew at a time, Infelise's having been the first. The strategy would reach its apex two years later when Lenny Patrick, who was two or three ranks above Jahoda in the mob hierarchy, followed the rat path to the witness protection program.

Even though Jahoda had snowed O'Brien and me, I never resented it. It was his job to lie.

FOURTEEN

...

COOL RUNNING

EVEN IN PAIRS, DRUG COPS ULTIMATELY ALONE
May 17, 1990

The undercover war on drugs was joined two or three nights a week next to a grease bin in a parking lot uptown.

The agents arrived one at a time in department-issued sedans with maroon velvet interiors or old Cadillacs leaking long trails of oil, pulling up to a grassy railroad embankment that hid the lot from view. Getting out of their cars, two women and six men looked relaxed in jeans and T-shirts, as though they had come for a barbecue.

They assembled for a drug investigation targeting a Jamaican bar called Cool Running that was believed to be the hub of a mid-level cocaine business on the Far North Side. Operation Cool Running was a local police matter, relying on the manpower of the Chicago police and intelligence gathered by the department. It typified the unglamorous but expanding covert war being fought by dozens of police agencies against narco-traffickers in their cities. Even small midwestern towns were suddenly inundated with drugs as supplies fanned out to suburbs and farm communities, where the biggest law enforcement problem had until recently been traffic offenses like speeding. Drug squads were in demand as much as SWAT teams had once been to fight real and imagined Arab terrorists. There was a hunger for something, anything, to be done.

Operation Cool Running had started out enthusiastically in late 1989 with hopes of victory and little blue police medals. Like most local drug probes, it grew from a tip. Often a telephone call from a cop or an alderman about a dangerous street corner in the neighborhood would set the gears in motion. The police system was not much more organized than that. By the late 1980s the drug business in Chicago had become so diffuse that police admitted they couldn't even name the top dealers.

In this case, an anonymous letter sent to the Cook County state's attorney's office complained about a group of "fellow Jamaicans" who were selling drugs way north on Broadway. The citizen enclosed a list of license plate numbers, car makes, and the names of "some of the evilest people out of Jamaica living right here in Chicago and other parts of America."

The letter was passed on to Commander Risley in narcotics, who handed it to one of his sergeants, Al Isaac, the leader of an undercover unit of seven or eight officers, depending on who was scheduled to work that day.

By national standards, the Chicago Police Department's commitment to the narcotics unit, even at the height of the drug war, was paltry. Less than 1 percent of the force was assigned full-time to drug enforcement, compared to 5 percent or more in other large cities. And though there was occasional public uproar over the shortage in manpow-

er—on most days there were fewer than fifty narcotics officers on the street—the situation never improved. That was
only one of the problems.

The sad fact was that the crude battle over dope in Robbins and other communities mirrored the plight of the Chicago police, whose officers got paid every week but who
faced the same overwhelming odds. They had a few more
men and women, more money, more cars, but hardly any
more success. Seizures of dope, for example, the primary
measuring stick, remained fairly steady despite increasing
supplies entering the city. The department vacillated between strategies, unsure whether to target common street
dealers or more sophisticated organizations. Cool Running
was in between, an eyesore with a hierarchy.

■ ■ ■

Isaac stood in the parking lot, cigarette smoke shooting out
his mouth like in the giant ad in Times Square, his brain in
a low boil. With his wavy black hair, grainy beard, and silver
hoop earring, he looked like Al Pacino in *Serpico.*

Ever since he was a sergeant in the Rogers Park neighborhood, Isaac was suspicious of certain Jamaicans on the
North Side. The hunch took hold when an officer under his
command was the subject of a misconduct complaint that
he had searched, allegedly without a warrant, the home of
a handsome twenty-five-year-old Bahamian named Phillip
Miller. Every time Isaac called Miller's apartment to look
into the complaint, a different Jamaican answered the
phone. With reflexive, police-style prejudice, Isaac associ-
ated the melodic Caribbean lilt with cocaine, Uzis, and the
nasty drug posses that used them. And there was something
about Miller, he thought, his arrogance and fine double-
breasted suits, that said he was involved up to his neck.

When Isaac returned to undercover work, the Jamaican
chorus stuck in his head. If there was a posse, it could make
a sexy, high-profile case that would keep him and his crew

away from the monotony of street busts for a long time. It would be a feather in his cap, a sign that local cops could handle the important cases, upstaging the federal agencies that held the Chicago rank and file in disdain. As in journalism, the long-term project was usually preferable to the short-term one because it offered greater rewards, carried greater status, and offered the hope of bigger, better assignments.

The police department's intelligence division had compiled a fifty-page report on the structure and hierarchy of what it called the Gold Star Posse. In the file were reports on several unsolved homicides linked to the group, its known hangouts, including Cool Running, and the requisite police glossary of Jamaican Rasta terminology ("Bring I self tool and machine," for example, translated as "Bring me a gun and a machine gun").

Isaac's plan was simple and by the book: His officers would become regulars at the bar, lure dealers into selling increasingly larger quantities of cocaine, expose the flesh and bones of their organization, and move for a conspiracy charge that would hold up in court. And if some of the suspects decided to cooperate, God bless them, who knew where the case would lead?

In the first three months of the operation the team had made roughly a dozen buys at the bar, which was located on a busy strip of upper Broadway, a few blocks west of the lake. Several of the buys were for more than fifteen grams, Class X felonies. One of the dealers who allegedly sold to the undercover cops was Phillip Miller.

But it had been three weeks since the last hand-to-hand buy, a long dry stretch that was making Isaac nervous. Had the officers been made? Were they in danger? Had the supply dried up?

It was here at the meet spot that Isaac conducted his last-minute strategizing, going from philosophical to dire in a matter of minutes, becoming the Man from U.N.C.L.E. leading F-Troop. He glanced at a commuter train as it clanked toward the city limit, the cars glowing an unearthly green, and then toward the dark blue heavens. He considered himself in the end to be the protector of his unit, a job he took very seriously, God forbid that any of his agents should get hurt.

"Oy veh," he muttered as the group gathered around him. A dozen buys are fine, but not enough, he thought to himself.

"They will have to start selling us dope again," he announced as another train passed. "This is spring. They are dealing. We know they have the dope. They always have. Press. Press harder."

Isaac directed his plea to the two female officers, Wendy Marrello and Patti Lockridge, who would be entering the bar in a few minutes to try to buy $1,200 worth of cocaine. "Spend some dough," Isaac said, suddenly sounding paternal and understanding. "That's what it's for. Okay?"

The women stood with their hands on their hips, straightening their posture in the absence of the .38s that usually dragged them down. They listened to Isaac, their faces expressionless.

The group split up as the officers began the two-mile trip to the streets and alleys around Cool Running. The bar was on "the B street," between a greasy burger joint and another small bar, this one favored by Nigerians. Across Broadway were a quick-oil-change garage, a transmission shop, a large dance club, and a Pakistani temple surrounded on most weeknights by idling cabs.

Once the buy officers entered the bar, the main responsibility was surveillance. Two cars continuously circled the bar while another vehicle, either a van or trailer, depending on which was available that night in the narcotics garage, was parked across the street.

The surveillance team communicated with two-way radios they kept hidden somewhere beneath the dashboard. Isaac also kept a cellular phone beside him so the undercovers, the "UCs," inside the bar could call him or respond to his pages. Wendy and Patti called Isaac every half hour or so to tell him how things were going, or paged him with a message: 00, nothing happening, be out soon; 2, bag is coming in; or 911, emergency.

Everyone was always on the lookout for 911, or a chair through the window, at which point the investigation ended and a rescue began.

■ ■ ■

My first night out, I took up my position in the back of a camper trailer with Tom Hitz. Another officer, Frank Pisterzi, had parked the van directly across the street from the bar and turned off the engine, leaving us in the rear of the trailer for as long as the night's incursion would last.

The seats were upholstered with scenes of vegetables growing and coated by a layer of dust. The dark wood cabinets were warped and wouldn't stay shut. All in all, though, it wasn't bad. Wisconsin-ready.

Scattered on a table were a police radio, binoculars, a one-way mirrored window facing the bar, a two-pound plastic bag of salted nuts, and an empty Maxwell House coffee can to pee in.

Five minutes into our surveillance Hitz was listening to a Blackhawks game over his yellow Walkman, chewing tobacco, when suddenly I heard screams. I looked out the window at the entrance to the bar; it was quiet. But just in front of the trailer a teenage boy had been struck by a cab. We could see through a small window at the front of the cabin that he was flat on the ground, his body half in the crosswalk, half out, his arms spread at two o'clock. We could do nothing but wait for an ambulance, or else blow our cover. Muted shouts penetrated the walls of the trailer. I thought the boy was dead. A great way to start off. Already I felt like bad luck.

By the time the ambulance arrived the boy was standing upright and walking toward the burger shack across the street, where video machines would neutralize the trauma. The paramedics found him behind Pac Man. Hitz observed the scene through the binoculars, let out a laugh, then resumed the lookout.

There wasn't much happening. Every few minutes Isaac would check in by radio, telling us where he was located and what, if anything, he had heard from the officers inside. Isaac's voice intermittently faded as the radio hissed with static.

"The goddamn radios don't work," Hitz complained. "They want us to fight a war and the goddamn radios can't transmit from a few blocks away. Once I went along with some DEA agents on a surveillance. They followed a guy to Milwaukee, and they were talking to their officer in Chicago. In Chicago! Can you imagine?"

There was no excuse for such shoddy equipment. I knew this to be the case because I had finally figured out where the drug money seized from drug dealers went.

Along with another reporter, Joel Kaplan, an honest and relentless investigator who could pick apart the lies of public officials as easily and naturally as he tied his shoelaces, I had spent the previous weeks going through a foot-high stack of vouchers and bank records relating to the drug fund. Virtually no one in the police administration was willing to discuss the money, and the inquiry caused considerable anger among some of my sources, who preferred slow-pitch press conferences about murders to hard questions about cash.

Our conclusion: The police department had amassed more than $5 million, $3 million of which was kept in a bank account hidden from City Hall. And what did the department do with the money? Not much. Less than half of it had been spent. Most of the funds hadn't earned interest for years. All the while, drug cops on the street could barely communicate by radio. At last I understood what they were so angry about.

■ ■ ■

In musty quarters like the trailer, from across the wide, torn-up seats of squad cars, in hallways and courtrooms and locker rooms, cops get to know their partners well, much more intimately than they know their own husbands or wives. Together they reviewed mistakes of the past, plans for the future, every important date, every important meal, so that eventually there were no secrets. That first night out there was plenty of time for Hitz and me to get to know each other, and we did.

Hitz was a large person, a tackle at birth, a gunner, an urban tunnel rat, bald with a goatee that made him look more sinister than he was. After working hours he ran a comedy club with his girlfriend.

He grew up in a "prejudiced family" on the South Side, barely setting foot in the North, the one memorable excursion being a visit to a girlfriend whose roommate answered the door naked.

"I said, 'Do all girls act this way up here?' "

He thought people were jerks by nature, most of them exhibiting the nosiness and arrogance of what he considered the lowest type of human beings—police internal affairs investigators. Though he hated and mistrusted the police bureaucracy, he had joined the department in 1981 because "police work isn't as routine as loading and unloading corrugated metal in Frankfurt, Illinois. You know what I mean?"

He took a tactical job in Englewood, where there was always an arrest to be made by him or his partner, Steve Haras, who also had joined Isaac's team. Now the two of them were learning another side of police work, a presumably subtler side, where the night wasn't over when you hauled in a few gang bangers caught tossing a .45 into the bushes.

" 'Just tell me you're not the police,' " Hitz said, mocking the toads who sold him dope undercover despite their suspicions that he was.

" 'Okay, I'm not the police,' " he'd answer.

" 'Okay, here's your bag.' "

This leap of faith was the engine of undercover work. Stupidity on the part of the seller made it go. As a cop, you had to be patient. You had to stay with it for months. You had to figure out the route the drugs traveled. You had to drive around in circles. You had to hold out for more, even when you were sick and tired of sitting in the back of a trailer, peeing and spitting tobacco into a rusty coffee can.

"The last couple of days have been getting to my girlfriend," Hitz confided as he emptied a handful of nuts into his mouth. "She knows what I do, but she doesn't know exactly what I do. She knows it from TV, where the good guys always win."

No chairs flew through the window of the bar, no drugs were bought or sold, no new friendships made. After about three hours, that was the message sent to Isaac over his pager, and he passed on the frustrating news to the surveillance team.

Pisterzi climbed into the cab of the trailer, started the engine, and drove us back to the meet spot for a short debriefing.

"For weeks the place has been hot," Isaac huffed in a pained voice. "Then, from the night of the president's speech about crime or some shit, they start saying, 'I can't sell you anything. I'm quitting the business.' Can you believe that?"

But Isaac smartened up, zeroing in on his own naïveté. Had he expected it to be easy? Had he believed for a second that he could deliver this gang of violent Rastafarians, these killers, in a neat package without some heartache? Why, he asked himself, as though it was one of the four questions sung on Passover, should this investigation be different from all other investigations?

"We'll get them next time," he said, and in a swift motion lit another cigarette.

■ ■ ■

LeRoy Martin had furnished me the box seat.

During one of our conversations in his office, I asked Martin for permission to follow an undercover drug unit from start to finish on one of its investigations.

These were the early days of the drug war, and there was heightened interest in the daily grind and perceived grandeur of undercover work. I promised not to compromise the unit's operation, would write about it only when it was completed, and agreed to abide by whatever additional ground rules were set by the news affairs director.

Martin said it would be fine with him. I can only guess that he saw a benefit in documenting what his officers were up against, and that they were doing their best.

My editors supported the idea but were understandably hesitant to cut me loose from the beat for a few months or even a few weeks to follow a bunch of undercover cops around. So I decided I would do it on my own time, after I had done my duty at Eleventh and State for the day and filed my stories. Undercover work was done mainly at night anyway, so what difference did it make?

■ ■ ■

The narcotics unit, still considered a plum assignment because of the autonomy allowed its officers, was headquartered in a two-story warehouse in the Bridgeport neighborhood, the islandlike nerve center of white ethnic Chicago and home of Comiskey Park. On game days the narcs would charge out the front door hauling bulletproof vests over their shoulders and shiny pistols in their belts as the fans shuffled toward the ballpark, oblivious.

The location didn't seem to be any big secret. White

Sox fans were not the enemy. The enemy was all around Bridgeport. Among law abiding citizens, among the past and future cops who hurried past their door, the narcs were invisible. Elsewhere, though, particularly in black neighborhoods that required black buy officers (of which there were few), this was less true.

It was always startling that you could just drive up to the warehouse and walk in off the street. You didn't have to ring a bell, enter a code, utter a secret password, or wear a laminated identification card around your neck. At the top of a long staircase sat an overweight cop who acted as gruff receptionist.

"Help you?"

"I'm here to see Risley."

"Straight back."

Narcotics was kept on a short leash by the police brass. Risley carefully monitored the ebb and flow of buy money, a maximum of $10,000 for a single deal, looked for the warning signs of burnout, and battled his bosses for more equipment and manpower, neither of which materialized. He also kept a wide eye on his career, wondering if he would ever get the top job. This was unlikely because he didn't have a strong political sponsor, and he was white.

With Martin's okay, Risley set me up with Isaac.

"He's got a team working on some interesting stuff. Why don't you talk to him?"

Isaac's office down the hall was crammed with metal filing cabinets. The walls were decorated with posters of Jamaican beaches, an Israeli flag, its blue Jewish star nearly covered by a pirate's mask, and a photo of Mayor Daley with a dart piercing his left nostril.

Isaac sat on top of a gray metal desk, smoking and drumming his legs against its tinny front panel. Then, with two deep drags on a cigarette, he launched into a soliloquy on the mechanics of deception, a speech he delivered seamlessly, as though he had been preparing it since the day he was issued a badge, turning it over like a pancake until done.

"If you're not just a bit frightened, then you're stupid. You don't belong in this business. You're playing chess with your life here. You have to be up by five moves. What if he says 'We're going to Milwaukee?' What if he says 'I want to sleep with you?' They move, you react."

He spoke intensely but calmly, as though he had just walked out of a hot shower, and refrained from a lot of cop talk about Teflon bullets and beating people up.

"Once you find something that works, you stay with it. It puts them at ease. They figure you can't be the police. Sex sells. Sex and drugs have always gone together. You sell the concept. You sell the fantasy.

"Wendy and I used to paint sexual pictures. We'd paint an illusion. Not only did we sell the drugs, we had a good time with it. I used to drape a cat-o'-nine-tails over the mirror. People would ask, 'What do you do with that?' All that sexual tension. It helps."

Here, I thought, was a group of cops I could easily spend a few months with.

■ ■ ■

I got into Isaac's car, a leased maroon Ford. We circled the bar, hoping the women would have some luck this night.

"This is mid-America at its best," Isaac said, gesturing at the sights and sounds of Broadway, which was nothing like New York's Broadway. At its northern end it was essentially a seedy commercial strip. The surrounding neighborhoods were mixed, ranging from downright dangerous to quietly middle-class. Denise Farmer had been killed just a few blocks from the bar, but her death had nothing to do with the drugs Isaac was chasing. These were different dealers, different suppliers, different users. At the McDonald's down the block, a young man was killed while sitting in his rented black Porsche. There was a rumor that the dead man had been a customer at the bar, but no one was sure.

Isaac planted the cellular phone on the floor and

wedged a police radio under his crotch. From behind the wheel the professor of undercover conducted surveillance in authoritative radio jive while drinking a diet Pepsi.

"Look at these people," Isaac said of his crew. "They're tired. They're beat. They could do absolutely nothing and still get paid for it. But they stick it out on the line to make things happen. Every one of these people is dedicated to the operation. They worry about it. . . . You want to come in and deal for the kilo. You want to shelve the mother load. You want to be remembered for doing something significant."

The drug supply would hardly be affected, even if everything went perfectly; that much was obvious. But Isaac was too wrapped up in the operation to consider its ultimate futility.

"You would probably drive yourself crazy if you told yourself that you're only looking at a small percentage of the drugs in Chicago. So you choose targets. Your main goal is to wreak havoc on that organization, decimate it. Then you pick another group. Little by little, with enough people doing it, maybe you'll have an effect."

That night ended like the previous one. No one wanted to sell any dope. Patti and Wendy sat at the bar telling each other jokes, slowly sipping vodka and orange juice.

At the meet spot, no one wanted to talk about it. So they went to a bar on the edge of Chinatown everyone called "the Two-Six."

It had once been a funeral parlor. The proscenium was painted in pink and blue pastels and framed a six-foot-wide television screen that dropped electronically from the ceiling.

The proprietor of the bar, "Cat," was its funky chaperone who prepared her own mole sauce and smiled and danced the lambada after midnight as though it was her wedding reception. The bar bought nearly every other round, which kept everyone happy and talked out.

The members of Isaac's unit rounded a table in the center of the room, shouting at each other across an army of empty beer bottles and overflowing ashtrays. The dim juke-box light cast shadows on the salmon-colored walls, across smoky mirrors and elaborate moldings.

Official introductions followed.

Wendy Sue, a tall blonde, was the divorced mother of two teenage boys. Her still youthful figure crammed into stone-washed jeans, she attracted attention and tongue wagging.

She clung to being a cop, raising the kids, adjusting to being alone for the first time. She relaxed by tanning for hours in her backyard in Bridgeport. In the Two-Six her eye shadow, a green and purple combination, shone in the juke-box light like a tropical fish.

To Wendy's right was Patti, a black University of Chicago graduate with a soft-spoken, gentle demeanor and an even gentler smile. She had grown up on the West Side with her mother, a librarian. They still went to storytelling conferences every spring. She had become a cop when she decided she didn't want to spend the rest of her life as a sales rep, her first job after finishing college.

Wendy and Patti were the lead officers of Operation Cool Running, working inside the bar, buying most of the coke. They were occasionally joined by John Matthews, a black officer who lived on the North Side with his wife and kids, but who could act like a dealer when he had to, fixing his gaze and lowering his voice so that he quaked. Now he was jovial, which was his usual mood.

The surveillance crew took up the remainder of the table. There was Jim Hennigan, who looked scholarly with his mustache and round glasses, and who was most interested in following the money and seizing assets, even if the system was a sham; Pisterzi, a graduate of De Paul University who wanted to become an alderman; and Isaac, the perverted, the ringmaster, the rabbi. He was an existential schmoozer, part salesman, part lecturer, part conspiracy theorist, part chicken soup. He looked as though he had never played a game of tennis in his life.

After becoming a sergeant in 1988, Isaac had gone to the Rogers Park district for a while, then came back to narcotics, where he felt most comfortable, his gritty and fatalistic imagination feeding on the edginess of the job.

Isaac was not a typical cop. For starters, he was Jewish. He went to synagogue every now and then, got together with his family at Passover and Yom Kippur, and though not observant, he was familiar with the nuts and bolts of Jewish law—you don't mix milk with meat, and so on.

Other elements of his upbringing did not exactly dictate that he enter law enforcement. His father was a gangster, Isaac said, a onetime member of Detroit's Purple Gang who was convicted in Florida in 1951 of attempted murder. When he was incarcerated, the whole family—Isaac and his sister and mother—moved to Florida, near Raiford prison outside Tampa.

Drafted by the army in 1972, Isaac was dispatched to Fort Polk, Louisiana, for two years, where he learned, he said, absolutely nothing. He bought a pickup truck and a horse, a butterfly-specked Appaloosa named Parnee Stardust, that he broke himself. His father used to have a horse in Chicago. And his grandfather had ridden one in Romania. He liked the idea of carrying on the tradition.

"I had a lot of help from the cowboys on the Texas border. 'Get up on that there horse I-sack. Don't let that horse throw you, I-sack. Get up there like John Wayne. . . . Hey, I-sack, you one of those Hebrew-lites? We always thought you guys had tails and horns.' "

When he was done with the army he sold the Appaloosa for $250 in overdue feed bills and returned to Chicago. The police department seemed an honorable profession after the military. His first undercover buy was in Humboldt Park, half a gram of cocaine from some gang members.

During his first stint in narcotics, other drug officers would ask him if he "took," which basically meant stealing money during raids, and he'd tell them he didn't, that he hadn't become a cop to get rich.

Then, one night in 1980 near Humboldt Park, during a traffic stop, he found himself staring into the barrel of someone else's gun. Pisterzi, who had been there, described the scene to me during a shift in the surveillance van.

"I was writing parking tickets on snow emergency streets in the district. In the Fourteenth at that time you were never alone. So there's a call for a stolen car and Al says he is right behind him. The next thing I hear is this icy voice, 'Shots fired at police. Shots returned by police. Offender is down.'

"I got out and it smelled like gunsmoke. Both windows were blown out and there were four shots in the driver's door. Al was over the body, reloading his gun."

Isaac never talked about the shooting with me, but it informed his understanding of the job. It was dangerous work, just as he'd imagined. Therefore one must be willing to kill. This was a requirement he didn't like, but accepted.

■ ■ ■

I was excited that I had hooked up with such a diverse group. Black, white, Jewish, gentile, college educated, streetwise, hardened, funny. They were made for TV. Deluded as I was about Hollywood, within weeks of meeting them I wrote an overblown movie treatment of the operation.

"Mariachi music and Spanish cursing ring out in the summer air. Five hundred thirty kilos of cocaine are loaded beneath the floorboards of a cattle truck. A layer of manure is spread around like cheap paint. Cows are herded aboard.

"The truck crosses the border at Juarez/El Paso, speeding up the interstate, past wheat fields and dairy farms until it arrives at its destination, a garage on the South Side of the city.

"Here is the story of the massive shipment, the undercover unit that tries to seize it, and the havoc— the corruption, betrayal, and violence—that invades the officers' lives."

Months later, carrying all sorts of illusions, I actually took the idea to L.A.

"I think you're talking about 'Crime Story' with stronger characters," an agent with slicked-back hair said from across the wooden table. He was enthusiastic but preoccupied, as though maybe one of his kids was an alcoholic.

"Exactly," I answered.

Here's what I needed to do: Slap on a couple of spiked haircuts and throw in a few helicopters, and I'd have myself a hit.

As for the treatment, there was a lot wrong with it, but not everything.

■ ■ ■

During the day, I was busy with the stories at hand.

On April 5, after he had finished his math homework, a ten-year-old boy was walking from his aunt's apartment in the Robert Taylor Homes to his grandmother's building a few yards away. It was a pleasant evening. Little girls were jumping rope; boys played tag. The next sound the boy heard was the pop of a .22. A bullet fired from the small-caliber gun pierced his left temple and blew out his right one. When he woke up in the hospital with two white bandages covering his eyes, he was blind.

■ ■ ■

"It looks like we have a go on the deal . . . a go on the deal," Isaac said into the radio he held less than an inch from his mouth.

It was to happen in an apartment a few blocks away from the bar. This made surveillance problematic, but Isaac decided to go ahead with it.

The van and three surveillance cars followed Wendy and Patti to an apartment building a short way north, where they covered the front and rear doors. They entered with another man and within minutes reappeared downstairs. They had bought a marble-size ball of cocaine packed in wadded plastic.

The crew drove to narcotics headquarters to weigh and inventory the drugs, then added the buy to their master list. A few recent deals I hadn't been a party to made the list about ten entries long. The scale said the girls had been shorted. They had bought less than an eighth of an ounce. Time to drink it off.

All around the Two-Six that night were cops, nurses, and loose-tie bureaucrats. We had walked in on a bachelor party.

A big-breasted woman in a faux leopard coat stripped to a G-string, ogled a bachelor until he surrendered his dignity, his pants twisted around his ankles as he chased her around the floor.

"I've never seen anything like that one," Cat said.

Cat weighed more than I did, but we danced together in a drunken fit, her hips moving in rapid, clockwise bursts. Isaac and Wendy sang early Elvis and held hands under the table. We exhausted ourselves complaining and drinking.

Cops opened up in bars, venting their anger and making room for more. Bosses took the worst hits. By this time I knew who they were talking about, the chiefs and deputy chiefs who had nothing on their minds but their next promotion. There was no brotherhood once you made it to an office upstairs at Eleventh and State.

After a few hours, I was ravaged with hunger. I didn't know how I'd navigate the expressways with all those headlights in my face.

"Hey, Al," Cat shouted from behind the bar. "Phone call."

Isaac stood near the bar, talking. After hanging up he walked back to the table slowly to announce the news: Phillip Miller had been shot by another Jamaican. The early reports said it wasn't about drugs, but nobody believed that.

"We're going to get killed," Wendy suggested calmly as she stared into her beer.

"I was born in a clean, sterile room in Jefferson Hospital," she said as she turned to me. "I don't want to die with my blood running into a dirty street."

"We're not going to," Isaac reassured her.

At the end of the night Isaac warned me, as he warned everyone else, "Be careful"—as though I was about to tumble into a deep, violent conspiracy. Of course, what he meant was that I should drive safely, which was difficult. I got to know the road from the Two-Six to my house, bleary-eyed, with the stereo on as loud as I could crank it just to keep me awake.

■ ■ ■

Steve Haras got married in a wedding factory in Bensenville, a suburb about forty-five minutes from the city.

Table 19 was the cop table, though you wouldn't know it by looking at its occupants. This was deep cover. Wendy wore an ivory top and skirt; a gold necklace dripped into her yard-tanned cleavage. She danced with her sergeant, cha-chas and disco numbers, Isaac making his shoulders sway in a rumba, Wendy just a fraction of an inch behind him. Old couples, relatives of the newlyweds, stopped by the table to tell them how nice they looked on the dance floor.

Although no one openly acknowledged their evolving relationship, they were now a couple, drawn to each other as the only comfort in these long and frustrating days.

■ ■ ■

On April 18 a student at Northwestern Medical School, a Thai woman named Lynda Singshinsuk, disappeared.

The carpeting in her dormitory room was stained with blood. Her wallet, credit cards, and checkbook were left behind. Though there was no suicide note, the police believed she had killed herself by wading into the choppy waters of Lake Michigan just across the street.

Within days, her father, a doctor in downstate Robinson, Illinois, who was certain she had met with foul play, offered a reward for information on her whereabouts.

"How much should I give?" he asked me.

"It's not for me to say, doctor."

"Is $25,000 good?"

This time the reward didn't matter. No one called with leads.

■ ■ ■

In May, cops were targets.

On Mother's Day, Raymond Kilroy and Gregory Hauser, who had been partners for more than a decade, were called to a Northwest Side home for a domestic disturbance involving a woman and her grandson. When they walked into the woman's garage, her lanky twenty-three-year-old grandson wrested Hauser's gun away from him and, at point-blank range, allegedly gunned down both officers.

Martin ordered that all officers on the street wear bulletproof vests, but not everyone in the field could.

A few days later, an undercover cop was shot in a stairwell during a drug buy.

I was in the Tribune Tower when the call came over the police radio, and I worried the officer was one I knew.

I was relieved when Isaac answered my page. "When it goes bad, it tends to go bad very quickly," he said with added pessimism. "Chances are it's going to be over before your backup gets there."

■ ■ ■

Operation Cool Running continued in fits and starts.

Later that month, Matthews had another deal.

"Mazel tov," Isaac shouted. "If you make this one you can have Thursday off. Is that what you want? And yesterday? You want two days? If you get his pager number you can have two days."

Matthews had paid $350 for a quarter ounce, a little high compared to the going rate. At the meet spot he turned the dope over to Isaac and began walking around, catching his breath.

A week later, the operation was falling apart. The cocaine had dried up again.

The team started working other assignments, partly to get their minds off their generally bad luck uptown, and also because they still had to generate some arrest figures.

Pisterzi wanted to work an airline employee suspected of smuggling dope through Midway Airport. So one night we all went bowling. Pisterzi met his contact at one end of the huge bowling palace. Isaac, Wendy, and I bowled at the other end.

I bowled the best game in my life, 165, and believed that I was suddenly close, as close as Wattley, to becoming a cop.

■ ■ ■

On a Friday afternoon, the witching hour, police disclosed a gruesome discovery made in a South Side apartment.

Inside a steamer trunk hidden at the back of a messy closet were the bodies of two children who were slain and then packed in plastic by their parents. For five years, and through five moves, the couple had kept the trunk with them.

At the Pullman Station we gathered around to see the photos of the trunk and its moist contents.

■ ■ ■

A father doused his five sleeping children with less than two dollars' worth of gasoline, then, one at a time, lit them afire. When he was done with his family, he stood in the middle of the living room and killed himself the same way.

At the cemetery, six identical silver caskets were lined

up in the sun. "The idea was to have everything the same, uniform," the funeral director told me. "The same with the hearses. You always do it that way for a family funeral."

The minister crushed six red carnations, sprinkling the petals over each coffin. A young man stood beside the casket of the oldest daughter, who had been his fiancée. Wiping tears from his eyes with his white pallbearer's glove, he watched as workers carted away her remains. Then he collapsed on the curb, whispering goodbye.

■ ■ ■

The last hope of salvaging Cool Running was pulling off an elaborate sting that the FBI had decided to fund after being convinced that the local cops had made valuable inroads. If everything went right, the investigation would close out with Class X felonies across the board, and everyone could share in the credit.

The FBI was a gold mine. The agency issued invitations, rented a dance club, paid for a long white limo, ordered a Jamaican buffet with red snapper and plantain and a lot of booze. All the dealers had to do was walk a few blocks, socialize, drink, and sell dope. This time the transactions would be captured on audiotape.

Everything was set for eight o'clock.

Hitz was wired. The Bureau of Alcohol, Tobacco, and Firearms sent a young agent. The prosecutor's office fielded an attorney.

Isaac was driving in the same surveillance pattern he had been driving for months.

"Don't be x-raying and charleying me," he shouted into one of three radios he was juggling, appalled by the Dick Tracy FBI chatter.

"They go to Quantico for six months to learn to talk that way," sneered a lieutenant who sat next to Isaac, observing the extravaganza.

Before the limousine arrived, Isaac's car phone rang.

"Oh, shit," Isaac exploded, sensing the course of events. "Fleming is burnt. Fleming is burnt. . . . Someone made him. He got lit up. He walked in front of a record store and someone recognized him from a raid and said, 'Hi, remember me?' "

Fleming was on his way to the meet spot. One down.

■ ■ ■

The limousine pulled up at eight-twenty, all six axles, a ridiculous-looking car that ballooned in the rear like a geometric pear.

"The bait is out there," the lieutenant said. "If these mopes aren't there by nine, they're not coming."

I was riding with Pisterzi, who marveled at the federal government's resources and its willingness, every now and then, to use them. The FBI had already spent something like $14,000 that night, and it was prepared to spend another $20,000 buying drugs.

Pisterzi may have looked like a vagrant, but he had a sharp mind, with the rhetorical flourishes of a good politician.

"The war on drugs is not pointless," he said as we sat in a surveillance car, staring at the entrance to the dance club. "But look at this vehicle. It's a piece of junk with a motor. There's no hubcaps on it. The T-top leaks. The city can't even afford patrol cars. This is some kind of shit you have to fight the war on drugs. Something is lacking.

"What effect is this investigation going to have on this community? How many people from this community go to Cool Running? Not many. But the police and the politicians can say, 'Here was a big problem and we tried to do something about it.' "

We were looking out the front window when something large and black scurried past the front of the car. It was a possum. "A fucking possum," Pisterzi yelled. It reminded me of the scene from *Apocalypse Now* when a roaring tiger suddenly leaps out of the bush. A possum was the right scale for this movie.

. . .

Inside the dance club were five cops working as security guards. They kept 9mm pistols and Smith and Wessons in their suits. One wore a tux.

By nine the bands were in full swing. But no one besides cops was there to hear them. The cops devoured the buffet anyway.

Hitz had gone all out. He wore an Eisenhower jacket and suit pants, which he had to go out and buy because he didn't own any formal clothes. He kept a blue steel 9mm in his ankle holster.

He had been wired in a hotel in Rosemont, with a large cassette player in his jock holder because he had too much hair to tape it to his chest. The wire ran up the inside of his shirt to his back, up his spine, under his armpit to the back of his neck. He cut a hole in the pocket of his only suit and put an on-off switch there that, like a windshield wiper switch, didn't click.

Neither did the sting.

Hitz spent the night discussing stereo equipment with one of the roadies. The only interesting talk he had that night was with himself.

We're going to have to close this out, he thought. We worked very hard on this and it's not coming around like it should. The FBI is here, the state's attorney. We're so close, but so far away.

. . .

By fall the chief of organized crime had canceled all long-term investigations, replacing them with quick street busts and reversals.

For Isaac's crew the shift in tactics meant at least a few nights a week in Englewood, where the violence never stopped. Already that year there had been thirty-seven murders and more than four hundred shootings in the district.

The narc cops were not there to do undercover work, to buy dope, work an organization. They were there to make an impression on the community, kick up some dust, kick in some doors.

There were no mirrored windows, no surveillance. The instructions were to run and gun. There was a code name for this operation too: Iron Wedge. The written directive said, "All members will wear their safety vests, raid caps and jackets."

The idea was to let the residents know exactly who they were. "Tonight the street belongs to us" was their motto. If they found kids with small bags of reefer, they'd give them a choice of eating it or going to jail.

Iron Wedge was a publicity stunt designed to respond to media reports about the bloodshed in the community. The chief of the organized crime division himself appeared on television. He wore a raid cap cocked to the side of his head like a gang banger; two guns dangled from his waistband. Where the press probed, the chief would follow. That seemed to be his strategy.

■ ■ ■

In early 1991, even though Operation Cool Running had stalled, twelve people were indicted for the sale of cocaine. Nine pleaded guilty. Two became fugitives. Phillip Miller demanded a trial.

He appeared in court wearing a stylish double-breasted suit, accompanied by his girlfriend and his lawyer. He had refused to plea-bargain with the prosecutors, but as he sat in the back of the courtroom, he could be overheard wondering aloud if he shouldn't have considered it. He had insisted he was innocent. His defense was that the buy officers were drunk when they visited the bar, and that everyone knew they were cops.

Wendy and Patti took the witness stand to describe their hand-to-hand buys from Miller. They denied they were ever drunk. That was the basic conflict in the case.

As the jury deliberated, Wendy, Patti, and Isaac went out for pasta at a nearby restaurant. About an hour into the meal, Isaac was paged. The jury had reached its verdict.

The gallery was empty except for Miller's girlfriend. The clerk glanced at the slip handed him by the jury foreman.

"Guilty."

The only sound in the courtroom was Miller's girl-friend, weeping.

The cops piled into the judge's chamber to congratulate themselves and the prosecutor, an assistant state's attorney; this was the first case he had won. One of his colleagues took a pair of scissors and cut his tie in half in celebration of the victory.

Isaac was ecstatic. He shook the hands of the members of the jury, thanking them as they exited the courtroom. The verdict didn't spell the end of a posse, as he had hoped. Nor did it mean the end of drug dealing on that strip of Broadway. But he felt proud that the work had led to a decent case, even if it didn't go all the way—that Phillip Miller and his buddies were going to jail, that the jury didn't succumb to a lie.

Miller was sentenced to eighteen years.

Some months later, in a ceremony at the Police Academy, LeRoy Martin pinned dime-size blue medals on the uniforms of everyone in Isaac's crew.

FIFTEEN

. . .

THE DESTRUCTION
OF THE TEMPLE

**Today we are here to rid the community of
the El Rukn blight once and for all.**
Richard Daley, June 6, 1990

O n a hot morning at Thirty-ninth and Drexel, victory
would be celebrated with a wobbly lectern and a six-
thousand-pound wrecking ball.

By the time I arrived at about ten, the intersection was
buzzing with activity, as though a giant wedding was to be
held in front of the Fort.

The lectern was wired from the grassy divide to television Minicams and portable radio transmitters. Unmarked
cars were parked on the sidewalks. Men in dark suits slapped
each other on the back and shook hands. Already in attendance were the U.S. attorney, the state's attorney, Martin,
Wodnicki, the head of the local FBI office, and dozens of

cops in sport jackets and ties. A few minutes later, Mayor Daley's entourage arrived.

They had come to mark a rare victory. They had come to destroy the Fort.

The building had been seized more than a year before following the indictment of sixty-five Rukns on a variety of racketeering charges, including twenty murders. It was the widest-ranging and potentially most damaging prosecution the gang, and perhaps any gang, had ever faced. Now the government was going to level the building, so that nothing but dirt and rocks remained.

I had never seen a more upbeat gathering of law enforcement officials in all my time at the Cop Shop. Even retirement parties were not this joyous.

About three hundred spectators gathered to hear the farewells. Among them were the gang task force members I had come to know, the prosecutors, the cops who had spent the better parts of their careers chasing the Rukns.

"They thought they could take on the government. They thought they could take on the community and get away with it," the recently departed U.S. attorney Anton Valukas said to open the ceremony.

Valukas, under whose tenure the major Rukn prosecutions were unleashed, looked at the Fort from the divide. The building was "a symbol of the evil the gang had represented. . . .

"They murdered people at will," he said.

When the wrecking was completed and the lot cleared, Valukas proposed, the city should build a park here, as a tribute to the community's victory over gang violence.

Then came Mayor Daley's turn to speak. He too glared at the ornate building, calling it a "symbol of destruction." And he praised the citizens who had had the courage to go to court and testify against gang members. At the end of his speech, he also made a pledge.

"It's not going to be just another vacant lot," the mayor said in the jumbled but sincere style of delivery that had become his trademark. Perhaps the city would build housing or a health center, a new symbol of hope.

LeRoy Martin, ever the police warrior, paid his respects to the late Officer Jimmy Alfano, who had died in a Rukn ambush. Never again should a building like this rise anywhere in the city.

"It is my vision," Martin bellowed into the microphones, "that with the removal of this building something can be put here that represents life."

The cops and agents standing on the grass applauded their boss.

A man who called himself Little Moe shouted in disgust as he tapped into a bagged beer bottle.

"Tell them to tear down Al Capone's house too. This is wrong. The disco inside was fun."

Only Father George Clements of Holy Angels Church a few blocks away seemed to grasp the decades-old cycle being played out that morning. He led a silent prayer for the "victims of gang crimes, law enforcement officials, and gang members who have died. . . .

"I can't tell you I hated the guys in that building, because I didn't. I loved them, and I'm sorry for what they did. Now it's up to us to do something positive, to make this a place where people want to live."

A few minutes after Clements had spoken, the crowd's attention shifted to where, across the street, a crane hoisted a rusty, pear-shaped wrecking ball above the weather-beaten cornice of the Fort. We waited like the crowd in Times Square on New Year's Eve for the signal from above.

I had always thought the crane operator winds up and swings the ball into the side of the building like a roundhouse pitch. Instead, the crane dropped the ball about fifteen feet onto one portion of the roof until it came loose. Lift and drop. A steady, tenacious motion.

Detective Richard Peck was reminded of how ugly and grinding the process had been.

He had been on surveillance at Sixty-second and Woodlawn when a group of eight Blackstone Rangers blew out the back window of his police car with a shotgun.

"There was one guy shooting with a banana clip. I had a bead on him and that's when I got hit in the back. Seventeen pieces of lead in me. Blood was coming out of every place. I drove to Billings Hospital and fell out of the car. After that, I felt I should do something to them."

Now he stared at the building in its last moments, feeling something akin to euphoria.

"This building has never been good for anything," he said as he watched the spectacle.

For the Rukn detail, for Dan Brannigan, Dave O'Callaghan, and Rich Kolovitz, who had recently retired from the department, the blows of the wrecking ball were the final act of revenge. There would be hundreds of court appearances and hours of testimony ahead to bring the most recent Rukn indictments to a successful conclusion, but nothing could be as emotionally cathartic as this ritual of destruction. The wrecking ball was payback for all the bus fights and name-calling and extortion for just walking the streets.

"It would have been nice if they used dynamite," Brannigan told me as he stared through dark aviator sunglasses.

■ ■ ■

After the fourth or fifth drop of the wrecking ball, chunks of the roof began falling to the ground. The scene was replayed countless times on television that night. The photo opportunity ended when the crane operator took a coffee break. The crowd surged toward the building to collect pieces of it as souvenirs and to pose for pictures in front of the debris. If the cameras hadn't been there, some of the cops would have urinated all over the wreckage.

"I'm gonna send a picture to Fort in Marion," one of the officers boasted.

I also took a piece of the building, a corner section, its

finish cracked in beautiful patterns like those of fine pottery. I put it on a shelf in my apartment, where it remains, a relic of an imagined victory and a piece of a much greater history of loss. In the end it had been a personal vendetta that kept the police interested, a desire to win, a need to set the record straight rather than to make it right. So much of what was accomplished by the cops happened for that reason and no other.

■ ■ ■

When the generals appeared in court to shed the secrets of the Rukn empire, it quickly became clear that the gang was not as sophisticated as the experts had imagined. The Rukns were not part of a well-oiled machine. They were, as the cops muttered, thugs. Their marksmanship stunk. After listening to Fort's elaborate instructions, after deciphering his code, they often killed the wrong person.

As for Fort, he was a hypocrite. He once swore, for example, that he would never sell heroin on the South Side. In 1981, he even told that to the mob.

According to court testimony, Fort went to meet a gangster named Frank Balistrieri in the back of a smoky Milwaukee bar. Balistrieri suggested to Fort that he might want to consider selling heroin as a way of raising cash.

Fort, enraged, shouted back, "If you ever bring heroin to the South Side of Chicago, around my people, I will come down on you so hard your forefathers in Italy will hear your bones rattling."

Balistrieri's bodyguards stood, but Balistrieri waved them off. He pleaded with Fort to calm down.

Realizing he had offended the don, Fort instructed his aides to present Balistrieri with two fur coats, a full-length ranch mink and a diamond mink. Balistrieri accepted them, blew into the mink, and handed the coats to his assistants. But as he walked out of the bar, Balistrieri dropped the coats on the sidewalk and left them there.

Three years later, in need of bond money for Fort, the Rukns turned to a Chicago businessman, Noah Robinson, for precisely the product Balistrieri had suggested. Through Robinson, the Rukns found two East Coast drug dealers to supply them with large amounts of cocaine and heroin for the South Side. If you wanted to buy some, you could go to Forty-seventh and Calumet, Sixty-first and Cottage, Forty-first and King anytime, any day, with anyone watching. By 1985, the Rukns controlled a good portion of the heroin business on the South Side.

■ ■ ■

The morning after the wrecking party, the story of the Fort's destruction appeared on the front page. It was hard not to be skeptical about the ceremony. The violence continued the same day, a drug murder in Englewood and another in Little Village.

As of noon that day there had been 339 murders in 1990, the highest homicide rate in sixteen years.

■ ■ ■

Within about a month the temple was completely gone, its debris carted off to a dump on the South Side, the earth beneath it flattened. Almost three years later, nothing but weeds had risen in its place.

E p i l o g u e
...

I know we're a democracy. But you know, I
don't think everything the communists do
can't be copied. . . . There are some things
they do that are better than what we do.
Police Superintendent LeRoy Martin, July 12, 1991

I came in from the cold just prior to the Persian Gulf War.
My editor told me I'd be coming back to the Tower to
join the general assignment staff to cover just about every
type of breaking story. The only drawback was that I would
now be in Aloysius Brooklyn's line of sight. Who knew what
that would bring.

It wasn't long after my return to the Tribune Tower that
a Polish immigrant suspected of having killed his wife tried
to slip me two crisp fifty dollar bills. He thought it would
improve my reporting.

A few weeks later, I interviewed a blind woman who had
accused a pudgy fourteen-year-old boy of raping her in the
basement of their apartment building. She had identified

him in a police line-up by the scent of his cologne and the feel of his hands. Though she was pleased to see me, she told me I would have to wait. That morning, she was transfixed by the sound of her voice reciting her story on the "Sally Jessy Raphael Show." The charges against the boy were eventually dropped.

Despite the subject matter, there was something lighter, more relaxed about my new assignments.

I had looked forward to the switch for months, if for no other reasons than not having to face the dregs at Eleventh and State every morning, and getting the two-way radio out of my car.

When I told Casey I was leaving, we said we'd have to go out for turtle soup at a restaurant called Binyon's, but we never did. The press room carried on at its own relentless pace, transmitting word of trouble to the city outside. City News recruits charged around in hopes of catastrophe. The "Charlie's Angels" poster kept watch from one of the walls. I had become a better reporter there, as I had hoped, but hard as I tried, I couldn't get too sentimental about the place.

My replacement would be an aggressive reporter who had previously covered the criminal courts and had a stomach for this kind of work. I told Casey he would like her.

I packed some files into a couple of boxes and drove them over to the Tribune Tower, where I was given a clean locker. I had moved to the North Side, just a quick ride from the comforts of Tower life.

I left the Cop Shop as I had found it, except it had become even busier. In the two and a half years since I first walked into the press room at police headquarters, the city had become as embattled as any other. This was confirmed one afternoon when another reporter, Bill Recktenwald, a ruddy-complexioned veteran of the paper whose cubicle backed up to mine, stood up after tapping away at a calculator for several hours.

Reck could squeeze numbers out of rocks. I often teamed up with him to write statistics-based stories documenting the rise or fall of the murder rate, the level of violence linked to handguns, or the overall crime rate. His calculator, perched on a pile of papers at the corner of his desk, had smudged keys, worn smooth as pebbles. The spool of calculator paper had long since run out.

The police department was perennially catching up with his analysis. This year the cops certainly weren't going to be in any rush.

Chicago had one of its highest murder rates in 1990: 851 killings. It was plain from Reck's calculations that more young people in the city were dying by homicide than from any other cause, including car accidents, cancer, or suicide. Nationally, young people between the ages of eleven and twenty accounted for a tenth of all murder victims; in Chicago the proportion was double.

To illustrate the statistics in human terms, Reck and I set out one bitter cold afternoon to give the story some life. Numbers alone would not do. Following threadbare police reports that listed the home addresses of victims and suspects, we traveled from one neighborhood to the next looking for a lead for our story.

At around noon we made our way to Forty-seventh Place, a gritty street sandwiched between a railroad yard and old factory buildings where, according to our reports, a sixteen-year-old boy had lived until he was slain. He had been shot nine times—six in the back of the head—after attending a party nearby.

The boy's grandparents welcomed us inside. At least they didn't set him afire, the way they did the boy next door, the woman said.

"The boy next door?"

"Yes, he was killed too, a few months before."

And so we went next door, one house to the west, and found a Hispanic couple who had lost their fourteen-year-old son. He had been beaten with a baseball bat and, as the neighbor had said, set afire by local gang members.

The two families mourned together. The Hispanic family brought *pan de dulce,* a sweet bread, next door. The white family left a check for a few dollars at their neighbor's wake.

We had a lead, one that expressed the idea that the violence did not recognize class or racial distinctions. There was no question that minorities bore the brunt of the loss, but the one-world proposition made it easier to get the story into print and onto the front page.

Explaining this trend was far more complicated. We were getting good at listing the possibilities, such as the availability of firearms. Chicago police were seizing nearly twenty thousand guns a year—two thousand more than their counterparts in New York City.

There were also the lack of jobs, the elimination of neighborhood youth programs, the shortage of role models, and the feeling of desperation bottled up in the underclass. Each explanation was correct.

During my last six months on the daily beat, the variety and intensity of violence seemed to expand with the grim numbers.

A rapist stalked the North Side, slipping through a nightly police dragnet. A mother and her two children were choked to death in their apartment in the Stateway Gardens project. A marine corporal on leave from his helicopter squadron in Tustin, California, was shot four times in the neck as he pulled into his parents' South Side garage. Another fourteen-year-old was killed in another gang shootout as he walked toward his building in the Abla Homes on the West Side.

His aunt Betty yelled into the phone when I called her.

"I tried to talk to him, telling him to stay out of the projects. There's nothing but death on those streets. You're nothing but a baby. Don't be messing with the drugs. He got in with the wrong people."

Then she stopped yelling. I remembered young Willie

in Robbins and the lecture he got from his mother. I wondered whether it had worked.

"Oh, it hurts so bad," Betty said, giving voice to the frustration and anger held inside by hundreds of people in the city.

Sollie Vincent was out as gang crimes commander, replaced by a marine named Bob Dart who proclaimed, "If we try to be sociologists, we're going to get ourselves in trouble." The simplicity of his words came as a relief, but the gang killings went on with added fervor.

■ ■ ■

The violence was even penetrating Little Italy, where the Mob traditionally kept it out.

On a crisp fall morning Lucien Senese, a Teamsters local official, pressed the automatic ignition starter on his key chain. He opened the door to his white Buick, threw his briefcase inside, stepped in, and was about to shift into drive when a huge blast tore the car to pieces. His hat on fire, his clothes burning, Senese ran to the steps of a church a hundred yards away, where he fell into the arms of a stranger. It was the first time in recent memory that an attempted hit had been carried out on Taylor Street, and on the same block as a school, no less.

Senese survived, though he was forced to wear a plastic body suit to keep his skin alive. No one was arrested for the bombing.

In time, big murder cases were solved. The boyfriend of Lynda Singshinsuk, the Northwestern medical student, was charged with her murder after he led a private investigator to her shallow grave.

Sixty-two of the sixty-five Rukn defendants were convicted. The organization was dead.

And, of course, it was still dangerous for cops. Though the number of officers slain on the job had decreased since the previous decade, a cop killing still occurred in Chicago two, three, four times a year. And when it did, the public was on their side again.

■ ■ ■

I had mixed feelings about the cops.

On the one hand, they were so dissatisfied and angry, you could feel it in the air around them. Uncorked, they were among the most dangerous people on earth.

I had seen the rage on several occasions.

Reporting a series on Chicago's illegal gun supply, I went to the busy Shakespeare district to seek the advice of some tactical officers.

Two or three cops were sitting around talking. One leaned back in a chair, compulsively tapping his foot and rocking back and forth. He lambasted a variety of city programs including the point system ("I need a certain number of points at the end of the month or I'm done"); the education system ("The schools are turning out idiots"); and the police promotion system ("If you don't got someone calling for you, you're nowhere").

In conclusion, he announced, "I hope someone takes an AK-47, sticks it up the mayor's ass, and blows his colon out."

Some months later I saw this acrimony vented on the street. I had dinner with a few plainclothes patrolmen on the South Side. For an hour they ate pizza and played "find the spy" on their paper placemats.

"Do you got the one under the window?" one of them asked.

"Yeah."

"How about the one where the willow tree turns into an evergreen?"

"Got it."

Every spy caught, they pulled on their bulletproof vests and headed for Englewood. When they found a teenage boy holding a bag of reefer, they unloaded. "If I find anymore I'll pull your dick off and stick it in your mouth," one of the cops shouted. Then they forced the kid to swallow the dope.

It was not hard to imagine how these encounters grew out of hand, ending in broken bones, bloodied lips, and soiled reputations.

Yet it was impossible to cover the crime beat without coming to respect the demands and dangers of the job cops were asked to do. Tagging along with Isaac's crew for months had reminded me of that, as had the funeral of Johnny Martin, who was gunned down off-duty while chasing an accused car thief in the alley behind his house.

That morning the street in front of the People's Church was closed to traffic. A dozen kilted, bagpipe-playing members of the police Emerald Society ushered the slain officer's white hearse down Lawrence Avenue.

Johnny Martin was a black cop, and the musicians were white Irish, but on this day the differences were invisible. Even the press was quiet, the only sound being the click and whir of camera shutters.

Pallbearers from his district removed Martin's flag-draped coffin from the hearse and carried it into the church. Programs stacked up at the doors captured Martin's fleshy cheeks and bright eyes. The church was decorated with finger paintings and bouquets of spring flowers. The pews were packed with family, friends, and fellow cops.

LeRoy Martin was the first to take the podium, delivering a short speech on the ultimate price paid by the dead officer. Then he surprised everyone by leading a round of applause for officers who had died in the line of duty, 403 all together. The church thundered. The superintendent had found the right tribute.

■ ■ ■

The police brass who were so convincing at funerals had sold out the rank and file with stupidity and greed. I had seen it with the drug money, and I had heard it in the back rooms of police headquarters. It was easy to understand why the bosses were hated; they certainly despised each other.

Consider the relationship between Martin and Wodnicki, which I once thought, perhaps naïvely, an example of racial harmony.

I was watching the TV news one night when the camera panned across a color photograph of the police brass hung in the lobby of headquarters. The reporter was describing a feud among top police officials allegedly caused by racial epithets uttered by one of them at a dinner. At about the same time, rumors were circulating in City Hall that Martin was planning to resign before his mandatory retirement date.

One evening before I left Eleventh and State, I went to see him. He sat behind his desk wearing a purple tie with neon orange and green spots. His top shirt button was open. He sprayed antihistamine into his throat.

"I was so pissed," he greeted me. "At a meeting today I told the deputies that I didn't plan on leaving. Where am I going to go? Unless the mayor asks me to go, and I don't think he will, why should I go? I plan on being here this November, next November, and the November after that.

"And it would be nice if you could print a story that I plan a little reorganizing too," he added.

"A shake-up?" I inquired.

"Not a major one, certainly not like the changes I made when I came in. Maybe ten to fifteen positions."

There wasn't much interest among the public in the internal workings of the department, especially when it came to promotions and demotions. At most Martin's warning was a brief, a list of names. But I had never seen the chief this angry or intense, and I hoped he would continue. He did.

"They're worried because they don't know who I'm talking about when I said I was going to reorganize. Everyone thinks it's them so they're laying low. Let me tell you, it's like with Brutus. Some people are blinded by ambition. Well, let me tell you something, this Caesar is going to slay his Brutus.

"I think these rumors of my resignation are coming from someone you know," he added.

"Does he have an Irish name or a Polish name?" I asked.

"Polish."

It was clear that Martin was talking about his onetime friend Eddie Wodnicki. He had it on good source, he said, that Wodnicki was after his job.

"You know, I'm just going to strike unexpectedly, see what he's made of, put him on the scale. The only way you can tell how much he weighs is by putting him on the scale. . . . I mean you've got to be a blockhead to even think that Daley would choose a white guy for the job."

Wodnicki denied he had ever wanted Martin's job, that he had ever insulted, bad-mouthed, or sabotaged his administration. By that winter they weren't speaking, and a few months later Martin, as he had implied, transferred Wodnicki to community relations, an obvious slap to the best-known detective in the department.

The humiliation didn't end there. In the summer of 1991, Martin demoted the fifty-seven-year-old Wodnicki, assigning him to the Town Hall district near Wrigley Field. Wodnicki announced his retirement the same day.

■ ■ ■

As the crime rate rose, Martin spoke out with uncharacteristic rancor. He was as quotable as ever, but his credibility was shot and his essentially good reputation was dissolving.

By the end of 1991, the murder rate, measured in relation to the city's population, had reached its highest level on record.

On returning from a trip to China, during a taping of a radio program, Martin suggested that the Bill of Rights be ditched to help confront dealers and gangs. He said he liked what he saw in Chinese prisons, their Spartan quarters and no-nonsense attitude, and didn't we need a little of that in Chicago?

Again, Martin was expressing Everyman's frustration with crime and killing. Gone, however, were the elements of lucidity, of amiability. He retired in early 1992 and was named head of public safety for the beleaguered Chicago Housing Authority.

Many people feared the city would just explode one night. Amazingly, it didn't. When the West Side went dark because of a power failure on a hot summer weekend, some thought that would be the spark. Nothing happened. Other than a looting rampage after the Bulls second NBA championship victory, unrest on a grand scale was unheard of. That summer, Carol Moseley Braun, the Cook County Recorder of Deeds, was on her way to becoming the first black female U.S. senator, and Bobby Rush, an alderman and former Black Panther, was waging what would be a successful campaign for a congressional seat. They would represent a city in crisis; in hundreds of less spectacular way, Los Angeles had already happened in Chicago.

■ ■ ■

The most innocent victim fell on October 13, 1992.

That morning, Dantrell Davis, age seven, was walking to Jenner Elementary School, a hundred yards from his home in Cabrini-Green, when a sniper's bullet struck his head. He was the third student from the school slain that year.

In a confession he later said was beaten out of him, the sniper said that he had been trying to scare rival gang members; he wasn't aiming for Dantrell.

This murder made news. Perhaps the image of a child gunned down while walking hand in hand with his mother finally rattled the city. Perhaps it was the early hour of the crime, which gave the press all day to package the tragedy.

Or perhaps it was the timing, in the heat of a presidential campaign indifferent to the inner city.

The press threw its full weight into the story. At the *Tribune,* we wrote about Cabrini with a heightened sense of compassion, passing on the words of residents who had seen too much bloodshed and too much waste. The stories made every zone.

Even the mayor reacted, sending in hundreds of police. Temporarily. Some buildings were closed down; others were fortified with steel doors and metal detectors. Teams of city workers hastily removed gang graffiti. The city's major black gangs declared a truce. We didn't know what to make of it.

In the newsroom, we promised not to forget. For a while at least, the taking of one life mattered. A new policy pledged to report the murder of children on page one.

■ ■ ■

I work in a broader arena now, covering stories not so much at street level, as I did at the Cop Shop, but in a subterranean form of journalism known as investigative reporting.

The AM radio no longer wakes me with the morning's morbid body count. I listen to FM. I don't have to run around with cops on Saturday nights.

I went back to Eleventh and State not long ago to show a new reporter around. She had worked in a small town in Oklahoma, where there were had been no murders in eighteen months. The biggest police scandal involved allegations that three cops had bribed a game ranger with $250.

When she walked into the press room she looked faint. Staring at her from one of the walls were the pictures of Sihanouk, Mayor Washington, and Ditka, each extending his middle finger. Welcome.

A layer of dust covered my old desk. The paper hadn't been staffing the pressroom regularly. There was only Casey and City News and the occasional reporter from the *Defender.*

The fire ticker had been mounted on a beautiful wood shelf. The vial of blood marked with Henry's name remained.

We walked down the stairs to the sixth floor and the Sheet. It seemed to be artificially stocked with violent crime. Every entry was either a murder or an armed robbery. I didn't remember things being quite that bad. Indeed, the latest crime statistics showed that the number of homicides committed in 1992 would surpass the 920 homicides of 1991.

"These numbers here are the district," I instructed my colleague, grabbing the clipboard from the counter, "and this is the time it was reported, not the time of occurrence. This is the manner, shot, stabbed, etc. . . .

" 'Juan Rivera, male, white, hispanic, thirty-three, DOA, gunshot wounds, shot during argument on the street, possibly by a rival gang member.' You have to look for something interesting, something out of the ordinary."

She shook her head.

A heavyset cop walked in to tell the keepers of the Sheet about his recent heart attack.

"A lot of times it's hereditary," one of the officers said from behind the counter to console him. On a television set next to him, Ross Perot was talking about MIAs.

" 'James Jones, male, black, nineteen. Drive-by. Witness stated black auto pulled up and questioned victim. Shots were fired and victim ran to hallway and expired.'

" 'Attempted rape on CTA. Suspect licked victim's breast and ran away.'

"There's a story in every one, really," I said.

■ ■ ■

We walked to Blackie's for lunch, and I bought. I figured she'd need it.